The Battle of Königsberg

*The Struggle for the East Prussian Capital,
October 1944 to April 1945*

THE BATTLE OF KÖNIGSBERG

THE BATTLE OF
KÖNIGSBERG

THE STRUGGLE FOR THE EAST PRUSSIAN CAPITAL,
OCTOBER 1944 TO APRIL 1945

BRIAN TAYLOR

THE BATTLE OF KÖNIGSBERG

Copyright © Brian Taylor 2012

Maps Copyright © Brian Taylor 2012

ISBN – 1-47767-629-5

First published in 2012 by Brian Taylor

Second Edition 2013

1 2 5 7 9 8 6 4 2

The right of Brian Taylor to be identified as the author of this work has been asserted by him in accordance with the Copyright, Designs and Patents Act 1988

All rights reserved. No part of this publication may be reproduced, stored in a retrieval system or transmitted in any form or by means, electronic, mechanical, photocopying, recording or otherwise, without prior permission in writing from *BRIAN TAYLOR*

Contents

Preface	7
Chapter One - Königsberg: A Brief History	9
Chapter Two - The War in the East	25
Chapter Three - The Frontier Battles	39
Chapter Four - The January Storm	101
Chapter Five - The First Battle for Königsberg	135
Chapter Six - Fortress Königsberg	175
Chapter Seven - The Final Battle: The First Day	201
Chapter Eight - The Second Day of the Assault	211
Chapter Nine - Encirclement Complete	221
Chapter Ten - The Bitter End	229
Chapter Eleven - After the Battle	247
Selected Bibliography	253
Index	255

THE BATTLE OF KÖNIGSBERG

Preface

During the final months of the Second World War a series of bloody battles were fought along the Baltic Shores of East Prussia, battles which culminated in the defeat of the German Army in a number of isolated pockets. One of these pockets was around the historic capital city of the province, Königsberg.

The Battle of Königsberg: The Struggle for the Prussian Capital, October 1944 to April 1945 recounts the story of the Soviet victory over the beleaguered German garrison, of the fighting in and around the city, from the attacks along the East Prussian frontier in October 1944, to the overwhelming offensive of January 1945 which saw the province overrun, and on to the final battle in April 1945 when the ruined city fell to Stalin's vengeful soldiers. The campaign against East Prussia was particularly brutal as Stalin had his eyes set not only on the defeat of the Germans, but the expulsion of the populace. Königsberg, like thousands of other East Prussian settlements, fell to the enemy from the East and its very name was wiped off the map, its people expelled from their ancestral homeland.

Given the redrawing of the map of Eastern Europe following the Allied victory, I have referred throughout to the towns and villages of the region by their original German names. Where possible the modern name of these settlements is given in the Notes.

To differentiate between the opposing armies I have used the following convention for the identification of the German and Soviet forces. The German armies are described in words, those of the Soviets in numbers. Thus we have the Germans deploying the Fourth Army while the Soviets deploy their 5th Army. German corps' are displayed using

Roman numerals, e.g. XXVI Corps, while the Soviet ones are again displayed using numbers (1st Tank Corps). The Germans tended to use the unconventional XXXX instead of XL for 40 and I have also adopted this throughout. Of divisions, both are referred to numerically (for example the German 1st Infantry Division and Soviet 236th Rifle Division). Most actions are described down to divisional level on the German side, and corps level on the Soviet. Where it is crucial to the understanding of the battle, lower level formations are included.

I must also make one final point, that being that this is a study of a military campaign. Many recent works have devoted much print to the terrible atrocities that were committed by Soviet troops as they advanced through German territory. While in no way wishing to denigrate the appalling crimes which did occur, this book does not relate these terrible stories, only giving them mention where they have a direct impact on the military aspects of the campaign. The harrowing tales of rape and murder which abound in other works are not discussed here. It must be kept in mind that as savage as the acts of some of the Soviets soldiers were, and they were appalling, these soldiers were crossing into the territory of an enemy which had killed over 13 million civilians in their own land, while another 8 million military personnel[1] had died expelling the Germans. Total German civilian losses in the Second World War were as high as 3.1 million, of whom 600,000 or more were killed by the Allied bombing of German cities. That the bulk of the remainder were killed in the Eastern provinces should come as no surprise given the terrors the German forces had visited upon the peoples of the Soviet Union. By 1945, revenge was the order of the day and the Soviet soldiers ensured that the Germans reaped in East Prussia what they had sown in the Soviet Union.

Chapter One - Königsberg: A Brief History

In 1255 AD, having concluded their successful campaign against the pagan Prussians and Sambians, the Christian Order of the Teutonic Knights established a fortified settlement on the site of an old Prussian town, building a castle on a modest mount close to the mouth of the River Pregel. The fort they built was named in honour King Ottokar II of Bohemia, under whose command the Knights had conducted their campaign. The new castle dominated the landscape and confirmed to all who lived there that the Germans had staked their claim to the region, a claim which was to last seven centuries. The castle was named Kings Hill, Königsberg in the native German. A small town quickly grew up around the castle, to later become known as the Old Town (Altstadt) area as Königsberg expanded. A Prussian uprising in 1262 saw the town destroyed and the settlers had to seek refuge behind the walls of the castle. Despite this setback the Knights renewed their efforts to pacify the area and after conquering the rebellious tribes, rebuilt Old Town and strengthened the castle defences. In its earliest years the settlement of Königsberg comprised three separate villages. The Old Town was situated to the south of the castle while to the east the village of Löbenicht quickly developed. On the island of Kniephof[2], which lay in the middle of the River Pregel to the south of the Castle, another village also grew. The Pregel was influential in the development of Königsberg, providing an avenue for trade to bring wealth into the city. East of the Kniephof the river flowed in two parts. The New Pregel was to the north and Old Pregel to the south and between them was a narrow strip of marshy and waterlogged land. From the Kniephof the river joined as one and flowed west to the Baltic Sea. Situated along the banks of the River Pregel, there gradually developed wharves and markets, with lively Fish and Meat Markets being a hub of activity. The citizens of the city eventually spanned the river with seven bridges. The Krämer Bridge, one of the first to be built, joined the western end of the Kniephof Island to the Old Town. The Green Bridge, also one of the cities oldest bridges, spanned the Old Pregel from the Kniephof to south bank, in the area where the Stock Exchange would later be built. Just a few yards downstream the Köttel Bridge was built. The eastern end of the north shore of the Kniephof was joined by another bridge which crossed into the Fish Market. The Holz Bridge crossed the New Pregel from the Meat Market, situated southeast of the castle, to the Old University buildings. The Honey Bridge, the last of the five Kniephof bridges, joined the island with the Lindemanstrasse to the east, where the New Jewish Synagogue had been built. Further upstream there was the Palmburger Bridge, which completed the seven bridges in and around the city. South of the Pregel the suburbs of Haberberg, Rosenau and Nasser Garten were established.

The city contained many fine buildings. The Castle had been build up over many years until it reached its final grandiose state, with its ninety metre main tower and four smaller towers around the perimeter. The Castle's main spire dominated the city skyline. The Cathedral was situated at the eastern end of the Kniephof and had been built in the 14th Century. It replaced a smaller structure that had originally been built in the Old Town. The new Cathedral took around fifty years to build and had spires at its north and south ends, although a fire in 1544 saw them both destroyed. In the subsequent repair work only the south spire was rebuilt. The Reichs Bank and Town Hall were also situated on the Kniephof. The original buildings of the University, known as the Albertina after their founder, Grand Master Albert of Brandenburg, were built in 1544 on the banks of the New Pregel to the east of the Kniephof. Other University buildings were built to mark the three hundredth anniversary of its founding. The new Albertina was situated north of the castle with the Paradeplatz, a wide open ornamental garden, to the front. This was where General Otto Lasch established his bunker headquarters during the final battle for the city. The construction of these buildings began in 1844, as did that of the University Library to the north, and Zoological Museum and University Botanical Gardens to the west. The University staff celebrated the four hundredth anniversary of the founding of their institution in July 1944 but just than a month later its buildings were destroyed by Allied bombing. On the south bank of the Pregel, between the Green and Köttel bridges, was the Stock Exchange. Further out, on the southern reaches of the Haberberg suburb, was the Main Railway Station. It had been developed in the late 19th Century and in the 1920's had had an impressive glass roof constructed above its platforms. To the east of the city, near the village of Lauth, was located the Königsberg-Devau airport, which had opened in 1922.

Figure 1 - Königsberg at the beginning of the war

The three separate settlements of Königsberg were walled around for mutual defence as early as the1370's but it was not until the 1620's that Königsberg was formally fortified with its 'First Defensive Belt', mainly in response to the threat posed during the Swedish Wars. The First Defensive Belt consisted of an eleven-kilometre long, fifteen-metre thick fortified earth bank around Old Town, Kniephof and Löbenicht.

With the continuing rise to power of the Duchy of Prussia the city quickly established itself as the foremost settlement in the region. On January 18th 1701 Frederick, son of the Elector of Brandenburg and Prussia, declared himself King Frederick III at a ceremony in Königsberg Castle, and Prussia became a Kingdom. However, it was not until 1724 that the three districts of the city were officially united. They developed steadily over the following years and many smaller surrounding settlements, such as Sackheim and Rossgarten to the east and Tragheim to the north, were absorbed into the urban area. During the Seven Years War of the 1750's, Königsberg fell to the Russians and was peacefully occupied until their withdrawal in 1763. The Partition of Poland that followed in 1772 brought the province of East Prussia into being, with Königsberg its capital. Some thirty years later the city had grown to a population of 60,000 with a military garrison of some 7,000 soldiers.

The Napoleonic Wars brought yet more change. Fleeing from Berlin and the pursuing French troops, King Frederick William III and his court sought refuge in Königsberg. Following Napoleon's defeat in Russia the war swept to the west and Königsberg was left to prosper once more, its population standing at 64,000 by 1820. As military technology advanced the First Defence Line fortifications fell into obsolescence, to be subsumed as the city grew outwards. Some two centuries after the original defences were built, when the Kingdom of Russia posed the primary military threat, newer and more advanced defences were begun. Between 1843 and 1859 the construction of the Second Defence Belt took place. This defensive system was built over the top of the First Defence Belt, except to the south where the defences were moved outwards to incorporate the expanding suburb of Haberberg. This new system included the latest in defensive emplacements, comprising twelve bastions in a ring around the city, together with two fortresses, three ravelins and seven spoil banks. It was this network of defences which comprised the Inner Defence Line in April 1945.

A third period of fortress building took place between 1874 and 1885 when the forts around the Ring Chaussee were constructed, relegating the defunct Second Defensive Belt to the role of an inner defensive works. This fortress line formed the main defences against the Soviet offensive in 1945. Originally eleven main forts were built but a twelfth fort and three smaller intermediate forts were added between 1887 and 1890 in order to plug some gaps in the fifty-tree kilometre long perimeter. Each of the standard forts was around 340 metres wide by 150 metres deep, encircled by a ten metre wide ditch which was up to five metres deep. The fortresses were substantial red brick built structures with hard-packed earth roofs up to four metres thick, concrete outer walls and stout inner defensive walls. There were cupolas for artillery pieces and howitzers and to aid communication a network of underground connecting tunnels. The forts were made from especially hardened bricks and had no openings to their front, having only a single exit and entry way to the rear. This configuration left them somewhat vulnerable if they were encircled, the garrison of between 200 and 500 soldiers having but one means of escape. By the time of the Great War the development of high velocity artillery and penetrative rounds made many of the defences vulnerable and so the fortresses lost their importance.

In 1914 the population of the city had reached 246,000 but its economy and that of East Prussia as a whole, was in steady decline. Unlike the western provinces of Germany, East Prussia had failed to industrialise, its economy still largely being based on agriculture. The city infrastructure continued to be developed though, being connected to Berlin by railway in 1860, while another line headed east to St Petersburg. The building of a canal to Pillau helped to increase trade but not enough to halt the general malaise. The isolation of East Prussia following the German defeat in 1918 merely hastened the economic decline. Nevertheless, by 1939 the population of the city had peaked at 372,000, making it the second largest German city west of the Oder-Neisse line[3].

THE BATTLE OF KÖNIGSBERG

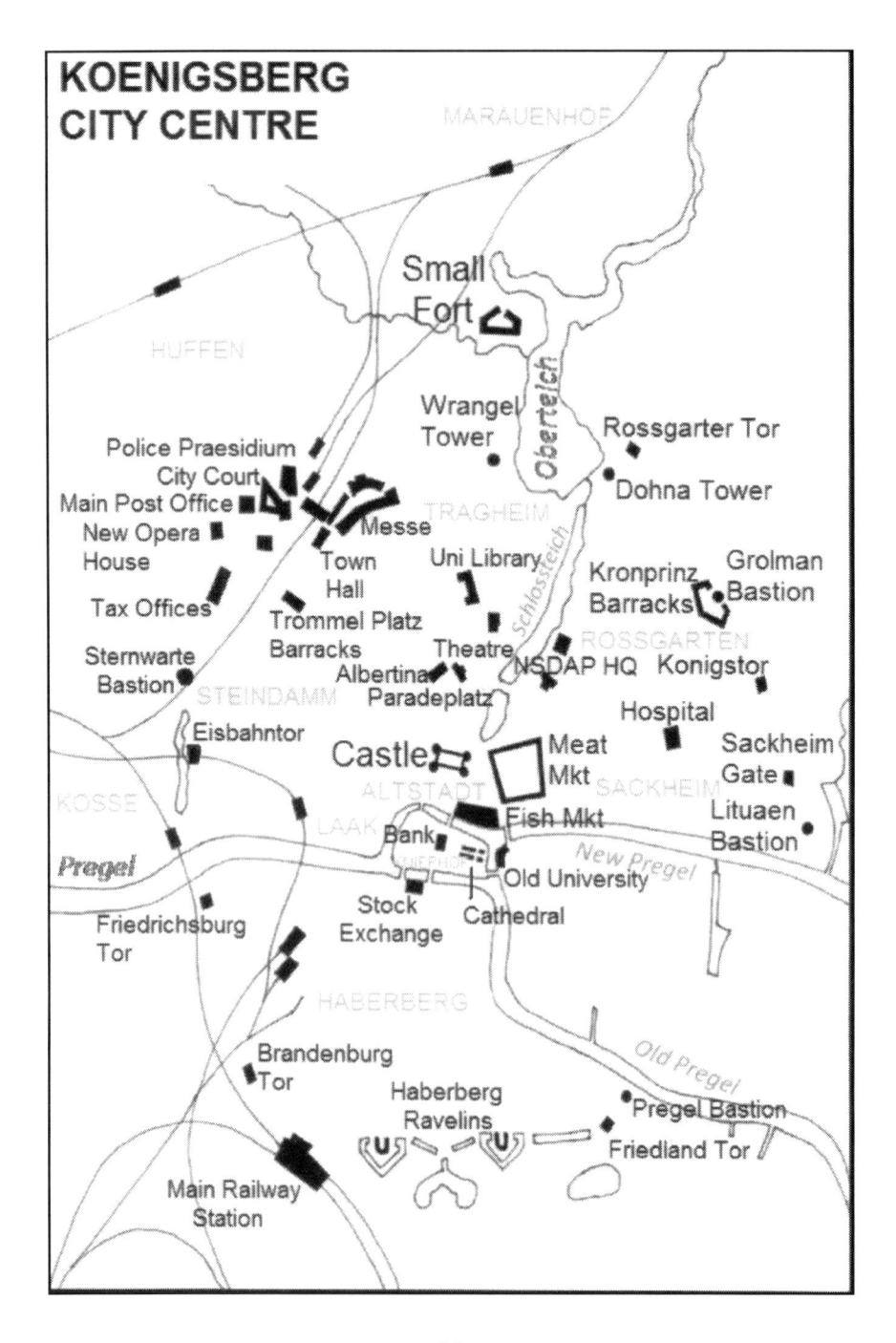

KOENIGSBERG CITY CENTRE

MARAUENHOF

Small Fort

HUFFEN

Wrangel Tower

Oberteich

Rossgarter Tor

Police Praesidium
City Court
Main Post Office
New Opera House
Tax Offices
Sternwarte Bastion

TRAGHEIM

Dohna Tower

Messe
Town Hall
Trommel Platz Barracks
Albertina
Paradeplatz

Uni Library

Schlossteich

Kronprinz Barracks

Grolman Bastion

Theatre
NSDAP HQ

ROSSGARTEN

Konigstor

STEINDAMM

Hospital

Eisbahntor

Castle

ALTSTADT

Meat Mkt

SACKHEIM

Sackheim Gate

KOSSE

LAAK

Bank

Fish Mkt

Lituaen Bastion

Pregel

TIEFHOF

Old University

New Pregel

Friedrichsburg Tor

Stock Exchange

Cathedral

HABERBERG

Old Pregel

Brandenburg Tor

Haberberg Ravelins

Pregel Bastion

Friedland Tor

Main Railway Station

14

The Nazi's made their mark on Königsberg, and East Prussia as a whole, from the late 1920's with the arrival of the ruthless Erich Koch. Koch, who came from Elberfeld in the Rhineland, had worked as a railway employee before joining the Nazi Party in 1922. He had risen through its ranks until Hitler appointed him Gauleiter of East Prussia in 1928. At the time of his appointment there were less than 100 Nazi Party members in Königsberg but the scheming and resourceful Koch quickly recognised the need to appeal to the agricultural classes while also promising employment through public works and industrialisation. From less than 1% of the East Prussian vote in 1928, the Nazi's went on to secure nearly a fifth in the 1930 elections and almost half in the elections of 1932. The rise in votes was accompanied by a corresponding increase in violence on the streets, as intimidation and gang warfare between the Nazis and Communists increased. Koch's success at the polls led to his representation of East Prussia in the Reichstag from 1930, and his appointment as Oberpräsident for the region in 1933. Koch and the Nazi Party did indeed bring jobs to the region and within a few short years the high unemployment rate had been significantly reduced through road building programs and limited industrial developed. His efforts to collectivise agriculture met with significant resistance from the conservative landowners of the region, and had a long lasting effect on Koch's popularity with the rank and file of the populace. Koch assiduously lined his pockets at the same time as he undertook his economic reforms, establishing the Erich Koch Institute to siphon off his ill gotten wealth. When the war began Koch's powers increased considerably. Initially he was appointed State Defence Commissioner for East Prussia and took under his control Polish territories which bordered the southern reaches of East Prussia. His rule here was harsh but events in Russia took him away from the region after he was appointed State Commissioner for the Ukraine in September 1941, and then also briefly for the Ostland region (Latvia, Lithuania and Belorussia) in September 1944. Koch's empire in the east was extensive. His brutal governance, with mass executions and severe reprisals against the most minor infraction, led to the deaths of thousands, and the persecution and extermination of the local Jewish populations. Many thousands more were sent to Germany, to work in her factories as slave labourers. Not for nothing was he known by the local populace as the Hangman of the Ukraine.

Figure 2 - Erich Koch, Gauleiter for East Prussia

Gauleiter Koch returned to his East Prussian stamping ground as Reichs Defence Commissioner and later also commander of the East Prussian Volkssturm, towards the end of the summer of 1944, after the Red Army had overrun much of his eastern fiefdom. As the fighting drew closer to the East Prussian frontier, the German High Command realised they needed to build defences to hold off any further Soviet thrusts. Responsibility for the construction of these defences prompted a power struggle within the Nazi hierarchy but In August 1944 Hitler decided that the construction was to be overseen by Martin Bormann and the Gauleiters. In East Prussia this responsibility fell to Erich Koch. Koch was supposed to oversee the provision of civilian labour while the army provided engineering officers to show the workers where to build their defences. Unfortunately a shortage of engineering officers meant the Party often dug its trenches in badly sited positions and the works they constructed proved to be of poor quality. The folly of digging in up-ended concrete pipes to make one-man defensive positions across the breadth of the frontier says it all. The defences, bombastically proclaimed the 'Erich Koch Wall', were situated twelve miles behind the frontier, and were supposed to protect East Prussia from the approaching Red Army, but proved instead to be a monumental and costly folly, being outflanked even before it was completed. They were nevertheless proclaimed as a great success by Koch, and declared a model for other Gauleiters to follow. In October 1944, as the fighting approached the frontier, the Army leadership urged the evacuation of civilians from what would soon become an operational zone. Koch absolutely refused to countenance any talk of evacuation and even went so far as to order that any civilians trying to flee the region without permission should be shot. The gruesome fate of thousands of civilians in East Prussia and Königsberg rests in no small part upon the shoulders of Koch, who denied them the opportunity to escape to the West in good time.

The war that had raged so long and hard in Russia since 1941 had largely passed Königsberg by. In the opening days of the invasion the Soviet air force had made an effort to bomb the city. On the night of the 23-24th June 1941 a small force of Soviet bombers had launched a raid but damage was negligible. For the next three years the people of the city only experienced the war through the loss of their fathers, sons and brothers in the battles that were raging around Europe and the trains of wounded who arrived in the city to rest and recuperate. The devastating area bombing raids of RAF Bomber Command and the daylight raids of the US Air Force, which wrecked cities across western and central Germany, largely left the eastern portions of the Reich unscathed. Being at the extreme operational range of their bomber aircraft, and lacking major heavy industry, Königsberg was a target of little value to the Allies. For this reason the city remained largely untouched until the late summer of 1944 when the RAF finally set its sights upon it. During the night of August 26-27th the war came home with a vengeance. A force of 174 Lancaster bombers, operating from bases in England, struck the city. The lead aircraft overshot their intended target, the city centre, and most of the bombs fell to the east, missing the industrial and port facilities to fall on residential areas. The German anti-aircraft defences, which had been assembled some time before the raid in a belt around the city, proved unprepared, only four of the British bombers being shot down. Civilian casualties were severe, around 1,000 were killed and a further 10,000 left homeless. This first raid brought home to the citizens of Königsberg that the war was coming closer.

The British returned to Königsberg just days later, during the night of August 29-30th 1944. On this occasion 189 Lancaster's did manage to hit the city centre, devastating Old Town, the Rossgarten and Kniephof. Nearly 500 tons of ordinance were dropped, which comprised a mix of high explosive and incendiary bombs. This proved a deadly combination. The timber framed buildings in the city centre burned fiercely, spreading the destruction far and wide. In the resultant inferno nearly 4,000 civilians were killed and 150,000 more made homeless. Damage to the city was extensive with thousands of residences being destroyed. The Castle and Cathedral were completely burned out and reduced to mere shells, their outer walls standing as a stark illustration of the devastation within. Many of the University buildings were also left in ruins, as were the warehouses along the Pregel and the main railway station left a corpse strewn, gutted wreck. Five of the city's seven bridges were destroyed and the Kniephof was cut off from the rest of the city. It was largely abandoned for the remainder of the war. Despite the devastation wrought, the German air defences had been more prepared for the British attack and fifteen RAF bombers were shot down, their wrecks littering the East Prussian countryside the following morning while the city continued to burn.

Figure 3 - Königsberg after the devastating Allied bombing raids

Königsberg had had a military garrison since the earliest days of its foundation and with the rearmament of Germany in the mid 1930's, it became the headquarters of the German Army's Wehrkreis I[4]. A number of army divisions held East Prussia as their home base and towards the end of the war many were to return there, including the 1st, 61st and 349th Infantry Divisions. General Otto Lasch took over as commander of Wehrkreis I at the beginning of November 1944. Lasch was not a native of East Prussia, having been born at Pless in Silesia in 1893, the son of the Master Forester to the Prince of Pless. By 1944 he had spent much of his career in the province. After serving as a soldier in the Great War he had joined the German Police Force before transferring back to the Army in 1935 with the rank of Major. He then served on the staff of the 45th Infantry Regiment before being appointed commander of the III Battalion of the 3rd Infantry Regiment in 1936. The latter was based at Osterode in East Prussia. Promoted to Colonel in late 1939 he was then appointed commander of the 43rd Infantry

Regiment (part of the 1st Infantry Division), which had its home base at Insterburg. When Hitler launched his invasion of the Soviet Union in June 1941, Lasch and his 43rd Infantry Regiment were deployed as part of Army Group North. While the panzer troops under General Reinhardt fought a hard battle at Daugavpils, Lasch, led an audacious attack in the van of the German Eighteenth Army in an effort to secure the important railway bridge across the River Dvina at Riga. His aim was to prevent the Soviets from pulling their 8th Army back through the city while also opening a way for the Germans to continue their push into Estonia. In bitter fighting Lasch's men secured control of the bridge only to see it blown up by the Soviets after heavy fighting. Nevertheless, Lasch's heavily outnumbered force put up a determined battle against the retreating men of the Soviet 8th Army, who launched repeated counter attacks. The Germans managed to establish a bridgehead which they later used to push on to the north. For these actions in July 1941 Lasch was awarded the Knights Cross with Oak Leaves. In August 1942 he was promoted to Major-General and appointed commander of the 217th (East Prussian) Infantry Division on September 27th 1942. He and his division remained in the Leningrad theatre until late 1943. In April 1943 he was promoted to Lieutenant-General and on November 20th of that year was appointed commander of the newly formed 349th Infantry Division. In April 1944 he and his new command moved to the southern sector of the Eastern Front and were involved in the bitter and costly defensive battles that were raging in the western Ukraine. The 349th was virtually destroyed in a bloody encirclement battle around Brody in July 1944, although Lasch led the remnants of the division on a successful break out attempt. The survivors of Lasch's former command, the 217th Infantry Division who had also been brought south into the Ukraine, were also destroyed in the fighting at Brody. The 349th Infantry Division was reformed in late 1944 as one of the new generation of Volksgrenadier Divisions, and went on to see action in its native East Prussia.

Figure 4 - Otto Lasch

At the end of August 1944 Lasch left the Eastern Front and was transferred to the Officer Reserve in order to recuperate. His period of rest was brief as on 31st August 1944, after just five days of leave, he was ordered to report to Hitler's headquarters at Rastenburg. Here he was met by Alfred Jodl, the Chief of the Operations Staff of the Armed Forces High Command (the OKW) and told of his appointment as commander of LXIV Corps, which was deployed on the Western Front in France. By early October 1944 Lasch had reported sick, being diagnosed with jaundice and so was granted five weeks sick leave. For a second time Lasch was not to see out his leave, being contacted at his quarters in Osterode after less than a week. Hitler informed Lasch in a terse phone call that he was appointed commander of Wehrkreis I with immediate effect. Lasch was somewhat surprised by this appointment, understanding that commander of a Wehrkreis was a largely administrative appointment. Being a frontline officer such a rear area appointment did not seem appropriate, but Hitler told him bluntly that the frontline was already on the boundary of his command. Unlike Erich Koch, Lasch was a professional soldier with a conservative outlook and deep sense of responsibility for those under his command, both military and civilian. His sense of right from wrong would guide him through the toughest decisions of his career when the Soviets attacked Königsberg in 1945.

Battered and bruised, and with a terrible sense of foreboding, in the autumn of 1944 the citizens and defenders of Königsberg nervously watched the approach of the Soviet armies. As the summer weeks waned, the low rumble of gunfire that came from the eastern horizon grew louder by the day. In August 1944 the dreaded news arrived that Soviet troops had crossed the frontier and entered German territory. The war was drawing ever closer, and the day of reckoning was fast approaching for the people of East Prussia.

[1] G. I. Krivosheev, *Soviet Casualties and Combat Losses*, 1997

[2] The Kneiphof is now known as Kant Island.

[3] Breslau in Silesia was the largest city in Eastern Germany at that time.

[4] A Wehrkreis was an army area command. It was not a combat command but an administrative organisation. Germany was split into a number of Wehrkreis, each responsible for raising new forces and training and sending reinforcements to the armies in the field.

Chapter Two - The War in the East

The fighting that drew closer to Königsberg in the autumn of 1944 had begun three years earlier, in the summer of 1941. On June 22nd 1941 Adolf Hitler had sent his armies against the Soviet Union, hoping to destroy Bolshevism for once and for all. Until this point the Germans and Soviets had appeared as unlikely Allies to the rest of the world, Hitler's Germany and Stalin's Soviet Union having signed a Non-Aggression Pact in August 1939. The Pact was one of convenience as Hitler had sought to secure his eastern frontier before beginning the war against Poland, lest the Western Allies launch a counter strike across the Rhineland frontier. In the invasion of Poland which followed, the German Army cut the Polish forces to pieces, seemingly unstoppable columns of armour, supported by dive bombers and swarms of fighters, ushering in the age of Blitzkrieg. In the aftermath Stalin and Hitler carved Poland up between them. This was just the first territorial adjustment which the Pact had recognised. In the winter of 1939-40 Stalin launched his invasion of Finland, but this backfired badly as the small but hardy Finnish Army inflicted crippling defeats on the Soviet colossus. To the rest of the world the gigantic army which Stalin could deploy seemed rotten to the core, unable to beat even the tiniest of enemies. Stalin's forces eventually prevailed through sheer weight of numbers and fire power, forcing the Finns to a negotiated settlement. In the spring of 1940 Hitler began his extremely successful conquests in the West and in a matter of weeks had defeated the French Army, and sent the British scurrying back across the Channel to their island redoubt. Despite a defeat in the skies over southern England, to all intents and purposes the War in the West appeared to have been won by Germany in a surprisingly short time, and for just a few thousand casualties.

Hardly had the battle of France ended, than Hitler turned his attention to the East, to his planned war against the Bolshevik giant. In an address to his generals he talked of German eyes being turned to the east. Ever since publishing *Mein Kampf*, Hitler had spoken of launching an attack against the Soviet Union, the reason being the need for 'Living Space' for the German people, all at the expense of the Slavs, who were deemed sub-humans in comparison. On July 21st 1940 Hitler ordered the Commander in Chief of the Army, Walther von Brauchitsch, to conduct a study on the practicality of a campaign against the Soviet Union. Hitler initially wanted to launch the operation in the autumn of 1940 but at the urging of his generals he accepted this was simply not feasible. Instead the invasion was to begin no later than May 1941.

In the spring of 1941 German preparations raced ahead. More and more divisions were moved to the east, the excuse being that they were undertaking exercises away from the prying eyes of the Royal Air Force. German reconnaissance flights repeatedly violated Soviet air space and yet still Stalin refused to believe that Hitler would betray the Pact. On June 22nd 1941, a month delayed after an unexpected series of events in the Balkans had prompted the German invasions of Yugoslavia and Greece, the betrayal of the Pact was complete. Hitler launched his long planned invasion. The invasion force was truly colossal in scale. The Germans had assembled 3,206,000 soldiers with 3,330 panzers and 250 assault guns, supported by 2,840 aircraft and 7,100 artillery pieces, and supplied by 600,000 motor vehicles and 625,000 horses.[1] This armada crossed the frontier from the Baltic Sea in the north to the Black Sea in the south, beginning a campaign that would end four years later in the ruins of Berlin.

The German forces which invaded the Soviet Union were split into three main groups, two attacking north of the vast Pripet Marshes while the third attacked to the south, into the Ukraine. Army Groups North and Centre, situated north of the Pripet Marshes, launched their attacks in the direction of Leningrad and Smolensk respectively, while Army Group South headed for Kiev. The Soviet forces in the centre, comprising General Pavlov's West Front, suffered a devastating blow at the hands of Army Group Centre, hundreds of thousands of its troops being cut off by the fast moving German armour of Heinz Guderian's Second and Hermann Hoth's Third Panzer Groups. The Germans first destroyed the Soviet 3rd, 4th and 10th Armies in a gigantic encirclement battle around Minsk and then again wiped out a new set of Soviet armies in yet another cauldron battle near Smolensk. On the road to Leningrad matters were less spectacular. The difficulty of the heavily forested terrain, bisected by river lines and interspersed with lakes and marshes, meant the troops of Kuznetsov's North West Front were able to pull back in stages to the Rivers Dvina and Luga and eventually to the outskirts of Leningrad itself, avoiding a costly encirclement battle with Army Group North.

With Army Group Centre firmly established east of Smolensk, in August 1941 Hitler decided to move his armour away from the centre and on to the flanks. This decision met with considerable resistance from his generals, who urged that the push towards Moscow be continued. Hitler's mind was made up though. The new objectives to the north and to the south were the cities of Leningrad and Kiev. During September 1941 the seemingly unstoppable panzer divisions met with yet more successes in the south. In a spectacular encirclement operation Guderian's panzers pushed down from the Bryansk area to link up with Ewald von Kleist's First Panzer Group, which was advancing north from its bridgeheads across the River Dniepr. The two forces met up to the east of Kiev, trapping almost the entire force of the Soviet South Western Front. In the fighting that followed more than 660,000 Soviet soldiers were either killed or taken into captivity. The Kiev pocket was one of the worst defeats the Red Army was to suffer, and saw the South Western Front virtually wiped out, its commander, General Kirponos, being killed while trying to break out. On the road to Leningrad, Army Group North's Eighteenth Army and Fourth Panzer Group had to batter their way through line upon line of fortifications which the Soviets had constructed before the city. The fighting eventually reached the suburbs of Leningrad in September before a combination of General Zhukov's stubborn defence and Hitler's orders to remove the armour terminated the German effort. Leningrad, though surrounded, remained free. What followed next were two and a half years of unremitting horror. Battered daily by artillery fire and bombing attacks, the Germans tried to starve a city of three million into submission. The battles which followed essentially comprised Soviet efforts to break the siege and German counter moves to thwart them, and would see the deaths of a third of the city populace.

In the late autumn of 1941 the focus of operations returned once more to the Moscow axis. Hitler threw his over-extended and increasingly exhausted troops upon the Soviet capital in a desperate bid to take the city before the onset of the feared Russian winter. More spectacular victories followed as the West Front was carved up and destroyed around Vyazma, another 650,000 Red Army soldiers marching into German captivity. German troops then pressed on to Moscow but the early arrival of a particularly ferocious winter crippled forward movement. For the Germans it now seemed that the very country itself was at war with them. Unused to such terrible conditions, equipment and men both broke under the strain. Tanks and guns became inoperable and soldiers froze to death at their posts. Zhukov, brought back from Leningrad, husbanded the shattered Soviet armies before the capital, conserving his reserves in order to launch a devastating counter strike. Men who had grown up in these winter conditions inevitably fared better when called on to fight in the open than those who had not. For the Germans it was worse than it needed to be. Winter clothing had failed to arrive and so the men of the German Army froze to death in their summer uniforms, thousands being incapacitated through frostbite. Soviet equipment also performed better in the cold weather, the T-34 tank was built to operate in extreme conditions and seemed to glide over the snow on its wide tracks. In contrast the German Panzer III's and IV's sank up to their bellies, the oil frozen solid in their sumps and their guns useless for lack of winter lubricants. Zhukov launched a well planned and executed counter offensive at the beginning of December 1941, at the very moment the Germans were at the end of their strength. In the biting cold the Soviet forces surged forward into the flanks of Army Group Centre and came tantalisingly close to encircling the Germans east of Smolensk. At the front the German generals made desperate calls for permission to fall back to the west but Hitler obstinately refused, instead ordering the troops to stand fast. Hitler's order in no small part helped stop the rot at the front. The danger of the whole line being overrun was averted but this success brought with it the seeds of the German defeats in the defensive battles of 1943-45. Hitler increasingly became convinced that sanctioning any retreat would lead to inevitable defeat, and began to believe that he above any other knew better than the officers of the General Staff. Stalin's over confidence also played its part in the survival of the German forces. His expectation that his armies could throw the Germans out of Soviet territory led to a series of offensives in the north, centre and south in January 1942, all of which ultimately failed as the thinly spread Soviet troops lacked the strength or equipment to break through the equally thinly spread Germans. Throughout the first six months of the campaign Stalin had refused to allow any retreats, and had sacked and in some instances executed unsuccessful generals mercilessly. His rigidity consigned hundreds of thousands of Soviet soldiers to German captivity, from which more than 3.5 million would never return, some two-thirds of those captured. It would take a brush with disaster along the banks of the River Volga for Stalin to change his approach.

During the spring of 1942 both combatants had time to recover their strength and rebuild their shattered armies. Both sides prepared to launch major new offensives in the summer that would knock their enemy out of the war once and for all. Hitler focused his efforts on the south, stripping Army Groups North and Centre in order to reinforce Army Group South, which was soon split into Army Groups A and B so that it could take on two objectives. The German plan was to push Army Group B to the River Don, encircling the Soviet armies in great cauldron battles in the bend of the river. Once this had been achieved the German armies would advance to the Volga and sever the vital river traffic with Moscow, and also capture the industrial city of Stalingrad which lay on the western bank of the river. Once this had been achieved, Army Group A would drive into the Caucasus to secure control of the vast oilfields of Baku and Grozny. Deception measures would ensure that the Soviets thought the German effort would be in the centre against Moscow.

Figure 5 - The T-34/76 tank. Armed with a 76.2mm main gun it cane as a great shock to the Germans in the summer of 1941.

Stalin and his generals had their own plans. Strong defensive positions were built up before Moscow but it was in the south that Stalin also saw the possibility of renewing the offensive. The attacks in the Ukraine in the winter of 1941-42 had seen the Soviet armies push a deep salient into the German lines south of Kharkov. Timoshenko, supreme commander of the Soviet South West and South Fronts which were deployed in the eastern Ukraine, proposed an offensive which would encircle the Germans at Kharkov and then drive them back across the Dniepr. In May 1942, while the Germans were still finalising preparations for their attack, Timoshenko launched his offensive. Initially the Soviets drove an even deeper bulge into the German positions, carving out a larger salient south of Kharkov, although their northern pincer nearer to the city was halted virtually on its start lines. Worse was to come though as within days the Germans unleashed their own counter-offensive and trapped the Soviet forces in another gigantic pocket. Despite being in danger of annihilation, Stalin obstinately refused to let his armies retreat, condemning another 170,000 men to death or captivity.

The debacle at Izyum was followed in June and July by the opening of the German offensive towards the Rivers Don and Volga. Shortly after the offensive began Hitler began to meddle in the operations of the attacking forces. First he diverted the panzers, which were driving quickly into the Don bend, for no purpose, then issued orders for both Stalingrad and the Caucasus to be conquered at the same time. The long and bitter attrition battle for Stalingrad changed the course of the war on the Eastern Front. From August 1942 General Paulus' Sixth Army bled itself white against the formidable Soviet 62nd Army under the command of General Chuikov. In September Zhukov and Vasilevsky, who we shall learn more of later, came up with a plan to destroy the Sixth Army in a great encirclement battle. As winter approached the Red Army concentrated its reserves. The offensive was aimed at the weaker Romanian armies which were deployed on either flank of the German Sixth Army. Three months of bitter street fighting sapped the strength of the German force until in November 1942, as the Russian winter took hold with a vengeance; the Red Army launched its massive and well planned counter offensive. The ambitious assault successfully caught the Germans in a pincer movement, trapping Paulus' army and part of Hoth's Fourth Panzer Army in the ruins of the city and on the Steppe to the west. In the days that followed the Soviet success Paulus' vacillation meant the army failed to make a decisive move to break out to the west, condemning it to a long slow death in encirclement. Hitler now took on the role Stalin had in 1941 and 1942, and refused to grant Paulus' repeated requests to break out. Despite bombastic promises by Göring that the Sixth Army would be supplied by his air force, the inadequate air lift that followed, hindered by the terrible winter conditions and facing concentrated Soviet anti-aircraft defences, saw the army starved and bereft of vital supplies. An attempt by Field Marshal Manstein to break through to the Sixth Army from outside was also repulsed after hard fighting. Manstein, now commanding the newly formed Army Group Don, had attempted to punch his way through from the south west, via Kotelnikovo rather than by the shorter route from the River Chir. By Christmas 1942 it was clear that Manstein's attack had failed, a Soviet counter attack throwing the Germans back to their start lines. The fate of the Sixth Army was sealed. New Soviet offensives along the Don then threatened to create a crisis of truly staggering proportions. As Army Group Don was pushed back towards the Dniepr, Army Group A, still deep in the Caucasus, was in danger of isolation. A hasty retreat followed in the New Year, while the Soviet armies surrounding Stalingrad threw the Germans back across the steppe and into the city. Resistance from inside the pocket was considerably greater than expected, the Soviet High Command had not realised just how great their success had been. The Stavka had conservatively estimated it had surrounded 75,000 Germans, maybe 100,000 at the most. In actual fact some 250,000 had been trapped. By the end of January 1943 the 90,000 weakened and sick survivors of Paulus' once powerful army surrendered in the frozen ruins of the city. The commander and his men marched into captivity, much to the disgust of Hitler who had promoted Paulus to Field Marshal just days before in the expectation that he would kill himself to avoid capture.

The defeat at Stalingrad saw the direction of the war in the East changed for good. No longer could the Germans expect to sweep the Red Army aside as it pleased. In growing numbers and with increasing confidence, armed with thousands of tanks, artillery pieces and aircraft, the Red Army began the long struggle to throw the Germans out of their territory and defeat them on their own ground. After the victory at Stalingrad, Stalin would take a more relaxed approach with his generals, directing in broad strokes rather than interfering in the minutiae of battle. Stalin and his generals grew in confidence with each new victory; the high level co-ordination of the Front's becoming more and more efficient with every new attack. Groups of Fronts were overseen by Stavka[2] coordinators, men like Zhukov and Vasilevsky, and finally in the closing days of the war, Stalin himself.

Figure 6 - Aleksandr Vasilevsky

Aleksandr Mikhailovich Vasilevsky would play a major part in the battles in East Prussia. As a young junior officer in the Red Army he had taken part in the Russo-Polish War and the Civil War of the 1920's before serving in the Training Directorate from 1931. Here he established important connections with powerful men in the regime, coming to the notice of Voroshilov and Shaposhnikov. He was one of the officers who came through the 1937 Purge unscathed, attending the General Staff Academy from 1937 onwards. After graduating he was promoted to the General Staff in October 1937. Following the German invasion of June 1941 he was promoted again, this time being appointed commander of the Operations Directorate. He had previously served as deputy in this department. Together with Zhukov he helped control the co-ordination of the Soviet armies in the defence of Moscow in October 1941, during which time he was promoted to Lieutenant General. Vasilevsky next helped oversee the counter offensive that threw the German forces back from the city. By April 1942 he was acting Chief of the General Staff due to the failing health of the incumbent Marshal Shaposhnikov, and was promoted to Colonel General. In June 1942 Vasilevsky formally took over as Chief of the General Staff, also holding his post as Chief of Operations until November of the same year. Vasilevsky's role in the defeat of the Germans at Stalingrad was crucial; from the planning stages alongside Zhukov, to the coordination of the offensives which rippled along the Don and into the Donbas. Vasilevsky was promoted to Marshal of the Soviet Union in February 1943. As Stavka representative he coordinated the actions of the Voronezh and Steppe Fronts during the Battle of Kursk in July 1943, and of the Fronts that went on the offensive through the Ukraine in the following months. During 1944 he helped control the strategic actions of the 1st Baltic and 3rd Belorussian Fronts during Operation Bagration before going on to do the same with the three Baltic Fronts as they pushed into the Estonia, Latvia and Lithuania.

On the German side of the lines matters deteriorated with each new defeat. Following Stalingrad Hitler took more and more control over events at the front, refusing to allow his commanders freedom of movement which a defensive war against an opponent with superior material and manpower resources demanded. Like Stalin in the early days, he sacked generals who he considered had failed him and appointed men who displayed Party loyalty and a will and faith in final victory in their place.

Following Stalingrad, Manstein was able to rescue the German southern wing from complete collapse in the spring of 1943 as the Red Army once again over-reached itself. A sharp counter attack saw Kharkov recovered by the Germans after a bitter battle for the city just weeks before. The ensuing thaw brought movement in the Ukraine to an end and left a threatening bulge in the German line, centred on the small Ukrainian town of Kursk. The stage seemed set for the next set piece battle on the Eastern Front. Thus far the Soviets had always attempted to attack first whenever the opportunity showed itself but on this occasion Stalin and the High Command held their nerve and made preparations to absorb the expected German attack before launching an offensive of their own. Line upon line of defensive positions were constructed by the Soviets, while reinforcements were grouped to the rear as a strategic reserve, ready to pounce once the Germans had exhausted themselves. For the Germans the attack was a worrying prospect. Manstein, commanding Army Group South, believed the attack could succeed if it was carried out without delay but unfortunately this could not be done. Hitler continually delayed the start of the offensive while more armoured forces were brought up. The Panther tank, which would go on to be a highly effective combat vehicle, was rushed into service for the battle without its teething troubles being ironed out. As May and June passed by with each side making their preparations, in the West the German forces in North Africa met their end, surrendering in Tunisia with a loss that exceeded that of Stalingrad. At the start of July the Germans were ready and so began the greatest tank battle in the world to that point. The resulting Battle of Kursk saw the Soviets wear down the German attacks from the north and south. After a week and a half of bitter fighting Hitler called off the attack, the excuse being the requirement to release forces to the west, where the Allies had launched their invasion of Sicily. The Germans believed the Soviet forces were as exhausted as they and were surprised when the Red Army delivered a counter blow of its own that began the long drive west to throw the Germans out of Russian territory for good. The hard and costly Soviet advance throughout the latter months of 1943 saw the Germans pushed back across the River Dniepr from Smolensk to the Black Sea, barely managing to prevent a total collapse of the southern wing. With the coming of winter the Soviet attacks did not stop but continued to roll on to the west. Kiev was recovered and the Ukraine all but cleared of German troops by the end of the year. While the German southern wing was bent further and further back, to the north, the siege of Leningrad which had cost the lives of a million of the city's inhabitants, was broken in January 1944. In a well planned and executed offensive, the German Eighteenth and Sixteenth Armies were shunted back to the frontiers of the Baltic States. In April 1944, on the extreme southern end of the front the German Seventeenth Army, trapped in the Crimean peninsula, was destroyed by an overwhelming Soviet attack.

These defeats in both the north and south left a bulge in the centre of the line in Belorussia, where Army Group Centre stood on the defensive. Stalin and the Stavka next turned their attention to this group of German forces. Operation Bagration was the codename for the Soviet attack whose aim was nothing less than the complete destruction of the German army group and liberation of the last great chunk of Soviet territory still in German hands. The offensive was launched in June 1944, just weeks after the Allied invasion of France and almost three years to the day since the Germans had begun their own invasion of the Soviet Union. A colossal force of 2,500,000 Soviet soldiers, supported by 5,300 aircraft, 5,200 tanks and 31,000 artillery pieces, sliced through the formations of the German Army Group Centre. Beginning with probing attacks on June 22nd, the main offensive began the following day and within a few days saw the LIII Corps of Colonel-General Georg-Hans Reinhardt's Third Panzer Army isolated and destroyed around Vitebsk while the XXXV Corps and XXXXI Panzer Corps of the Ninth Army were wiped out around Bobruisk. Between these two attacks lay the German Fourth Army, which was drive back by the 2nd and 3rd Belorussian Fronts and, at the beginning of July, was encircled east of Minsk. In just a few days the Soviet forces had achieved a remarkable victory. Between June 22nd and July 4th some 300,000 German soldiers were killed, wounded or captured, a force of twenty-five divisions wiped off the German order of battle. In the ensuing follow up offensives the Germans lost another 100,000 or more troops as they were pushed back into the Baltic States and Poland.

Shortly after the defeat of the German forces in Belorussia, Colonel Count von Stauffenberg made his attempt to kill Hitler. The attempt failed but had terrible effects on the relationship between Hitler and his generals. Hitler became increasingly paranoid and his distrust of the army plumbed new depths. As Heinz Guderian, the Chief of the Army General Staff from July 1944 until early 1945, related after the war:

> [Hitler] *quickly recovered from these physical effects [of the assassination attempt]. His already existing malady, plain for all to see in the trembling of his left hand and left leg, had no connection with the attempt on his life. But more important than the physical were the moral effects...the deep distrust he already felt for mankind in general, and for the General Staff Corps in particular, now became profound hatred....He often lied without hesitation, and assumed that others lied to him....He frequently lost all self-control and his language grew increasingly violent.*[3]

The success of Operation Bagration led directly to further Soviet operations in the Baltic States and Poland, operations which would lead to the battles that brought Soviet troops to the very frontier of East Prussia. It is to these battles that we shall now turn.

[1] Taylor, *Barbarossa to Berlin: Vol. 1*, p27

[2] The Stavka was the main command of the Soviet Supreme Command, responsible for the military and exercised control of planning and operations.

[3] Guderian, *Panzer Leader*, p342

Chapter Three - The Frontier Battles

The disaster in Belorussia had serious repercussions for the German forces in Lithuania, Latvia and Estonia. The collapse of the Third Panzer Army had left Army Group North's right wing, comprising the Sixteenth Army, hanging open around Polotsk. Attacks by General Ivan Kristoforovich Bagramyan's 1st Baltic Front had secured control of Polotsk at the beginning of July but then had met increasingly strong resistance as the Sixteenth Army brought more forces onto its southern flank in order to blunt the Soviet thrust. The Sixteenth Army then came under renewed attack as the Soviet armies strove to complete yet another grand encirclement by pushing northwest towards Riga, the Stavka plan being nothing less than to isolate the whole of Army Group North in Latvia and Estonia. The German flank was pushed ever further back as the Soviets extended their attacks until at the end of July 1944 the leading elements of Bagramyan's 1st Baltic Front reached the Gulf of Riga to the west of the city. The success that Bagramyan had achieved was only temporary however, as Colonel-General Ferdinand Schörner, commanding Army Group North, hastily transferred more divisions from his left wing in Estonia to the right flank near Riga. While the battle on the road to Riga intensified, other elements of the 1st Baltic Front pushed to the west, liberating Siauliai in central Lithuania as it drove the remnants of the Third Panzer Army back.

At the beginning of August the Third Panzer Army had been partially reformed and given a new commander[1]. It concentrated its forces to the north and west of Siauliai in an effort to punch a corridor through to Army Group North and also to recapture Siauliai. The new commanding officer was Colonel-General Erhard Raus. He had an excellent pedigree as a commander of armoured troops.

Figure 7 - Erhard Raus

An Austrian by birth, Raus had commanded a motorised brigade of 6th Panzer Division in 1941 and with this division led a battle group that had pushed towards Leningrad during the opening phase of Operation Barbarossa. He was appointed commander of the 6th Panzer in September 1941 and remained on the Eastern Front with this division until April 1942, when he and his men went to France for a period of rest and to take in drafts of replacements and new equipment. The disaster at Stalingrad brought Raus and his division back to Russia in November 1942. After hard fighting during the ultimately unsuccessful relief attack towards the Sixth Army, and in the subsequent retreat, the division both suffered and inflicted heavy losses. In early 1943, when the German southern wing lay in tatters, Raus took command of a composite corps formed from the remnants of a number of divisions. This formation, known as Corps Raus, fought bitter battles in the Donets Basin against the advancing Soviet armies who were trying desperately to cut off Army Group Don. On the conclusion of these battles, and following Manstein's well planned counter attack around Kharkov in the spring of 1943, Raus was involved in the battle of Kursk in the summer of that year. His corps suffered severe casualties and then conducted a difficult retreat through the Ukraine during the autumn. His skilful leadership saw him promoted to command of the Fourth Panzer Army in November 1943. He was instrumental in the planning and execution of the successful German counter attack at Zhitomir, west of Kiev, at the end of the year. Command of the First Panzer Army and Third Panzer Army followed later in 1944, Raus taking command of the latter on August 16th, the day after his promotion to Colonel General.

On taking command of the Third Panzer Army Raus urged that any counter attack to relieve Army Group North be carried out close to Riga so that the distance the armour had to cover was as short as possible. This would have the dual advantage of demanding the stockpiling of less fuel for the mobile troops and also decrease the likelihood of a Soviet counter stroke. Raus' commander, Colonel-General Reinhardt, who had been promoted from command of Third Panzer Army to that of Army Group Centre[2], argued in Raus' support but Hitler refused to listen to their sensible arguments and insisted that the attack be launched in both the north toward Jelgava, and the south toward Siauliai.

The counter attack began on August 16th with General Otto von Knobelsdorf's XXXX Panzer Corps attacking from the south, from the Kelmy area, with the aim of recovering Siauliai, and General Dietrich von Saucken's XXXIX Panzer Corps beginning its assault from the north toward Jelgava in order to rejoin the main combat front with Army Group North while also destroying the Soviet forces which had penetrated close to Riga. By August 18th the XXXIX Panzer Corps had made contact with the Sixteenth Army at Tukums and thus reopened the lines of communications between the two forces. More than a week of heavy fighting followed but the Germans failed in their efforts to recover

Siauliai and destroy the Soviet pincer which continued to pose a threat to Riga.

Figure 8 - Georg-Hans Reinhardt

This setback in Latvia prompted the Stavka to pause and regroup its forces. Reinforcements were sent to the northern group of fronts and a new plan developed which would see the Leningrad Front, together with the 2nd and 3rd Baltic Fronts, pin the Eighteenth Army frontally while General Ivan Bagramyan's 1st Baltic Front drove through the narrow German corridor near Tukums, isolating the Germans and completing the capture of Riga.

THE BATTLE OF KÖNIGSBERG

Figure 9 - Ivan Bagramyan, picture taken after the war

Bagramyan was an ideal commander for such an operation. A seasoned veteran of the campaigns against the Germans, he was an aggressive and talented general. Having survived Stalin's Purge of the Red Army in the late 1930's, he had a rough time in the early months of the invasion. At the opening of the attack he served as deputy Chief of Staff of the South West Front under Kirponos and was involved in the disastrous Kiev encirclement, barely escaping from the pocket when his commander was killed. Bagramyan then served as Chief of Staff of the South West Theatre under Timoshenko from April 1942. He was involved in the planning of the catastrophic Izyum offensive in May 1942 and following its failure was scapegoated by Stalin, being demoted to Chief of Staff of the 28th Army. At his own request, Bagramyan was transferred from his staff role to a front line command. In July 1942 he took over as commander of the 16th Army, replacing Konstantin Rokossovsky who had moved on to command the Bryansk Front. His command of the 16th Army proved extremely successful, his men being rewarded by having their formation elevated to Guards[3] status in April 1943. The 16th was redesignated the 11th Guards Army. Bagramyan was heavily involved in the fighting in the Orel salient following the Battle of Kursk in the summer of 1943. In October 1943 the 11th Guards were transferred north, to join the 2nd Baltic Front fighting on the frontiers of the Baltic States. In November 1943 Bagramyan was promoted to General and appointed to command the 1st Baltic Front, which was deployed south of the 2nd Baltic. Bagramyan led his 1st Baltic Front in the bitter battles around Vitebsk during the winter of 1943-1944 before then preparing to take on his part in Operation Bagration in the summer of 1944. His victories during Bagration brought his front deep into the Baltic States, where we will now return.

The new Soviet offensive against Riga began in the middle of September 1944, the attack rippling along a 300-mile front and saw the commitment of 900,000 troops, 3,000 tanks, 17,000 artillery pieces and 2,600 aircraft. Bagramyan's primary objective was the capture of the Latvian capital and to achieve this, his front had taken the lion's share of the reinforcements. The 1st Baltic deployed 1,300 of the 3,000 tanks that had been amassed for the offensive. Bagramyan made slow but steady progress during the first two days of the offensive, advancing ten miles from his start lines, and closing to within twenty-five miles of Riga by September 16th. To the north Soviet progress was even slower. With rigid frontal attacks being made against the entrenched Germans, the advance was very costly. Despite continuous attacks the Germans were able to pull the bulk of the Eighteenth Army back upon Riga, avoiding encirclement to the east of the city. Hitler finally gave permission on the 16th for Schörner to abandon Estonia and much of Latvia in order to reinforce the defensive positions around the city. The next day the 1st Baltic Front was struck unexpectedly in its left flank by yet another counter attack by the Third Panzer Army. This latest

German assault saw the Germans renew their earlier attacks around Siauliai. By September 18th the XXXIX Panzer Corps had managed to push a ten mile salient into Bagramyan's flank but was then itself hampered by the demand that it send reinforcements to Army Group North. Two days later Raus' force was transferred from Army Group Centre to Schörner's Army Group North so that it could better co-ordinate its actions. Unfortunately it was clear that the panzer army lacked the strength to halt the Soviet attacks. Nevertheless, Raus' attacks gave Schörner the breathing space he needed to pull the Eighteenth Army back through Riga, effectively negating the entire Soviet plan to isolate Army Group North east of the city. The Stavka also realised this and on September 24th it called off the offensive. Bagramyan's men were by that time just ten miles from Riga, but they simply could not get through the last stretch of formidable German defences. Yet again the Stavka issued new orders which changed the whole axis of the offensive. Bagramyan's front was to redeploy so that its major thrust was made to the west, isolating the Germans in the Courland region of Latvia in order to separate Army Group North from the rest of the German forces in the east.

The Stavka issued revised orders to the 1st Baltic Front within days of the offensive against Riga being halted. Bagramyan had much to do, moving his armies along the heavily used and muddy roads of Latvia and Lithuania so that the attack could be renewed from around Siauliai. By concentrating their main forces in the Baltic on the southern wing, the Soviets would push west towards the Baltic coast near Memel. A breakthrough here would not only isolate Army Group North, but also prevent the Germans from establishing a line of defence along the East Prussian frontier. During the last week of September and first few days of October Bagramyan's men were hard at work, hundreds of vehicles traversing the forest roads to redeploy into the Siauliai area. To the north and south of the town the 1st Baltic Front amassed four armies in its first echelon and another two in the second. Yet another two were deployed on the northern flank of the offensive to harry the Germans back into Courland.

The general plan called for the main attack to strike west toward the Baltic coast, fanning out to the northwest, in order to drive into the deep flank of Army Group North, and south west in order to push Army Group Centre back into East Prussia from the north. The first echelon of the breakthrough attack would be conducted by the Lieutenant-General Petr Malyshev's 4th Shock Army, with four rifle corps deployed on the northern flank of the offensive, Colonel-General Ivan Mikhailovich Chistyakov's 6th Guards Army with three guards rifle and one regular rifle corps and General Afanasii Pavlantevich Beloborodov's 43rd Army, also with four rifle corps which were in the centre, and Colonel-General Porfirii Grigorevich Chanchibadze's 2nd Guards Army with four rifle corps and the support of Lieutenant-General Vasily Vasilevich Butkov's 1st Tank Corps on the southern flank. General Yakov Grigorevich Kreizer's 51st and Colonel-General Vasily Timofeevich Volsky's 5th Guards Tank Armies were held in the second echelon, ready to exploit any breach of the German positions. Chistyakov's 6th Guards was to attack from the area between Kurseinai and Siauliai and would push through Tryskiai to then head northwest in order to reach the coast at Libau. To the south, Beloborodov's 43rd Army would push directly west from Siauliai, aiming to reach the Baltic coast near Memel. Beloborodov would later play a major role in the battle for Königsberg. At the beginning of the Russo-German War he had served as a rifle division commander before taking command of the 5th Rifle Corps and 2nd Guards Rifle Corps. He was appointed commander of the 43rd Army in May 1944 and with this force took part in Operation Bagration. The 43rd had been formed in July 1941, in the opening weeks of the German offensive into Russia and had fought on the Moscow axis from autumn 1941 through to 1943 before advancing into Belorussia in 1944. On the southern wing of the offensive, Chanchibadze's 2nd Guards Army, with Butkov's 1st Tank Corps operating in the lead, would drive south west through Kelmy and toward the mouth of the River Niemen and, further inland, to Tilsit.

Once a breakthrough had been achieved by the rifle armies, Volsky's 5th Guards Tank Army would be committed from the second echelon to operate through the lines of either the 6th Guards or 43rd Army. It was anticipated that the tank army enter the battle during the first day of the offensive, and by the end of the second day should be sixty miles into the German rear areas. Its objective was to reach the coast at Palanga and Memel. Kreizer's 51st Army would also enter the battle as part of the second wave, reinforcing the attack northward into the deep flank of Army Group North. Bagramyan's attack would be supported by the aircraft of Lieutenant-General Nikolai Filippovich Papivin's 3rd Air Army. It was to concentrate on operational support of the ground forces while also preventing the Luftwaffe from interfering in the course of the battle.

Supporting the southern wing of the assault was Lieutenant-General Ivan Ilych Lyudnikov's 39th Army, the most northerly unit of Chernyakhovsky's neighbouring 3rd Belorussian Front. The 39th was situated between the town of Rasieniai and the River Niemen. Lyudnikov would also aim to reach the River Niemen at Tilsit, bringing Soviet forces across the East Prussian frontier to conquer the Memelland region. Like Beloborodov, Lyudnikov had also held a number of divisional commands during the early part of the war until being appointed commander of 25th Rifle Corps in 1943. He was made commander of 39th Army in 1944.

Marshal Vasilevsky was to co-ordinate the actions of the Baltic Fronts for the Stavka. Since the dark days of 1941 the senior commanders of the Red Army had learned how to handle their considerable forces with skill, flexibility and imagination. Operational planning and its delivery, that peculiarly Soviet concept known as the *operational art*, was undertaken on a grand scale and was well executed. At the tactical level, the junior commanders and their troops, while inordinately brave, remained rigid in their approach to battle. As Major-General von Mellenthin, who experienced battle against both the Red Army and Western Allies, wrote after the war:

> ...the higher commanders and staffs learned much from the Germans and from their own experience. They became

adaptable, energetic, and ready to take decisions...The junior officers, and many among the middle command group were still clumsy and unable to take decisions; because of draconian discipline they were afraid of shouldering responsibility. Purely rigid training squeezed the lower commanders into the vice of manuals and regulations, and robbed them of the initiative and originality which are vital to a good tactician.[4]

Often heavily outnumbered German units were able to inflict crippling losses on attacking Soviet formations. With sufficient ammunition the Germans would repel wave after wave of attacks. Soviet troops made this mistake right to the very end of the war, attacking the same point, time and time again until either the enemy was overrun, or the supply of replacements for the attacking units ran out. This desire to simply batter the enemy down with repeated frontal assaults remained a key factor in the approach of the infantry forces. Such tactics brought with them staggeringly high casualties, but the Soviets accepted such losses as a necessary part of winning the war. Severe casualties could not be absorbed for ever though, even by a nation with such seemingly inexhaustible supplies of manpower as the Soviet Union. By 1944 the problem of finding replacements was growing acute. Boys in their teens were enrolled into the army, while it also became common practice for the advancing units at the front to press newly liberated civilians and recently released prisoners of war into their ranks. These men either lacked military experience or were weak from their long periods of ill treatment at the hands of the Nazis, but were eager for revenge. Often without even a new uniform, they were handed a weapon and integrated into the rapidly advancing armies. The simple fact remained though, that despite its brutality and the lack of sophistication in its methods, the Red Army was hammering the German Army into the ground.

The tough Soviet infantryman who was lucky enough to have survived until 1944 had fought his way across hundreds of miles of devastated territory. Many had seen their families killed or taken away to slave labour in Germany and understandably thirsted for a chance to give the Germans a taste of their own medicine. Discipline among the rank and file was draconian, with the slightest infringement of the military rules bringing on severe punishment. Despite their combat experience Soviet troops could still prove unpredictable, fighting tenaciously one day and retreating under the slightest of pressure the next. With ample supplies and munitions the Soviet soldiers were truly formidable. As the Germans learned to their cost during many encounters, if Soviet troops were able to gain a bridgehead, unless it could be destroyed immediately it would be reinforced and strengthened to a point where it could no longer be removed. In defence he was extremely capable, fighting stubbornly even though he had been surrounded and, according to Western standards, should by rights have surrendered. Now on the offensive across the whole length of the front, the infantry marched across Europe much as their forebears had in the wars against Napoleon. Columns of ragged men, with mismatched and threadbare uniforms pushed continually westward, forcing back the once proud divisions of the Wehrmacht. Particularly successful army units, whether infantry or armoured, could be elevated to Guards status. These formations received a higher level of pay and were generally better equipped, looking more like the modern mechanised army that the Red Army was developing into. Rifle divisions, both regular and Guards, generally comprised three rifle regiments, each of three battalions, supported by an artillery regiment and anti-tank battalion, giving them a significant level of firepower and protection against German armoured attacks. Theoretical strength was around 9,600 men although often they would number 6-7,000, sometimes, after hard fighting, as few as 3000, but many of these men were armed with automatic weapons, which were produced in their hundreds of thousands by Soviet industry. The lavish supply of the tough and versatile American Studebaker trucks did much to put the Red Army on wheels, increasing the success of their offensives. The trucks ensured that supplies could be brought forward in sufficient quantities to keep an offensive moving. Without the thousands of trucks the US shipped to the Soviets, the great offensives of 1944 would have been a great deal less spectacular.

Soviet armoured forces had been transformed since the early days of the war when they had been destroyed piecemeal by German attacks. The Soviets began to experiment with larger armoured formations during 1942 but it was not until the Stalingrad offensive that they really learned to use them to their advantage. Initially the armour suffered from the same failures as the infantry, an inflexibility which led the rigid attacks against pre-determined objectives. As the tank force developed, and radios began to be fitted to all vehicles rather than just command ones, the leadership of the armoured corps, and armies became significantly more flexible. Soviet tank commanders gradually learned to bypass points of resistance rather than attack them head on, learning that they could spread disorder in the enemy rear areas and gain far deeper penetrations with fewer casualties. By 1944 Soviet armour was generally grouped into tank armies, although separate tank brigades and tank corps also operated in support of the infantry forces. Tank corps, numbering 11,000 men with over 200 tanks and 1,600 vehicles, generally comprised three tank brigades and a motorised rifle brigade of three battalions, together with self propelled artillery and self propelled anti-tank regiments plus a mortar regiment and a battalion of the feared Katyusha rocket launchers. Tactically, Soviet tank troops were generally inferior to their German counterparts but sheer numbers would often win the day. The ability of the Red Army to return damaged vehicles to combat, together with the prodigious numbers of new vehicles rolling off the production lines each month, meant the Germans were never able to make a serious inroad into the numerical advantage of their enemy. Soviet equipment was also robust when compared with the highly engineered German vehicles. The truly outstanding T-34 was the mainstay of the tank units. Entering service with the Red Army in 1940, this vehicle had come as a major shock to the Germans when they encountered it in the summer of 1941. With its revolutionary sloped armour offering excellent protection, wide tracks, Christie suspension and powerful engine, gave great cross country performance

THE BATTLE OF KÖNIGSBERG

Figure 10 - The T34/85 with 85mm main gun and larger turret. It was produced in prodigous numbers

Figure 11 - The IS-II Stalin tank with its massive 122mm main gun

and a 76mm, later 85mm, main gun, meant it could outfight all of the early generation German tanks. The up gunned T-34/85, which started to enter service from early 1944, had an improved interior layout with larger turret and offered the Soviet tank troops at least a fighting chance against the formidable German Panther and Tiger models. The T-34 was produced in prodigious numbers, some 35,000 earlier model T-34's and 29,000 T-34/85's being manufactured between June 1941 and May 1945. Soviet losses were also considerable though, the loss of 13,000 tanks in combat during 1943 and a further 10,000 in 1944 meant production at this level was a necessity to both replace battlefield losses and increase the size of the tank arm. Such heavy losses in vehicles also had a telling effect on the personnel required to man them. As the war progressed the Red Army would make increasing use of women to fulfil the radio operator role.

To take on the heavier German tanks the Soviets introduced the IS-II Stalin tank. Weighing in at forty-six tons it was larger in size to the T-34 but also sported a considerably bigger 122mm main gun. This weapon, which fired a heavy round, gave it the punch to knock out the Panther and Tiger tanks, even the Tiger II which was encountered during the final months of the war.

The God of all Soviet weapons was their artillery. Soviet industry produced artillery pieces in prodigious numbers, in excess of 510,000 being produced between 1939 and 1945.[5] With rifle, tank and mechanised units all having their own organic artillery support, for offensive operations the High Command would often make available special divisions and corps of artillery. An artillery division of 9,700 men could add another 100 heavy mortars and 180 artillery pieces, with calibres ranging from 76mm up to 152mm, to the weight of an attack. The Katyusha rocket launcher was another highly effective area bombardment weapon used widely by the Red Army. Often mounted on a truck chassis for mobility, it consisted generally of two rails of rockets, numbering up to 48 devices. The rockets were launched in salvoes, normally a battery of four trucks discharging their rockets within a ten second period. Their resultant fire dropped over four tons of high explosive across a wide but concentrated area, their explosive power being enough to plough up most defensive positions. The characteristic whine of the rocket as it was launched prompted the Germans to nickname the weapon the Stalin Organ, and proved as frightening to the German infantryman, both in sound and result, as the sirens of a Stuka did to the Allied civilians and soldiers during the early days of the Blitzkrieg.

Figure 12- Katyusha rockets being launched from the back of trucks.

By the latter period of the war Soviet offensives often took a very similar pattern. In simplistic terms a large scale Soviet operation would begin a few days before the main offensive was to start with reconnaissance in force by infantry and armour units. Normally of battalion size, the purpose of these attacks was to search out weak spots in the German defences and gain control of locally important positions. Depending on the success of the reconnaissance attacks the main assault that would follow would be preceded by a powerful artillery barrage, generally lasting from one to three hours. Soviet artillery control became very sophisticated as their inventory developed. Rolling barrages and box barrages among other forms of targeted fire enabled the Soviets to isolate areas of the battlefield from enemy interference. An opening barrage would usually concentrate on the German front line positions, striking trenches, artillery positions and headquarters and communications facilities. Again we can turn to Mellenthin for his comments on the use of Soviet artillery:

> For large scale attacks the Russians normally had 200 guns on every half-mile of front. If thought necessary the number was increased to 300 but never went below 150 guns. The preliminary bombardment usually lasted two hours, and their gunners had a standing order to fire off the ammunition ration for one to one and a half days during that period. Another day's ration was held ready for the first phase of the assault, and ammunition reserves were kept further back. Under such concentrated fire the thin German lines were usually ploughed upside down in a very short time. Heavy weapons, in particular antitank guns, were soon shot to bits, however carefully they were sited and however well they were dug in.[6]

The barrage would then generally switch to rolling fire in support of the infantry and armour attacks. If a breakthrough was not achieved with the first attack the Soviet forces would often repeat the process until they managed to overrun the German positions, or ran out of resources to continue their attacks. When a breakthrough had been achieved the main concentration of armoured forces, the tank armies or tank corps, would be pushed through to begin the exploitation phase of the battle. Speed was essential to keep the enemy off balance and envelopment manoeuvres were used to isolate and then destroy pockets of German resistance. The exploitation phase would normally continue until the Soviet spearheads had used up their supplies or their losses had become so great their striking power had been blunted.

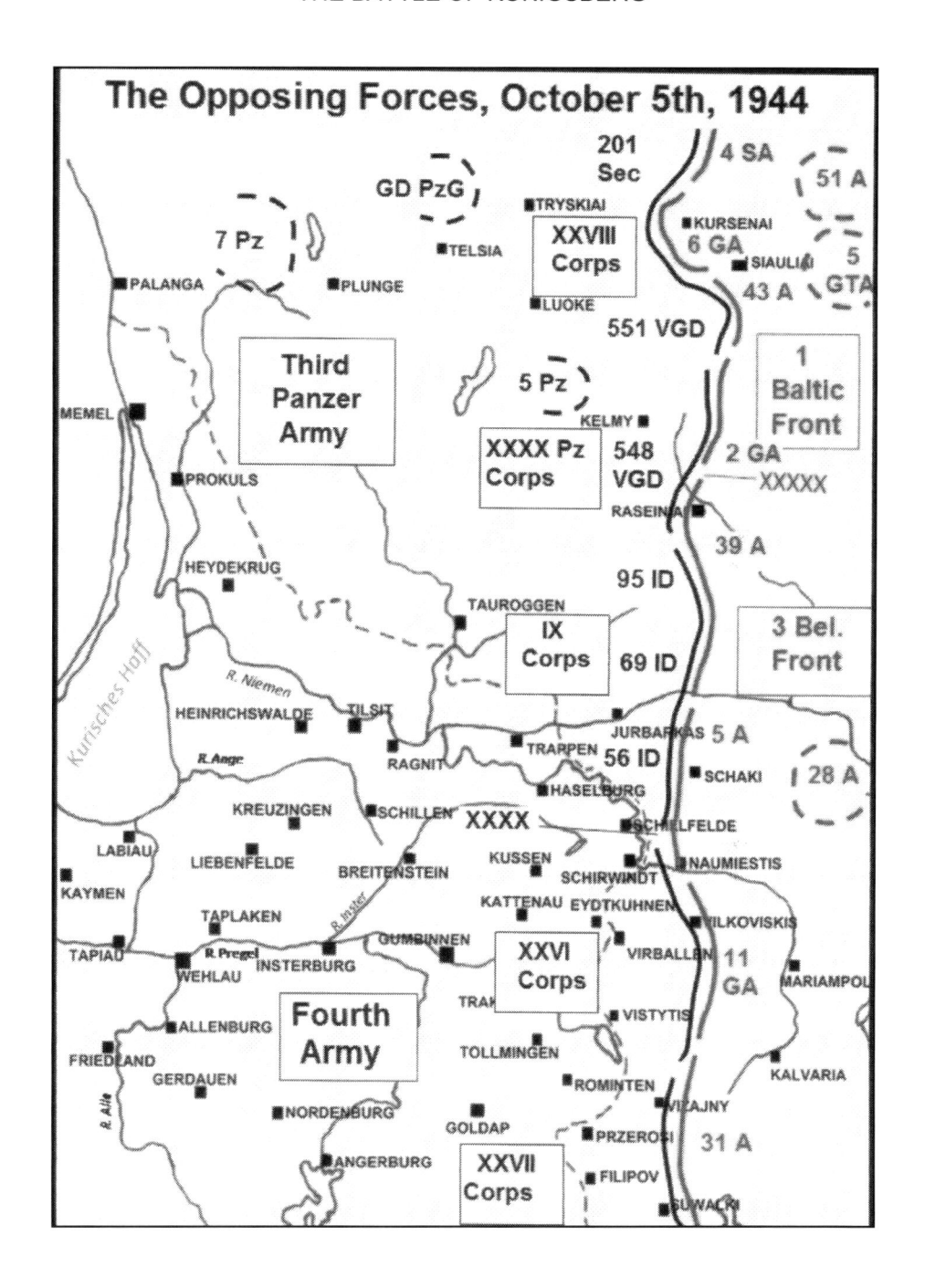

THE BATTLE OF KÖNIGSBERG

The Soviet air armies had become an extremely effective weapon in support of the land units and were used extensively in every offensive in the latter stages of the conflict. Soviet planes were grouped into formations which replicated that of the land forces. Three squadrons, usually comprising twelve aircraft each, would form an air regiment, three to four of which then formed a division. Up to four divisions could be grouped together into an air corps, a number of which were co-ordinated by an air army. Used mainly in the ground support and interdiction roles, Soviet aircraft would wreak havoc upon the German rear areas, striking command centres, artillery positions and interfering in the movement of reserves. So effective did Soviet attacks become that most German movements were undertaken at night in order to avoid bringing down an attack from the skies. Counter attacks and other movements undertaken during daylight hours were often disrupted by the ever present *Jabo's*[7]. Like the ground forces, on a tactical level the Soviet pilots were generally inferior to their German counterparts but once again their sheer weight of numbers, and the crippling lack of fuel being suffered by the Germans, sufficed to enable the Soviets to achieve aerial superiority over the battlefield.

Facing the Soviet forces around Siauliai were the widely spread divisions of the Third Panzer Army's XXXX Panzer Corps and XXVIII Corps. The left wing of the army was held by the XXVIII Corps. General Hans Gollnick's XXVIII Corps had just two weak divisions in the front line. Major General Siegfried Verhein's newly formed and inexperienced 551st Volksgrenadier Division held an extremely long twenty-eight mile section of front line on the right wing of the corps while the worn out and severely depleted 201st Security Division commanded by Lieutenant-General Alfred Jacobi was to its north. These two divisions would bear the brunt of the Soviet drive upon Memel. So long were the sectors held by the infantry that a continuous front line could not be manned, and instead the Germans relied on strong points with a thin screen of troops in between. It was very easy for the Soviets to send patrols into the German rear areas through these screens. To support the two infantry divisions was Major-General Karl Lorenz's

Grossdeutschland Panzergrenadier Division, which began to arrive in the XXVIII Corps sector and deploy around Tryskiai from October 4th.

Figure 13 - Hans Gollnick

The *Grossdeutschland* was one of the premier units of the German Army, a powerful, highly experienced, and well equipped division. Unlike a normal panzer or panzergrenadier division, it comprised a panzer regiment with its own Tiger battalion, as well as normal panzer battalion, a panzergrenadier and a fusilier regiment, plus tank hunting, armour reconnaissance, assault gun and anti-aircraft battalions plus an artillery regiment. Like many other armoured units, it was employed in a fire-brigade fashion, being rushed from one threatened sector to another to restore the positions of hard pressed infantry units. This inevitably led to a rapid loss of effectiveness as its elements became spread out all along the front, being used in small pockets as opposed to packing a powerful punch as a single unit. Unfortunately for the Germans, such was their weakened state that they had no other option than to use their armoured forces in this manner. Shortly after the Memel Offensive began, elements of Lieutenant General Dr. Karl Mauss' 7th Panzer Division also arrived from Latvia to provide support to the XXVIII Corps[8].

Figure 14 - Sigfrid Henrici

In the centre of the Third Panzer Army's long front was General Sigfrid Henrici's XXXX Panzer Corps[9] with just one division, Major General Erich Sudau's 548th Volksgrenadier. This division had only been formed in July 1944 and comprised the 1094th, 1095th and 1096th Grenadier Regiments plus supporting units. Like other German divisions at this stage of the war, it was under strength in both personnel and equipment. It was helped by the arrival of General Karl Decker's 5th Panzer Division from Estonia at the beginning of October[10].

Figure 15 - Rolf Wuthmann

On the southern wing, facing the 39th Army of the 3rd Belorussian Front was General Rolf Wuthmann's IX Corps with the 69th, 95th and 21st Infantry Divisions. These divisions would have a limited role in the fighting to come, mainly becoming involved due to the collapse of the combat line to their north.

Raus had been planning to launch a renewed counter attack upon Siauliai in the middle of October and to this end had begun to build up armoured divisions in the area. The early signs of an impending Soviet attack had been detected by the movement of forces onto the Siauliai axis but the Germans did not think the Soviet armies could attack until the middle of the month at the earliest, by which time their own strength would have improved considerably and their counter attack may have already begun.

The German Army suffered from a catastrophic shortage of replacements ever since it had gone to war in Russia, but particularly from 1944 onwards. That the army had come to this state was in part a response to the failed attempt on Hitler's life in July 1944, but also due to the draining losses suffered on the Eastern Front. Since the beginning of the campaign in 1941, to the autumn of 1944, the campaign had cost the Germans in excess of 1,400,000 killed with another million missing and five million more wounded. From a strength of 3.3 million men in June 1941, the Army had been bled white, fielding as few as 2.7 million just a year later. This situation was not to improve despite the ruthless trawling of the country for replacements. Following the assassination attempt on Hitler, Reichsführer-SS Heinrich Himmler had been appointed commander of the Replacement Army, replacing General Fromm who had been implicated in the plot. Instead of ensuring the regular supply of replacements to the Army units in the field, Himmler's chaotic command saw him concentrate his efforts on rebuilding burnt out infantry divisions as a new generation of Volksgrenadier Division. These units were based around the remnants of old divisions which had already been shattered in the fighting on the Western or Eastern Fronts. Each rebuilt division comprised three, two-battalion regiments, a theoretical strength of around 10,000 men although few ever achieved anywhere near this. Their experienced cadres were fleshed out with a collection of Hitler Youth, Luftwaffe ground staff, middle-aged businessmen from reserved occupations, recovering invalids and naval cadets. Training was brief at best, sometimes as little as six weeks but they did receive some of the newest infantry weapons and were lavishly equipped with both light and medium machine guns. This ensured their morale was relatively high, and if they held together under combat conditions, they could pack a powerful defensive punch. The Volksgrenadier divisions were intended for holding and defensive operations rather than offensive action and as such lacked the mobility of the Soviet units opposed to them. Alongside this program, Himmler also massively expanded his Waffen SS, creating a plethora of new divisions. With the demands on the limited German manpower pool being made by Martin Bormann, who was in charge of the Volkssturm, and Himmler for his Volksgrenadier Divisions and Waffen SS divisions, the Army struggled to secure enough replacements to make good the steady losses it suffered. That it managed to maintain a defence at all was a testament to the strength of the men and officers of the German Army at that time, despite all of its setbacks.

The Regular German Army units had been transformed after three years of fighting in the Soviet Union. The divisions of 1941 which had begun the invasion, well equipped and with up to 17,000 men, were a thing of the past. The increase in the number of divisions fielded in the succeeding years had been at the expense of their strength. By 1944 many infantry divisions no longer comprised three battalion regiments as they had originally, but instead had been reduced to just two battalions in order to concentrate their strength and cut down on support services. The strongest units would number just 12,000 men although like their Soviet opponents, many were often considerably lower than this and were starved of replacements. Towards the end, divisions numbering in the hundreds of men rather than thousands were all too common. One factor which had not changed was the mobility of the German infantry divisions. Even from the earliest days of the war, the German infantry had relied heavily on horse drawn transport to move itself across the battlefield. The image of the German Army as a highly mechanised force which motored across Europe is inherently false. Motorisation was largely restricted to the few panzer and panzergrenadier divisions, the many infantry using their feet, as their forebears had before them. This was one of the major factors which hindered the Germans in their cauldron battles during the early days of Operation Barbarossa. Quite simply, the infantry simply could not keep up with the armour and as a result many Soviet troops were able to escape from encirclement.

The panzer divisions, the pride of the Wehrmacht, had suffered equally as badly as the infantry formations and by 1944 many comprised just a single panzer regiment with two panzer battalions, plus a panzergrenadier brigade of two regiments (each with two battalions), a force of 13,000 men with around 120 tanks when at full strength.

Figure 16 - The Panzer IV. This example has the long barrel 75mm main gun and is fitted with side skirts and spaced turret armour.

The mainstay of the German panzer division was the reliable Panzer IV medium tank. Originally armed with a short barrel 75mm gun, it had been upgraded a number of times. By 1944 it sported a long barrelled 75mm gun, had been given additional armour plating on the hull and was protected by armoured skirts against shaped charge anti-tank rounds. The Panzer IV was a popular tank, although it was only just a match for the T-34 rather than superior to it. In an effort to overcome the scourge of the T-34 the Germans rushed into service in 1943 the Panzer V Panther.

Figure 17 - Germany's response to the T-34, the Panther tank.

This vehicle turned out to be one of the finest tanks of the war, despite its initial teething troubles. Armed with a long barrel 75mm gun and protected by sloped armour copied from the T-34, it could knock out the Soviet tanks at great ranges. Unfortunately it was over-engineered and often struggled in the harsh conditions experienced on the Eastern Front.

In late 1942 the heavy Panzer VI Tiger I tank entered service with the Army. This vehicle was armed with the formidable 88mm gun which had wrought great havoc as an anti-tank weapon. The Tiger was an effective weapon and could knock out the T-34 at distances where the Soviet tanks could not fire effectively in return. In 1944 the Tiger II appeared, a truly formidable machine, although too slow and heavy, and in too few numbers to make a real difference to the course of the battles to come.

Despite their technical superiority, the Germans simply could not produce enough vehicles to take on the masses of Soviet tanks that opposed them. In an effort to redress this balance they increased production of assault guns. Assault guns, grouped into brigades, were

Figure 18 - The Tiger I heavy tank with its fearsome 88mm main gun.

crucial anti-tank formations supporting the hard pressed infantry. Under the command of the artillery service rather than the panzer arm, they were equipped with turretless versions of the Panzer III and IV, and the formidable little Hetzer's which were based on the reliable Panzer 38(t) chassis. These vehicles were considerably cheaper and easier to produce than tanks, and offered an excellent defensive capability in the place of wheeled anti tank guns. The assault gun brigades were used widely, supplementing the infantry's lack of anti-tank weapons in many instances.

Fighting a war on a number of fronts had a crippling impact on the German war effort. The demands of the Western and Italian Fronts, together with the Allied bomber offensive against the industrial heartland of the Ruhr and other areas of western Germany, and in particular the terrible damage done to the supply of fuel, drew badly needed men and weapons away from the Eastern Front.

Figure 19 - The Stug III assault gun, essentially a turretless Panzer III

The Allied bombing of the oil refineries and fuel storage facilities across Nazi occupied Europe had a devastating effect on the armies in the field. From late 1943, and particularly after the Normandy invasion in the summer of 1944, German fuel production collapsed. The operations of the Luftwaffe were severely curtailed, the most insignificant use of fuel becoming heavily monitored. For the men at the front, air support was often just a dim and distant memory. The greater part of the Luftwaffe had been pulled back to protect the Homeland and what few units were left at the front were desperately short of fuel. Army units suffered too, often finding they were left immobile, with perfectly usable tanks being lost to the enemy for want of a few drops of petrol. To counter the threat of the Allied bomber fleets, thousands of the deadly 88mm anti-aircraft guns[11] were used in air defence rather than in their ground role again Soviet armour.

Figure 20 - The Jagdpanzer IV assault gun

Hitler's refusal to accept a policy of flexible defence, which would have taken advantage of the space available in the east, merely exacerbated the problems the Germans faced. His stubborn refusal to allow any form of withdrawal had seen the Ostheer smashed in a number of encirclement operations, culminating in the catastrophic defeat in Belorussia in June and July of 1944. Through sheer necessity a defence policy was adopted by the armies at the front, which proved successful only when sufficient forces and strong defensive positions were in place. In general outline the German defensive plan meant establishing forward, main and reserve defence positions. The forward lines were lightly manned and designed to absorb the weight of a Soviet offensive, soaking up the bombardment. As many troops as possible would be pulled back from this position to the main defensive position in the event of an enemy attack so that their barrage fell on empty positions and vacated artillery sites. This would ensure that the main defence line remained largely intact. Effectively, the Germans intended the Soviets to punch into thin air at the forward position, and then they would launch their own counter attacks from the main defensive position to disrupt further attacks and derail the Soviet timetable. The Soviet tendency to undertake reconnaissance attacks before an offensive began gave the German commanders ample warning that an attack was imminent. It was then just merely a question of timing in pulling out of the forward defence position. Many generals became adept at judging the correct moment to do so. This policy provided a sensible defence but experience showed that when the Germans were pushed out of their entrenched positions, their lack of mobile forces, anti-tank and armour reserves generally meant that a collapse of the front would quickly follow.

As the war had approached the Reich frontiers in late 1944, and with the huge manpower losses suffered both in the West and East, the Germans had been forced to consider the mass employment of civilians in defence of their Homeland. Guderian, by now Chief of the Army General Staff, had suggested the formation of a *Landsturm* in the eastern provinces in a discussion with Hitler in early September 1944. Guderian's idea had been to establish formations made up of men from reserved occupations, probably from the ranks of those registered with the SA. Hitler initially agreed with him but just a day later he changed his mind and gave responsibility for the raising of these troops to Martin Bormann and the Nazi Party. The Volkssturm, as this civilian defence force was named, was officially created by the Führer Decree of October 18th 1944. Rather than just being an organisation for the defence of the eastern provinces, the Volkssturm was now to be a national defence force, and Bormann envisioned it numbering in the millions. All males between the ages of 16 and 60 who were capable of bearing arms were liable for conscription. Volkssturm units were organised into battalions, a battalion generally numbering around 600 men and being commanded by the equivalent of a Major, although battalions of up to 1,000 men were not unknown. Once part of a unit many men found themselves with just a Volkssturm armband for a uniform. Sometimes even the Volkssturm armband was not available which meant they went into combat in civilian attire only, in contravention of the Geneva Convention. Following the disaster at Stalingrad and the continual heavy losses on the Eastern Front there had been many trawls for reinforcements for the army. Himmler's tenure as commander of the Replacement Army made an already difficult situation even worse. The result was that by October 1944, when the Volkssturm was raised, it comprised mainly young Hitler Youth and the elderly; those fit enough to fight having already been called upon.

Figure 21 - A Volkssturm member with his Volkssturm armband showing, being trained in the use of the Panzerfaust anti tank weapon

The problem of arming the Volkssturm units was also considerable. Stocks of captured weapons were issued widely but there was no central control over their distribution. An even greater problem was the supply of ammunition. Many Volkssturm members were handed a foreign or obsolete rifle with just a handful of rounds apiece. Weapons from the Great War were brought back into service to try to flesh out the firepower of the Volkssturm battalions. Perhaps the most deadly weapon the Volkssturm employed was the Panzerfaust, which cost the

Soviets many hundreds of tanks destroyed throughout the final months of the war. Quickly manufactured and relatively easy to use, the one shot Panzerfaust comprised a hollow charge warhead propelled by a small rocket, and proved extremely effective at knocking out tanks. Unfortunately for the user, the effective killing range of the weapon was between thirty and one hundred metres, depending on the model employed. This meant that once a hit had been achieved, a safe retreat from any accompanying infantry or other tanks was unlikely. Training for the new recruits was often rushed and inadequate, many men and boys having to master the use of their weapons when they entered combat for the first time. For the older members a familiarity with military life from the First World War was common, and younger members had grown up under a Nazi regime which had militarised most aspects of their lives. With this mixture of forces the Germans waited for the next round of Soviet attacks, attacks which would push across the eastern frontiers of the Reich and bring the war to the German people.

In preparation for the Memel Offensive the 1st Baltic Front began large scale reconnaissance attacks against the German forces on the Siauliai axis throughout October 4th. The attacks, which were supposed to be supported by the 3rd Air Army, were hindered by thick fog, which blanketed the landscape and remained through to the next day. The situation on October 5th was no better and so Bagramyan waited, hoping the visibility would improve as the day progressed. By 1100 hours the fog had thinned a little as a gentle breeze got up, enabling the Soviets to start sending their forward detachments toward the German lines. At 1110 hours Bagramyan finally decided to begin the assault. The thousands of assembled artillery pieces opened fire as one. As Bagramyan wrote:

At 1110 hours the ground beneath us trembled from the volleys of the Katyusha's and artillery, and over our heads was a dull roar as the shells swept past. Heavy shells could even be seen in flight. For twenty minutes there was a growing roar...a pleasing 'music' to our ears!...As the minute hand reached half past the rumble of the artillery and mortar barrage intensified even more[12].

The fog kept the planes grounded again and also meant that the artillery had to fire at predetermined targets, their spotters being unable to see where the rounds were landing. Despite these problems, Bagramyan pressed home his attacks, the concentrated fire striking the XXVIII Corps west of Siauliai. Unbeknown to the Soviet commanders, the Germans had identified the build up of enemy forces at the eleventh hour and had pulled their forward line back to escape the barrage. The initial attack by the Beloborodov's 43rd Army and Chistyakov's 6th Guards Army seemed to go well until they reached the main line of resistance, where the Soviet troops came under a hail of fire. The XXVIII Corps beat off the first wave, the 551st Volksgrenadier Division launching vigorous counter attacks of its own. A second wave of attacks followed and was also beaten off, but a third wave managed to penetrate the positions of the hard pressed and increasingly thinly spread Volksgrenadiers. Soviet troops swept to the west, pushing back pockets of German soldiers and encircling particularly stubborn pockets of resistance. Yet another hastily organised counter attack, this time by the reconnaissance battalion of the *Grossdeutschland* Panzergrenadier Division, brought part of the Soviet attack to a halt and even pushed them back to their original positions. The panzergrenadiers were able to link up with those elements of the 551st Volksgrenadier Division which had been bypassed but were still fighting hard in isolation near their original positions. Despite this localised success, the sheer scale of the Soviet assault meant the Germans could not hold everywhere. The 43rd Army and 6th Guards Army managed a modest advance of five miles by the end of the first day of their attacks, successfully crossing the River Venta which lay in their path. To the south the 2nd Guards Army had also met with similar resistance but it also managed to claw its way forwards and threw elements of the 1st Tank Corps into the battle, the tank troops successfully crossing the River Dubissa by the end of the day. The intensity of the German resistance, together with the difficulty of movement on the rain soaked roads, meant that Bagramyan held back from committing Volsky's tank army during the first day of the offensive, contrary to his original plan. It was anticipated that the German line would be breached the next day, so that the armour could be committed to pass through the infantry and push on to the coast. Nevertheless, Bagramyan was satisfied to be able to report to Stalin that during the first day of fighting his troops had managed to penetrate up to five miles into the German positions across a fifty-mile front.

On October 6th the Soviets renewed their attacks, the 6th Guards Army bypassing the *Grossdeutschland* Division's armoured reconnaissance battalion at Tryskiai. Forward units of the 7th Panzer Division had also begun to arrive here but they too were placed under intense pressure by waves of attacking Soviet infantry and armour. Soviet forces pushed deeper into the German rear, penetrating the second defensive zone to reach Luoke, where a hastily assembled battle group from the *Grossdeutschland*, 7th Panzer and 551st Volksgrenadier Divisions was outflanked and forced to withdraw. An improvement in the weather also brought Soviet aircraft aloft, and their ferocious attacks helped to hinder the German defence. In the face of incessant ground and air assault the hard pressed German front line began to crumble. Seizing on this opportunity, Bagramyan pushed Volsky's 5th Guards Tank Army through the hole torn in the German positions. Soviet tanks, with infantry riding on their rear decks, drove forwards, crushing nests of resistance beneath their tracks while bypassing more determined groups. These would be mopped up by the infantry which marched along behind the tanks. The leading vehicles quickly passed through the attacking infantry of the 6th Guards and 43rd Armies and pushed on to the west. Units spearheading the advance quickly reached Seda and captured the town, fending off a counter attack by more disparate elements of the *Grossdeutschland* Division.

The breakthrough by the Soviet armoured forces made it abundantly clear to the German commanders that the enemy forces intended to make for the Baltic coast and isolate Army Group North. Almost as soon as the Soviet attack had commenced, Schörner had begun to pull the divisions of the Eighteenth Army out of their positions south and east of Riga and place them on to the exposed right wing. In an effort to stop just such a movement of enemy forces, the 2nd and 3rd Baltic Fronts opened their attacks upon Riga, although once again they were of limited success given the strong defensive positions the Germans continued to hold. By October 7th it was also clear to Raus that his army was in danger of being torn apart. Gollnick's XXVIII Corps was conducting a fighting withdrawal towards Memel, having lost contact with the forces on each flank, while to the south the XXXX Panzer and IX Corps were being forced back to the southwest, towards the River Niemen. The weakness of the German divisions, which were severely overextended, meant that any reserves which came up were quickly sucked into the general conflagration and were unable to concentrate in order to close the gaping hole in the front line.

On October 8th, another rain-soaked day, the leading elements of the 5th Guards Tank Army reached the Memel defensive perimeter, which had been established some distance east of the town. German troops tried in vain to halt the Soviet advance but were outnumbered and outgunned, and compelled to fall back. Meanwhile, the 43rd Army continued to slog its way forward through the mud behind the tank troops, fighting pockets of German resistance as it advanced. With Soviet spearheads reaching as deep into the German rear as the town of Plunge, Raus was left with no option other than to try to pull what forces he could back to Memel, and left the rest to retreat to the Niemen. Effective German control over the course of events had by this time ended, the Soviet forces dictating the flow of the battle. Fortunately for the civilians of Memel an evacuation had begun just days earlier and virtually everyone had left the town, just the Army, Police troops, young Hitler Youth and old men remaining to defend the city. Elements of the German 58th Infantry Division, which had been shipped down from

Courland, had begun to arrive as the last civilians left. Without any respite the German soldiers marched through the town and on to the defensive perimeter in an effort to halt a Soviet advance into the urban area. The *Grossdeutschland* had also pulled many of its widely scattered elements back and was fighting to hold off the Soviets at Salantai, to the north east of Memel.

It was with some satisfaction that Bagramyan was able to report to Stalin during the evening of the 8th that his forces had smashed open the German line across a 120-mile front and penetrated to a depth of more than fifty miles. German losses had been severe, the Soviets counting more than 190 tanks and assault guns destroyed and a further sixty captured.[13]

The isolation of Army Group North in the Courland peninsula was completed on October 9th when Palanga, situated on the Baltic shore north of Memel, fell to the 306th Rifle Division of Kreizer's 51st Army. Kreizer's force had been released from the second echelon some days earlier to support the advance of the 6th Guards Army. After reaching the Memel defences yesterday, Volsky's tank army also sent units to the coast, reaching the shore south of Palanga after sweeping aside the *Grossdeutschland* Division in fierce fighting near Krottingen[14]. The unexpectedly swift Soviet advance saw the headquarters of the Third Panzer Army, which was transferred back to Army Group Centre that day, overrun by elements of the 5th Guards Tank Army. Raus and his staff had to fight their way through to Memel, from where they were later evacuated. With Soviet forces already in the outer defences of the town, Hitler declared Memel a Fortified Place[15] and ordered it to be held as a bridgehead from where to launch a counter attack that would recover Lithuania and link up with Army Group North. Inside the deserted port the 58th Infantry Division completed its deployment, taking up positions on the northern perimeter of the defence lines, the 7th Panzer, which had conducted a difficult retreat from the east, was in the centre and the *Grossdeutschland* Division was to the south.

As the 5th Guards Tank Army completed its drive to the sea, to the south the 2nd Guards Army and 39th Army advanced towards the River Niemen, driving back the XXXX Panzer Corps and IX Corps. Henrici's XXXX Panzer Corps' 5th Panzer and 548th Volksgrenadier Divisions had been attacked west of Rasieniai, where they had tried to hold off the attacks of the 2nd Guards Army which pushed towards Tauroggen. As with the XXVII Corps to the north, pockets of resistance were bypassed on successive positions. On October 6th the 5th Panzer, which had still not yet arrived in full, tried to make a stand at Kelmy with its anti-aircraft battalion and some panzergrenadier troops but they were soon forced to retire as their left flank was hanging open and Soviet armour was seen to be driving past without interruption. The next day the 548th Volksgrenadier Division lost contact with the most northerly unit of Wuthmann's IX Corps and so it and the 5th Panzer Division, whose 31st Panzer Regiment, commanded by Lieutenant Colonel Hans Herzog, had just arrived[16], formed combat groups and began a fighting withdrawal to the Niemen. The remnants of the 548th Volksgrenadier Division, fighting in isolation to the south of the 5th Panzer, undertook a similar move. These engagements were fierce, with repeated Soviet attacks being beaten off only for the German flanks to be turned. While the XXXX Panzer Corps struggled in the face of these attacks, Wuthmann's IX Corps was trying in vain to fend off the assaults of the 39th Army. Major-General Joachim-Friedrich Lang's 95th Infantry Division, which had been virtually destroyed during Operation *Bagration*, and Lieutenant-General Götz's 21st Infantry Division, which had been withdrawn from Riga at the end of September and brought south to reinforce the Third Panzer Army, were pushed back along the road to Tauroggen. Lieutenant-General Siegfried Rein's 69th Infantry Division, holding the southern wing of the corps was less affected by these attacks but nevertheless had to pull back upon Jurburg[17] to avoid its left flank being exposed. The 69th, which went on to fight its final bloody battle in Königsberg, had been raised in August 1939. Following the successful conclusion of the Polish campaign, the division formed part of the occupation force until in April 1940 it was redeployed to Norway.

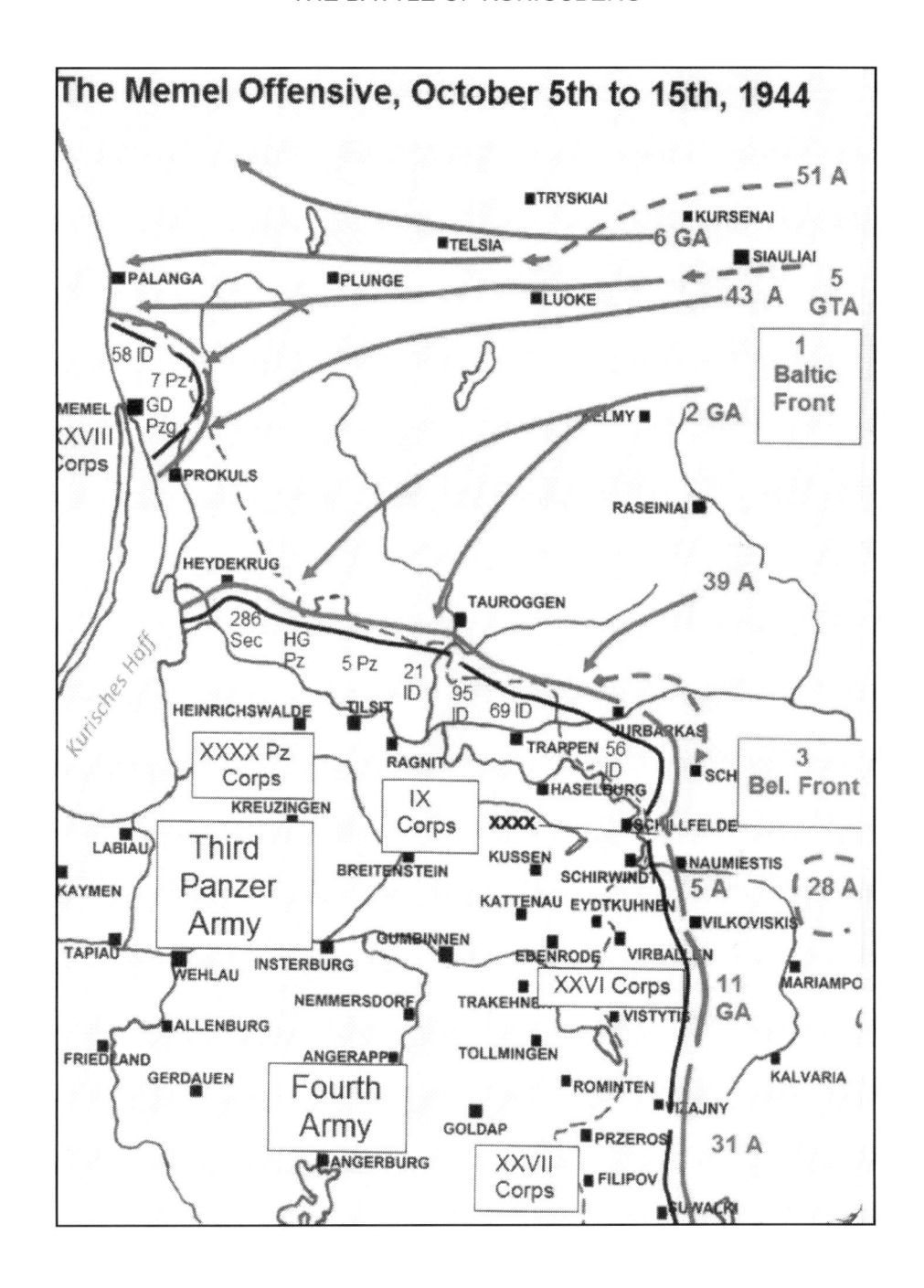

THE BATTLE OF KÖNIGSBERG

The Memel Offensive, October 5th to 15th, 1944

There it took part in the battle to capture Stavanger and Bergen. The division stayed in Norway throughout 1941 and '42 before being committed to the Eastern Front in the spring of 1943. It joined with Army Group North in the fighting around Leningrad. From here it was forced back by the Soviet offensive of January and February 1944 and saw action around Pskov. By the summer of '44 the division had been moved south to come under the command of Army Group Centre. In late 1944 its main combat elements comprised the 159th, 193rd and 236th Grenadier Regiments under the command of Colonel Grimme, Lieutenant-Colonel Heuer and Lieutenant-Colonel Schunk respectively.

Returning to the action at the front, on October 8th the positions of the 548th Volksgrenadier were pierced by new Soviet attacks. The 2nd Guards Army and 1st Tank Corps were able to penetrate the third German defensive zone and pushed their leading elements across the River Jura. The 5th Panzer and 548th Volksgrenadier Divisions, together with Major-General Hanns-Horst von Necker's newly arriving 1st Parachute-Panzer Division *Herman Göring* spent the next few days undertaking a fighting withdrawal to the northern bank of the Niemen, where the Tilsit bridgehead was formed. Troops of the 2nd Guards Army reached the mouth of the Niemen near Heydekrug on the 9th October, hastening the German retreat. Prökuls was also lost to the Soviets on the 9th and Tauroggen was given up on the 10th. Between October 11th and 13th the Germans beat off repeated attacks as the 2nd Guards Army tried to destroy the Tilsit bridgehead. The German defence was very strong due to the arrival of fresh forces, strong counter attacks being launched which troubled the Soviets considerably.

After a brief lull, the fighting around the Tilsit bridgehead erupted once more on October 17th as the Soviet armies launched a renewed assault whose aim was to tie the Germans down and prevent them from transferring forces to the south, where Chernyakhovsky was now attacking. This they failed to achieve as by October 18th the 5th Panzer Division had been pulled back, followed shortly afterwards by the 1st Parachute-Panzer Division *Herman Göring*. An orderly evacuation by the infantry units to the southern bank of the Niemen followed over the next few days. Wuthmann's IX Corps then took over responsibility for holding the south bank of the Niemen against Soviet incursions. The tenuous bridgehead on the northern bank was finally abandoned on October 22nd.

Although isolated, the German forces in Memel continued to resist repeated Soviet attempts to capture the town. The fighting continued until late January 1945, when the town was evacuated and the divisions defending it marched along the Frisches Nehrung to Samland. To all intents and purposes the Soviet command had achieved the goals it had set for the Memel Offensive. Army Group North had been isolated and a force of thirty-three badly needed divisions hived off from the rest of the Ostheer. Soviet forces now stood poised to break into East Prussia. It is to these battles that we now turn.

* * *

After the Memel Offensive had reached its successful conclusion the Stavka planned a new operation to destroy the German forces in Courland. To prevent the Germans from attacking northward from both their Niemen bridgehead and from Memel, General Ivan Danilovich Chernyakhovsky's 3rd Belorussian Front was to begin an offensive further south. The Soviet plan was simple and relatively unsophisticated; calling for the attack to drive along the obvious invasion route through Gumbinnen and Insterburg. The offensive, code-named the Gumbinnen Offensive Operation, was to secure control of a wedge of the East Prussian frontier districts between Gumbinnen and Goldap. Before the offensive began Chanchibadze's 2nd Guards Army of the 1st Baltic Front took over responsibility for the northern bank of the Niemen, where the Germans maintained their shallow bridgehead. This deployment freed up the 39th Army for operations on the south bank, between the Rivers Niemen and Scheschupe (now the Sesupe).

At the age of 38, Chernyakhovsky was the youngest officer to hold a Front command in the Red Army. He had begun the war as commander of a tank division and rose to command a tank corps by July 1942. In late 1942 he was appointed commander of the 60th Army and then of the 3rd Belorussian Front in April 1944. During Operation Bagration his Front played a crucial role in the destruction of the German Fourth Army. It was during this operation that he received his promotion to General of the Army. Chernyakhovsky was an extremely capable and imaginative general, possibly one of the best the Red Army possessed. He had a knack of being able to quickly identify the weakness of an enemy position and was comfortable redeploying his forces mid-offensive to exploit an advantageous situation. This ability to shift the main focal point of an offensive did much to unbalance the Germans.

Figure 22 - Ivan Danilovich Chernyakhovsky

THE BATTLE OF KÖNIGSBERG

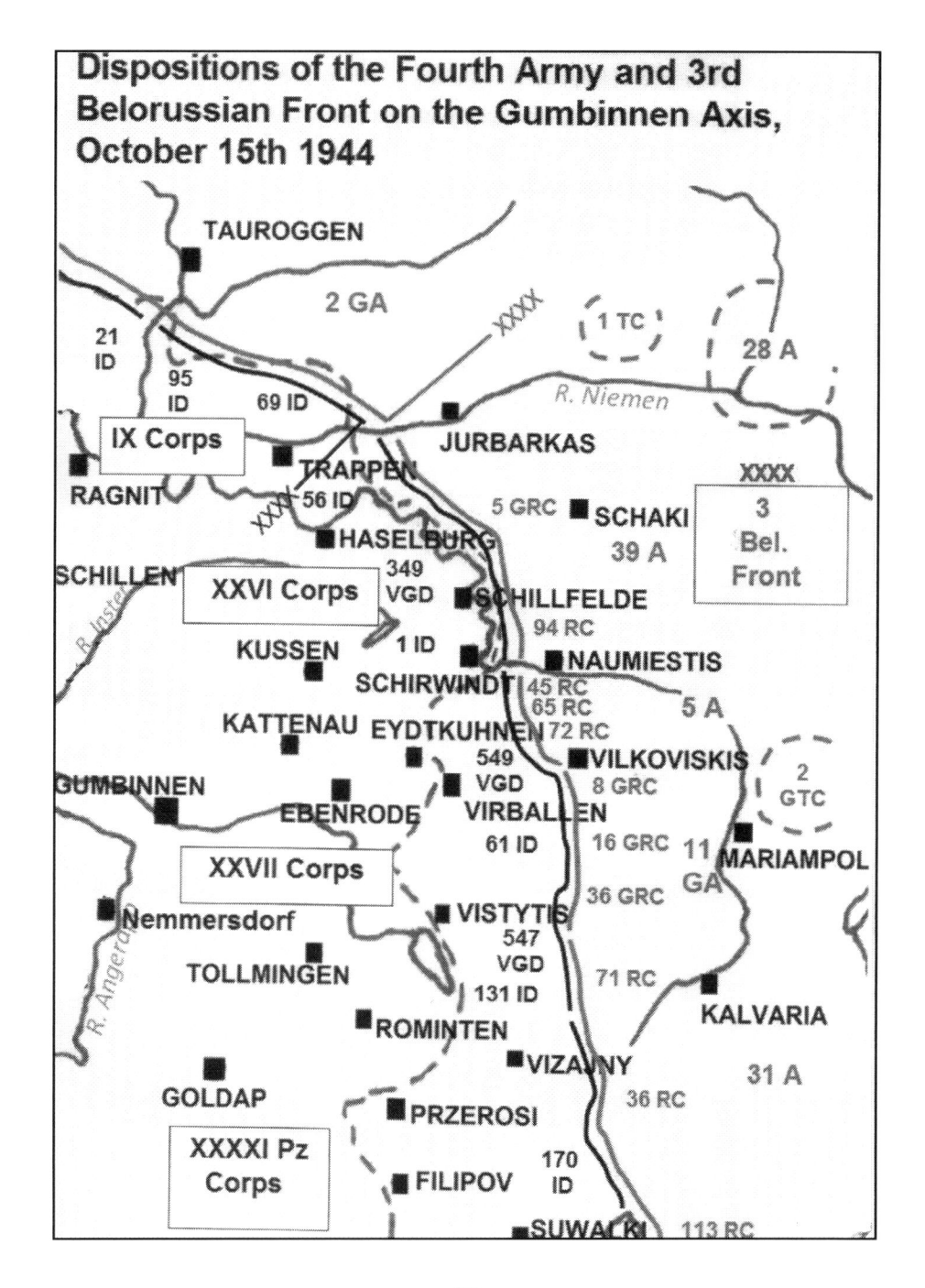

Dispositions of the Fourth Army and 3rd Belorussian Front on the Gumbinnen Axis, October 15th 1944

To smash through the German lines Chernyakhovsky planned to use the 39th Army, 5th Army and 11th Guards Army. Lyudnikov's 39th Army comprised two rifle corps', Major-General Bezugly's 5th Guards Rifle Corps and Major-General Prokofiev's 94th Rifle Corps and was deployed on the right wing of the Front.

Colonel-General Nikolai Ivanovich Krylov's 5th Army held a very narrow section of the front line after the redeployment of Lyudnikov's 39th Army. Krylov had held various staff posts during the early and mid stages of the war, serving as Chief of Staff to General Chuikov with the 62nd and 8th Guards Armies during the harrowing Stalingrad campaign and its aftermath. He achieved his first army command in 1943, taking over the 21st Army before later being appointed 5th Army commander. In October 1944 the 5th Army comprised Gorokhov's 45th, Perekrestov's 65th and Kazariev's 72nd Rifle Corps, and was situated south of the River Scheschupe. To the left was the 11th Guards Army, deployed between Vilkaviskis and Graziskiai. General Kuzma Nikitovich Galitsky commanded this army. He had commanded the 24th Rifle Division at the start of the Russo-German War and in September 1942 was appointed commander of 3rd Shock Army. He moved to the 11th Guards Army in 1943, taking over from Bagramyan, who had been promoted to Front commander. Galitsky's 11th Guards Army comprised three corps; Major-General Zavodovsky's 8th Guards Rifle Corps on the right wing, Major-General Vorobiev's 16th Guards Rifle Corps in the centre and Major-General Shafranov's 36th Guards Rifle Corps on the left wing. Chernyakhovsky would commit his armoured reserve, Major-General Alexei Semionovich Burdeinyi's 2nd Guards Tank Corps, to exploit the breach that the infantry armies were to punch through the German line. Burdeinyi had commanded the corps since 1943, having previously served as Chief of Staff on 24th Tank Corps before it was elevated to Guards status in 1943, becoming the 2nd Guards Tank Corps after its epic battle at Tatsinskaya as part of the Stalingrad campaign. Lieutenant-General Aleksandr Aleksandrovich Luchinsky's 28th Army, with Perkhorovich's 3rd Guards Rifle Corps, Shvarev's 20th Rifle Corps and Batitsky's 128th Rifle Corps, was in the second echelon during the initial stages of the attack, being held back to enter the battle in the most advantageous sector. Lieutenant-General Vasily Glagolev's 31st Army secured the southern wing of the front, holding an extremely long portion of the front line from the area west of Kalvarja and east of Augustow. It deployed the 71st, 36th and 113th Rifle Corps. Like Bagramyan to the north, Chernyakhovsky could call on his own air force, Colonel-General Khryukin's 1st Air Army being allocated to support the operations of the 3rd Belorussian Front.

Figure 23 - Friedrich Hossbach

The Soviet attack was aimed at General Friedrich Hossbach's Fourth Army. Hossbach, who had taken command of the Fourth Army on July 19th was well aware of the danger posed by a Soviet thrust toward Gumbinnen and had already alerted the divisions in the path of the expected offensive to the danger. Hossbach was well known to Hitler, having served as his military adjutant shortly after he came to power. In 1937 he was dismissed from this post after he warned the Commander-in-Chief of the Army, General von Fritsch, of the plot the Nazi's were forming to dismiss him. Despite crossing Hitler, Hossbach went on to command the 82nd Infantry Division and LVI Panzer Corps before taking over at the Fourth Army. Hossbach was certainly not a Nazi general like Schörner or others who rose to high command late in the war. He was however a skilful commander, and like many of his contemporaries who had served their time on the Eastern Front, had developed a keen sense of when a Soviet offensive was imminent. In October 1944 his Fourth Army held a 210-mile portion of the Eastern Front. The northern wing comprised General Gerhard Matzky's XXVI Corps[18], which was to the south of the Niemen from Sudargas, through Slavikai and on to the area west of Vilkaviskis. Matzky, who had previously commanded the 21st Infantry Division and XXVIII Corps, took command of the XXVI Corps in July 1944 in the aftermath of the fighting in Belorussia, where the unit had suffered crippling losses and had to be rebuilt. In October 1944 it had under its command a number of reformed and reconstituted formations. Major-General Blaurock's 56th Infantry Division was on its northern wing. The 56th Infantry Division had had a turbulent operational history and its shattered remnants would end their days at Königsberg. Involved in bitter fighting on the Eastern Front from June 1941, the division had suffered such heavy losses at the Battle of Kursk and its aftermath that in November 1943 it was absorbed into Corps Detachment D, a conglomerate formation which included the 56th and 262nd Infantry Divisions. As a Corps Detachment the former division fought in the bitter battles in Belorussia in summer 1944. It was reconstituted as a full division in September 1944, comprising the 171st, 192nd and 234th Grenadier Regiments, each with two infantry battalions. It was again reformed in late 1944, losing the 192nd regiment in this reshuffle.

Figure 24 - Gerhard Matzky

Major-General Karl Kötz's 349th Volksgrenadier Division was situated on the southern wing of the 56th Infantry Division and was deployed before Schillfelde. The 349th Volksgrenadier had been formed in September 1944 out of the remnants of Otto Lasch's 349th Infantry Division which had been destroyed at Brody in August 1944. The new unit had the 911th, 912th and 913th Grenadier Regiments under its command but many of its personnel were fresh from the replacement program and untried in combat. The backbone of the division was the combat hardened cadre who had survived the Eastern Front battles from April to August 1944.

Major-General Hans Schittnig's[19] 1st Infantry Division, another East Prussian formation, was just east of Schirwindt[20] across the East Prussia frontier. Schittnig was a veteran officer, having fought in the First World War and served in the Reichswehr in the 1920's before holding a number of staff appointments in the 1930's and early part of the Second World War. He only took command of the 1st Infantry Division on 1st October 1944. When he took over his new command, the division comprised the 1st Grenadier Regiment, 22nd Fusilier Regiment, 43rd Grenadier Regiment, 1st Artillery Regiment and 1st Fusilier Battalion. The division had originally been formed in 1935, when the Wehrmacht had begun to re-arm, and had its headquarters in Königsberg. It fought in Poland in 1939 as part of the XXVI Corps and then took part in the invasion of France in 1940. From 1941 onwards the division was on the Eastern Front, seeing action around Leningrad with the Eighteenth Army until October 1943 when it was transferred to the Ukraine to join the First Panzer Army. It returned to Army Group Centre in May 1944 and was pushed back into East Prussia by August, deploying close to Schirwindt and Schlossberg[21] as the Soviets approached the frontier.

General Helmuth Priess's XXVII Corps held the front line to the south of the XXVI Corps. Priess' formation would face the initial attacks of the 11th Guards Army and later of the 28th Army as well. It was deployed west of Virbalis and Wizajny. Priess had previously commanded the 121st Infantry Division in its battles around Leningrad from November 1942 until March 1944, then again from June until July 1944 when it suffered severe losses in Operation Bagration. He was appointed commander of the XXVII Corps as the German High Command tried to rebuild the armies in the centre of their shattered front. The new XXVII Corps, the original having been destroyed at Minsk, comprised four infantry divisions. Lieutenant-General Karl Jank's 549th Volksgrenadier Division was deployed to the east of Virbalis. It had been formed out of the 549th Grenadier Division, which had itself only been created in July 1944. The division was converted to a Volksgrenadier formation in early October 1944 and comprised the 1097th, 1098th and 1099th Grenadier Regiments together with the 1549th Artillery Regiment. Jank had commanded both the 549th Grenadier and 549th Volksgrenadier Divisions. These were his first divisional commands, Jank having served in mainly staff roles until July 1944. To the south was Major-

General Walter Gorn's 561st Volksgrenadier Division. The 561st, which would take a major role in the later battles for Königsberg, had been formed just days before the Soviet offensive was due to begin, on 9th October 1944. Like the 549th, it had originally been created as a grenadier division in July 1944 but then converted to Volksgrenadier. It comprised the 1141st, 1142nd and 1143rd Grenadier Regiments. The 561st was also Gorn's first divisional command and his men were fresh and untried in combat. Major-General Ernst Meiner's 547th Volksgrenadier Divisions and Lieutenant General Friedrich Weber's 131st Infantry Division were to the south of the 561st and completed the deployment of Priess' XXVII Corps.

General Helmuth Weidling's XXXXI Panzer Corps was south of the XXVII Corps, from the area east of Wizajny to just south of Augustow. It was a panzer corps in name only, largely comprising infantry divisions with only armoured brigades in support. It was opposed along most of its front by Glagolev's 31st Army. Lieutenant-General Wilhelm Schmalz's Parachute-Panzer Corps *Herman Goering*, which had only been activated at the beginning of October 1944, was behind the main front line at the start of the battle but its units would become involved in the fighting as the Soviet offensive developed. The combat front of the Fourth Army was completed by General Friedrich Herrlein's LV and General Horst Grossmann's VI Corps held the remainder of the Fourth Army sector to the junction with Weiss' Second Army.

To bolster the German infantry defences were three assault gun brigades, each held in reserve behind the front line. The 277th was assembled near Schlossberg and the 276th around Ebenrode under the command of Matzky's XXVI Corps. The 279th Assault Gun Brigade was attached to the XXVII Corps as was Colonel Mummert's 103rd Panzer Brigade, which was deployed behind the junction of the 549th and 561st Volksgrenadier Divisions south of Virbalis.

Hossbach had identified the build up of Soviet forces opposite his positions and carefully monitored the situation. The German defences along the frontier were better than along most sections of the Eastern

Front. The divisions in this portion of the front line had spent a relatively quiet few weeks from late August 1944 building extensive trench systems. They thus benefitted from strong prepared defences stretching as far back as Insterburg. While spread out more thinly than would have been liked, the availability of assault guns brigades and the arrival of armoured reserves during the battle made a breakthrough such as had happened at Siauliai unlikely. Recognising the warnings signs of an approaching attack, on October 14th Hossbach ordered his forward units to abandon their positions and pull back to the main defensive zone. The XXVII Corps pulled back without any problems during the night of the 14-15th but Matzky's XXVI Corps was held up in its redeployment and was still in the process of pulling back to the main defence line when dawn came.

Chernyakhovsky's offensive began at 0400 hours on October 16th with a two-hour artillery barrage against the XXVI and XXVII Corps, striking the German lines from the River Niemen to Suwalki. Damage to the German forward line was severe, communications and artillery positions to the rear also being badly hit. The Soviets made extensive use of their air units to interdict the German forces behind the front and add to the weight of the artillery bombardment, striking emplacements as far to the rear as Gumbinnen. After this fire storm, at 0600 hours the infantry and armour of the first attack wave moved off. The 39th Army struck in the 1st Infantry Division sector, the sheer weight of their repeated attacks with tanks and infantry supported by artillery and mortar fire swamping the German positions and forcing Schittnig, after an hour of bitter fighting, to order his men to begin a slow, grudging withdrawal. Hardly had the Germans begun to pull back than a new, equally fearsome artillery barrage struck them, inflicting crippling losses on the exposed infantry. To the right of the 1st Infantry Division, the men of the 549th Volksgrenadier Division also came in for a terrible pounding from Krylov's 5th Army. It too gradually pulled back under intense pressure, but managed to keep the line together to prevent a breakthrough. They were helped in their efforts by the arrival of the 279th Assault Gun

THE BATTLE OF KÖNIGSBERG

Brigade, whose fire halted the attacks of the Soviet tanks supporting the infantry. To the south, between Virbalis and Graziskiai the 561st and 547th Volksgrenadier Divisions of the XXVII Corps were struck by Galitsky's 11th Guards Army but here also Soviet progress was slower than expected in the face of ferocious German resistance. The 36th Guards Rifle Corps was held up around Graziskiai while the 16th Guards Rifle Corps only managed a limited advance in the centre.

Despite the overwhelming weight of the artillery bombardment, and repeated assaults on the German positions, Chernyakhovsky had failed to achieve a break through during the first day of fighting, instead merely shunting the German positions to the west while inflicting heavy casualties. However, the Soviets could absorb their casualties much more easily than the Germans.

At dawn on October 17th the Soviets unleashed a second crushing barrage on the German positions. Once again the men of the XXVI Corps were able to repulse the initial enemy attacks, launching their own counter attacks to disrupt the Soviet advance. In a repeat of the previous day's fighting the Germans continued to slowly give ground, the 1st Infantry Division losing control of Schirwindt to the 5th Army during the evening, but only after a day of bloody house-to-house combat and after the German units was threatened on either flank. As the Soviets attempted to push west of Schirwindt they were stopped by the arrival of the 277th Assault Gun Brigade, whose fire halted the Soviet tanks in their tracks. The 11th Guards Army was faced with a determined German counter attack along much of its front, beating off an attack by the 561st Volksgrenadier Division south of Virbalis, while the 547th Volksgrenadier Division counter attacked around Graziskiai. On the northern wing of the army, Zavodovsky's 8th Guards Rifle Corps continued its attacks towards Ebenrode[22] in conjunction with the southern wing corps of the 5th Army. Despite repeated attacks with masses of tanks and infantry, the 549th Volksgrenadier Division was able to use its well established defensive positions to break down each new attack and slow the Soviet advance to a crawl. Undeterred, the Soviets renewed their attacks and a strong thrust by Krylov's 5th Army managed to inflict severe losses on the right wing formations of the 549th Volksgrenadier Division. A complete collapse of the German line was only averted by the timely arrival of Mummert's 103rd Panzer Brigade, whose fire brought the Soviet advance to a halt. A little further south, Galitsky's 11th Guards Army renewed its attacks and started to make progress as the day progressed. The 8th Guards Rifle Corps remained stuck in heavy fighting near Virbalis but Vorobiev's 16th Guards Rifle Corps managed to tear through the overstretched and exhausted 561st Volksgrenadier Division. They pushed towards Eydtkuhnen, capturing the town after a difficult battle with further elements of the division. Schlossbach was also taken amid bitter fighting. The Germans, under intense pressure, were compelled to fall back upon Ebenrode. On the left wing of the 11th Guards Army, Shafranov's 36th Guards Rifle Corps was held up by further stiff resistance from the 547th Volksgrenadier Division. Galitsky's partial success prompted him to immediately change the focus of his attacks. Instead of continuing to bludgeon his way directly towards Ebenrode, he would move the weight of his attacks south of the town to exploit the attack in an area of marshy ground where the Germans would not expect a major assault.

On October 18th, which dawned clear and bright, the Fourth Army continued to struggle under Chernyakhovsky's attacks both from the air and on the ground. The hard pressed 1st Infantry Division was struck hard yet again. These attacks destroyed a number of vehicles from the 277th Assault Gun Brigades and killed the unit commander. Despite these successes the Soviet forward progress was still very slow. To the south the situation was improving as Galitsky pushed his forces forward to the south of Ebenrode. The 103rd Panzer Brigade, trapped in bitter fighting before Ebenrode, was unable to intervene. Galitsky's men captured Grosswaltersdorf on the River Rominte and began to push forward to cross the Rominte Heath, aiming to reach the River Angerapp in order to outflank Gumbinnen from the south before driving on to Insterburg. This expected development sent panic through the German rear areas, with the newly created Volkssturm being hastily mobilised to try to defend their homes.

Fortunately for the Germans, October 19th was overcast, which helped to limit the number of Soviet aircraft operating over the battlefield. The absence of air support meant that the fighting during this day proved even more difficult for the Soviet ground forces. Bloody fighting continued before Ebenrode and Schlossberg during the 9th and 10th, the 1st Infantry Division holding back repeated attacks at Schlossberg while the 549th Volksgrenadier Division beat off the attacks of the 5th and 11th Guards Armies towards Ebenrode. The defenders of Ebenrode were attacked by infantry supported by heavy IS-II Stalin tanks. An assault gun brigade was able to hold off the Soviet attack, but only with the greatest of difficulty. The fighting in front of Ebenrode was part of the Soviet effort to tie the Germans down and prevent them from transferring forces south against the rest of the 11th Guards Army. Galitsky now committed Burdeinyi's 2nd Guards Tank Corps to the centre of his drive across the Rominte. The Germans only had scattered units to oppose the Soviet advance in this area. A little further south Vystytis fell to the 11th Guards while the 31st Army captured Przerosi to the south. As General Grossmann, commander of the German VI Corps, recorded:

> ...the fire of the enemy artillery and mortars pounded the German defenders with even greater strength, and opened the way from attacks by masses of tanks and infantry. Villages were lost and retaken only to fall to the enemy once more. Eydtkau remained in enemy hands. The enemy fire crushed the defending forces and only remnants were able to make their way to the west. The Fourth Army situation on both sides of the Rominte Heath had become extremely threatening.[23]

The threat posed to the Fourth Army by Galitsky's advance prompted Reinhardt to request permission that the Tilsit bridgehead be evacuated in order to release the deployed divisions here for operations on the Gumbinnen axis. Permission was unexpectedly granted by Hitler and immediately the withdrawal of the armoured units in the bridgehead was begun.

With the 2nd Guards Tank Corps in the vanguard, on October 20th Galitsky was able to deepen the penetration, taking Tollmingen on his southern wing while also reaching the second German defensive zone south of Gumbinnen. With the redeployment of the 1st Parachute-Panzer Division *Herman Göring* and Major General Günther Sachs' 18th Flak Division to Gumbinnen, the Germans managed to put up a hasty defensive screen around the town. The regular units here were supplemented by the deployment of Volkssturm troops who had been quickly mobilised following the Soviet breakthrough. Farther south the 31st Army was also making good progress and secured control of Suwalki as it forced back the 170th Infantry Division of the XXXXI Panzer Corps. The stiff German resistance on the northern wing of the offensive prompted Chernyakhovsky to adjust his plan. Not averse to taking advantage of developments, he realised that in the north the attack had essentially stalled and so moved to exploit Galitsky's gains in the south. The limited progress prompted a revised order early on the 20th that Luchinsky put his nine divisions into the line between Krylov and Galitsky, thereby reinforcing the attacks of the 11th Guards Army. Luchinsky's force was to strike at Gumbinnen, on Galitsky's northern flank, while the 11th Guards Army fought to exploit its corridor to the Angerapp and anchor its southern wing on Goldap with the assistance of the 31st Army. Galitsky though, despite his localised success, was beginning to struggle. His army had taken heavy losses in the fighting since the 16th and the move forward to the Angerapp had seen the army leave much of its heavy weapons lagging far behind the front line units. Supplies were also beginning to run down and, combined with a stiffening of German resistance, the prospects of further major successes seemed to be receding.

THE BATTLE OF KÖNIGSBERG

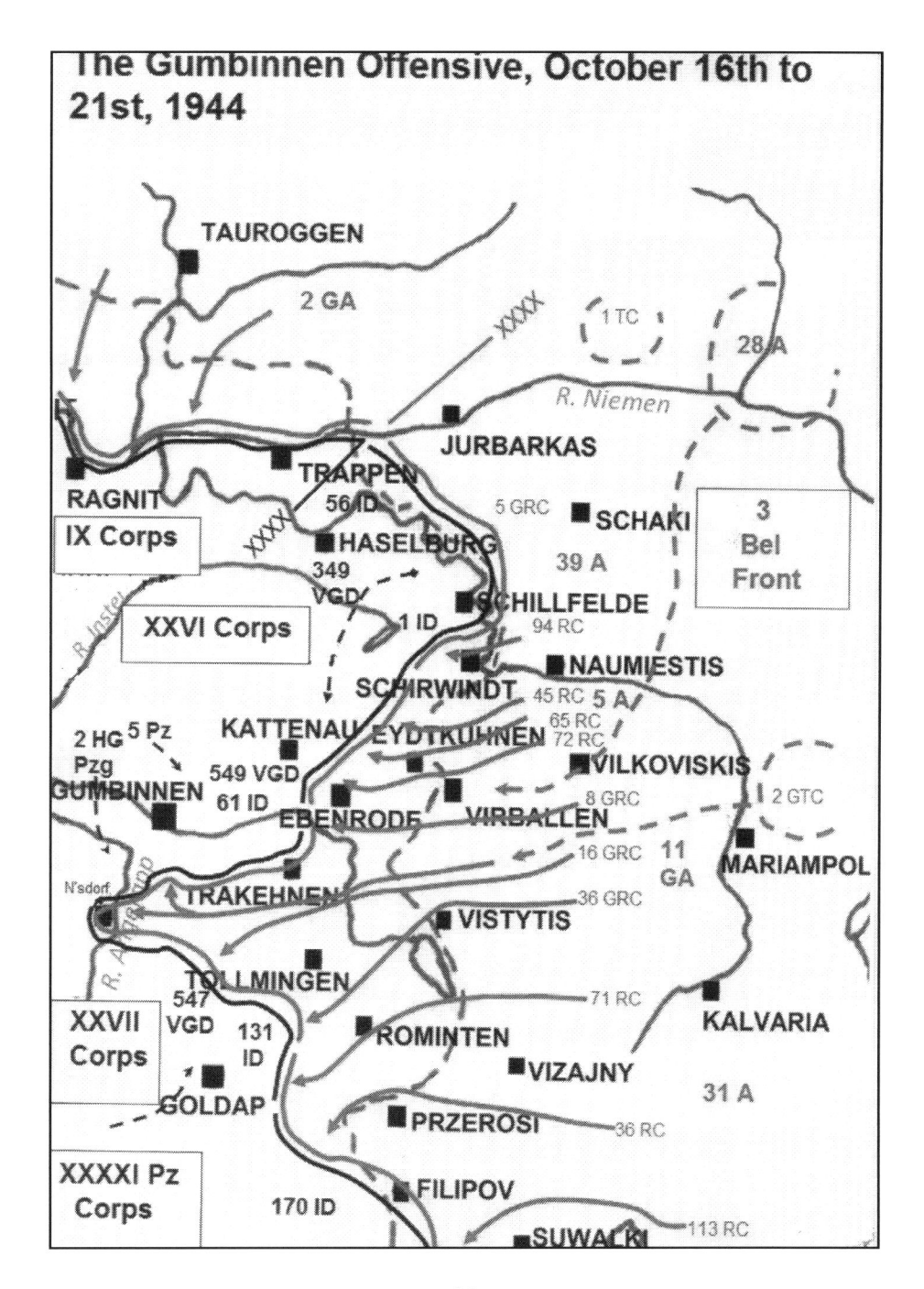

The Gumbinnen Offensive, October 16th to 21st, 1944

Bitter fighting continued around Gumbinnen during the 21st. By the evening Galitsky's leading units south west of the town had crossed the River Angerapp, Burdeinyi's 2nd Guards Tank Corps taking the village of Nemmersdorf[24] to secure the bridge across the river there. Other elements of the 11th Guards Army captured Trakehnen on the northern shoulder of the salient while the fighting also spread further south around Goldap, where the XXXXI Panzer Corps, supported by the Volkssturm, put up a good show against the 31st Army.

For the Germans it was critical that the Soviets be prevented from breaking through the second defence belt. The penetration between the XXVII Corps and XXXXI Panzer Corps had prompted them to transfer forces south from the Third Panzer Army's front. Raus had been able to pull much of the XXXX Panzer Corps, including Major General Erich Walther's newly arriving 2nd Parachute-Panzergrenadier Division *Herman Göring* and the 5th Panzer Division, out of the Tilsit bridgehead and moved them south to assist Hossbach. The 2nd *Herman Göring* had not yet been fully formed and lacked much heavy equipment. The veteran 5th Panzer, which was immediately thrown into action to stabilise the front near Trakehnen, remained significantly under strength after the heavy fighting it had seen over the last three weeks. Other newly committed units also arrived to bolster the German position. One such was Colonel Hans-Joachim Kahler's Führer Grenadier Brigade, which was lavishly equipped but lacked combat experience. It reinforced those elements of Hossbach's Fourth Army which were already fighting around Goldap. Fortunately for the Germans, these forces reached the front just in time to confront the fresh 28th Army. Hossbach considered it imperative that the Soviet salient at Nemmersdorf be eliminated so that the stability of his front could be restored. To achieve this, the 5th Panzer Division formed up a battle group on the northern shoulder of the salient. The battle group was under the command of Captain Alfred Jaedtke of the 14th Panzergrenadier Regiment. He was supported by the thirty Tiger II tanks of Captain Werner Freiherr von Beschwitz's Heavy Panzer Battalion 505. Their task was to push south from Gumbinnen to link up with the Fuhrer Grenadier Regiment as it drove north from Goldap, trapping the Soviet spearhead to the west where it could then be destroyed.

October 22nd was a day of confused fighting across the fluid front between Gumbinnen and Goldap. The leading elements of Luchinsky's 28th Army began to enter the line east of Ebenrode and launched a fierce attack into the positions of the 549th and 561st Volksgrenadier Divisions. Between Gumbinnen and Ebenrode the Germans gathered together a mixed collection of battle groups and composite units. Immediately south of Gumbinnen was the 2nd *Herman Göring* Division while to the east, near Gross Trakehnen, were elements of the 1st *Herman Göring* Division and 103rd and 102nd Panzer Brigades. Between these two groups was the 5th Panzer Division and Heavy Panzer Battalion 505 which were about to counter attack. Protracted fighting ensued as the Soviets tried repeatedly to take Gumbinnen, but it remained in German hands for the time being.

With the battles around and east of Gumbinnen increasing in intensity, the 5th Panzer Division began its counter attack. Battle Group Jaedtke launched strong attacks from Schweitzertal and drove into the extended right flank of the 2nd Guards Tank Corps and 11th Guards Army. The severely overstretched positions of the tank corps were easily broken through and the Germans quickly gained control of Grosswaltersdorf, threatening to isolate the tip of the Soviet salient. While the 5th Panzer Division moved down from the north, the Führer Grenadier Brigade began its attack from the south. The inexperience of this newly formed unit showed as it attacked in uncoordinated groups which took heavy fire and suffered a high number of casualties. Starting west of Lake Goldap, the Germans moved north towards Daken and Grosswaltersdorf. After midday the Führer Grenadier Brigade had reached Daken but between the two German pincers stretched a two mile gap which the Soviets fought desperately to keep open. Both the 5th Panzer Division and Führer Grenadier Brigade renewed their attacks throughout the afternoon and, after difficult fighting, the latter captured the town of Tellrode, just a few hundred yards from Grosswaltersdorf.

Despite the German counter attack being on the verge of success, the Soviet attacks on Gumbinnen and Goldap continued. After being repulsed earlier in the day, the 11th Guards Army and 2nd Guards Tank Corps resumed their attacks and finally managed to push into Gumbinnen from the south. In bitter fighting they pushed the Germans out, taking control of the ruined and burning town by the end of the day. Further south the attacks by the 31st Army at Goldap also continued. The remnants of the 131st Infantry Division, supported by the 279th Assault Gun Brigade, put up a stiff battle north east of the town and held up the Soviet attack, inflicting severe losses in men and armour. To the east the 170th Infantry Division was pushed back into Goldap itself, and after ferocious fighting Glagolev's men finally succeeded in taking it from the Germans. During the bitter fighting Soviet artillery fire had struck the armoured vehicle in which Priess was travelling, killing the general.

The following day, October 23rd, Battle Group Jaedtke at Grosswaltersdorf linked up with the Führer Grenadier Brigade at Tellrode and completed the isolation of the forward elements of the 11th Guards Army and 2nd Guards Tank Corps. The Germans struggled to hold the corridor intact, coming under fierce attack from both west and east as the Soviet units trapped inside tried to escape. The Germans were able to mop up the pocket throughout the day but many Soviet troops were able to escape to the east through the thinly held German lines. German soldiers who moved in to secure the area found to their shock the murdered bodied of the inhabitants of Nemmersdorf and the surrounding villages. While the Nazi leadership tried to exploit this as a propaganda coup, the men at the front had to make preparations to retake both Gumbinnen and Goldap. The 5th Panzer Division, still supported by the Tigers of Heavy Panzer Battalion 505, recaptured Gumbinnen on October 24th and the Führer Grenadier Regiment, aided by the 102nd Panzer Brigade took Goldap on the 25th. Bitter fighting would continue for the remainder of the month as the 39th and 5th Armies renewed their attacks around Schillfelde and Schlossberg. The armies on the southern wing of the 3rd Belorussian Front continued to attack around Gumbinnen and Goldap into early November.

THE BATTLE OF KÖNIGSBERG

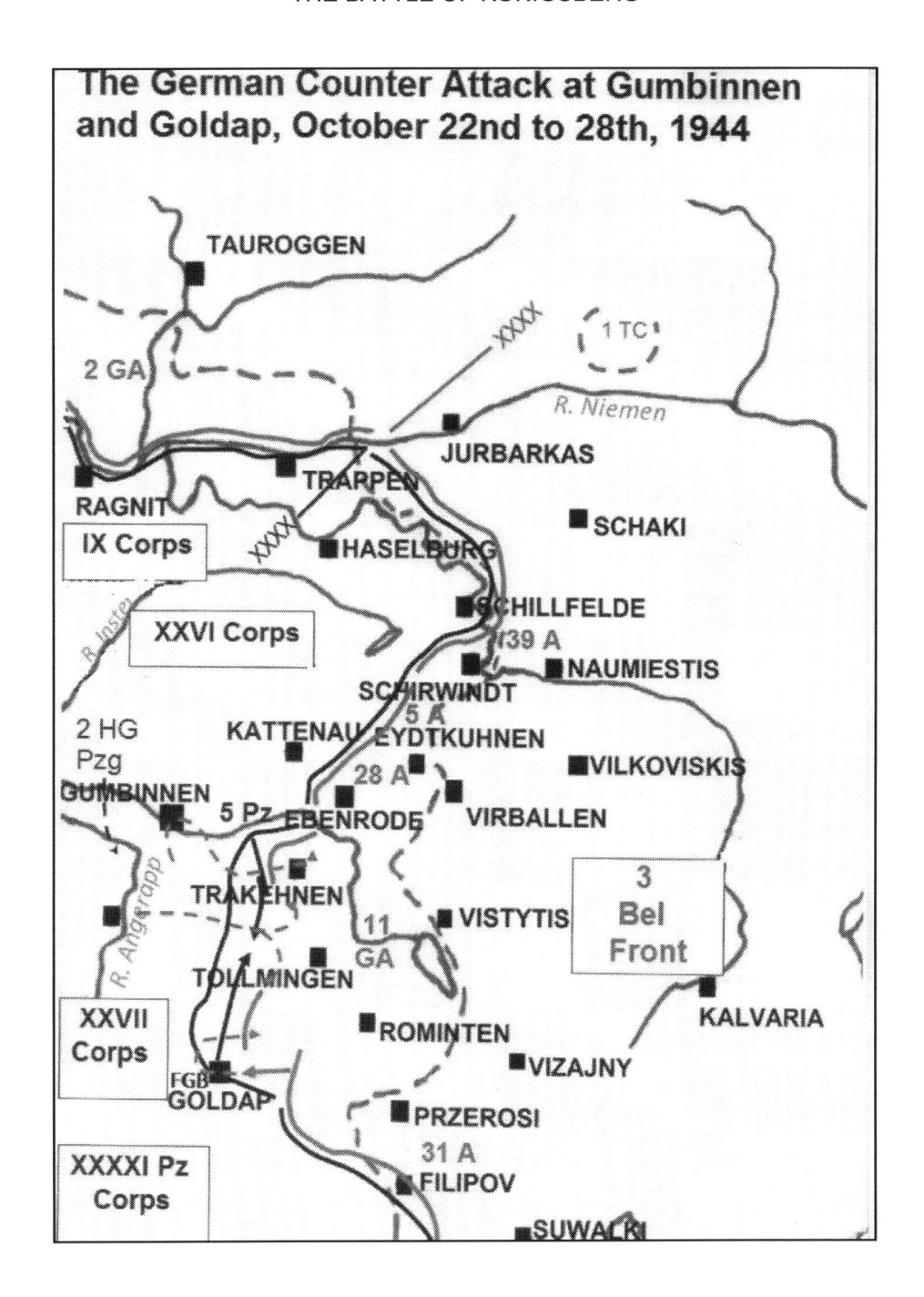

The German Counter Attack at Gumbinnen and Goldap, October 22nd to 28th, 1944

It was clear that as the fighting died down towards the end of October that the threat of a Soviet penetration through to Insterburg and even Königsberg had been averted. Tenacious German defence at the frontier had held up the Soviet troops and inflicted severe casualties. With deeply echeloned positions, the Germans had been able to blunt the Soviet thrusts and build up sufficient reinforcements to nip off the only breakthrough the Soviets had achieved. This difficult battle had cost the 3rd Belorussian Front dear, and given Chernyakhovsky much to think about.

At the beginning of November the Soviet forces along the East Prussian frontier went on the defensive. From June 1944 the Soviet armies had fought their way across Belorussia and the Baltic States and succeeded in clearing the Germans from Soviet territory. Casualties during these campaigns had been very severe; the fighting during the Gumbinnen Offensive alone seeing the 3rd Belorussian Front lose around 16,000 killed and 62,000 wounded. Time was now needed to replenish the armies, to replace losses and rebuild the road and rail network so that supplies, equipment and fresh troops could be brought forward.

The battles of August through to October 1944 had brought Soviet troops onto German territory for the first time, and given them their first taste of revenge. Nemmersdorf, the little village on the Angerapp, which was held by Soviet forces for just a couple of days, was the scene of an atrocity which Josef Goebbels, the German Propaganda Minister, used to try to outrage World opinion. Bringing in observers from Sweden and Switzerland, the mutilated bodies of seventy murdered civilians in Nemmersdorf and another ninety or more in the surrounding villages, were photographed to show the depths of Soviet brutality. Given the millions of Russian, Polish and Ukrainian men, women and children the Germans had killed during their occupation; and the recent discovery of the horrors of the Majdanek concentration camp, such claims had no effect on the outside world. The main impact of the Nemmersdorf massacre, and the publicity Goebbels gave it, was on the German citizens themselves. Goebbels propaganda machine made much of the inhumanity of the Soviet troops. His news films and constant reference to the fate the German people could expect if the Soviets conquered Germany had a profound impact on the German civilians. The alarmist stories from the East, although rooted in fact as it turned out, contributed to the massive numbers of refugees who fled before the Soviet attacks in January 1945, clogging the roads and hindering the movement of the German armies. This was a problem made worse by the ignorant attitude of Erich Koch and his cronies, who refused to even consider the timely evacuation of the threatened districts.

THE BATTLE OF KÖNIGSBERG

[1] At the end of August 1944 the Third Panzer Army comprised the XXVI Corps, IX Corps, XII SS Corps, XXXX Panzer Corps and XXXIX Panzer Corps under command.

[2] Reinhardt was appointed commander of Army Group Centre on August 15th 1944, the previous incumbent, Field Marshal Model, having been transferred to the Western Front. As former commander of the Third Panzer Army he was well aware of the situation on the Siauliai axis.

[3] Guards status was given to particularly successful army and air force units. It brought with it great prestige and better levels of uniform and equipment.

[4] Mellenthin, *Panzer Battles*, Oklahoma Press, p295

[5] Ellis, *The World War Two Databook*, Table 83, p277

[6] Mellenthin, *Panzer Battles*, Oklahoma Press, p299

[7] Jabo was the German slang term for the Soviet ground attack aircraft. The Illyushin Il-2 Shturmovik was a real menace to the Germans during the latter half of the war, being both heavily armed and well protected, and available in great numbers.

[8] The 7th Panzer Division comprised 25th Panzer Regiment, 6th and 7th Panzergrenadier Regiments, 42nd Tank Hunting Brigade and 78th Artillery Regiment, plus support services.

[9] Henrici had taken command of the XXXX Panzer Corps from September 1st, 1944.

[10] The 5th Panzer Division comprised 31st Panzer Regiment, 13th and 14th Panzergrenadier Regiments, 53rd Tank Hunting Battalion and 116th Artillery Regiment plus other services. The division arrived piecemeal and would be committed to the forthcoming battle as it arrived rather than as a concentrated force.

[11] The 88mm Anti-Aircraft gun had been adapted for ground defence in an Anti Tank role early in the war. It was a formidable anti-tank weapon, as had been proven by its use in the Tiger I tank.

[12] Bagramyan, *So We Went to Victory*, p445

[13] Bagramyan, *So We Went to Victory*, p460

[14] Krottingen was renamed Kretinga when it reverted to Lithuanian control after the war.

[15] In early 1944 Hitler had issued a directive on Fortified Places (Fester Platz) which dictated that any town declared a fortress must be held to the last man, the commander being responsible in many cases with his life for ensuring the defence of his particular town. Towns would be declared fortresses without any of the requisite defences or supplies, and merely trapped German troops in pockets where they could be destroyed at will by the Soviets.

[16] The 31st Panzer Regiment was considerably under strength, fielding less than 30 operational tanks when it entered the fighting.

[17] Jurburg – renamed Jurbarkas after the war.

[18] Matzky's XXVI Corps was transferred to the Fourth Army from the Third Panzer Army at the end of September. After Operation Bagration the Fourth Army had had to be reformed completely. At the end of September it had under command LV Corps, VI Corps, XXXXI Panzer Corps, XXVII Corps and XXVI Corps.

[19] Schittnig was promoted to Lieutenant-General on January 1st 1945.

[20] Schirwindt is now known as Kutusovo in the Kaliningrad Oblast.

[21] Schlossberg was formerly known as Pilkallen. In 1938 the Nazi's renamed the town, and many others in the frontier regions, deeming there name insufficiently German. The town is now called Dobrowolsk.

[22] Ebenrode was formerly Stalluponen. When the Soviet Union took control, it was renamed Nesterov.

[23] Dieckert & Grossmann, *Der Kampf um Ostpreussen*, p76

[24] Nemmersdorf is now known as Mayakovskoye

THE BATTLE OF KÖNIGSBERG

Chapter Four - The January Storm

The winter of 1944-45 was severe. East Prussia and Poland lay under a thick blanket of snow as temperatures plunged far below zero degrees, turning the ground as hard as concrete and freezing the lakes of Masuria as solid as the ground around. In the stark forests which ran along the frontier of East Prussia masses of Soviet tanks and artillery pieces began to assemble, surrounded by carefully camouflaged piles of ammunition and supplies. The build up had been preceded by weeks of activity and planning.

As early as the end of October 1944 the Soviet High Command had begun planning for the next phase of operations that, it was anticipated, would take them to the gates of Berlin and Königsberg. On November 16th Stalin had reshuffled the front commands in Poland in preparation for this final drive against the Germans. Pride of place went to Marshal Zhukov, who took command of the 1st Belorussian Front. Zhukov, the saviour of Moscow in the dark days of 1941, and architect of many of the victories since, was awarded the honour of leading the Soviet Front which was to crush the German forces in their capital. Rokossovsky, who had commanded the 1st Belorussian Front up to this point, was shunted sideways to take command of the 2nd Belorussian Front. Rokossovsky's move was largely due to his Polish heritage. Stalin wanted the victory over the Germans to be an undeniably Russian one and a general of Polish descent could not be left in command of the forces which would strike directly into Berlin. Zhukov's usual role as Stavka co-ordinator was taken up by Stalin, who was keen to present himself as the personal victor over Hitler. With the war clearly in its final stages Stalin was intent that none of his generals should outshine him. Marshal Vasilevsky was left to co-ordinate the operations of the 1st and 2nd Baltic Fronts against Army Group North in Courland, a mere sideshow at best.

THE BATTLE OF KÖNIGSBERG

The Soviet front line now ran everywhere, excepting Courland, on foreign soil. Chernyakhovsky's 3rd Belorussian Front stood in the eastern frontier districts of East Prussia. His next move appeared obvious, a drive west to take Königsberg, then on to the mouth of the Vistula to push the Germans from East Prussia entirely. To the south the 2nd and 1st Belorussian Fronts and 1st Ukrainian Front were deployed in the southern regions of East Prussia and along the Vistula in eastern Poland. A westward advance by these forces would clear the Germans from Poland and lead them on the road to Berlin.

The concentration of forces and supplies in Poland and along the East Prussian frontier began in earnest at the end of November and continued throughout December 1944 and into early January 1945. During this time the Soviet plan continued to evolve. It became clear that the strongest resistance would be expected from the German forces concentrated in Poland and with this in mind the emphasis of the attack on East Prussia was also amended. East Prussia could not be ignored. The presence of sizeable German forces on Zhukov's right flank as he pushed through Poland meant that the Germans there would need to be neutralised. The amended plan therefore called for the offensive, which would begin between January 15-20th, by Chernyakhovsky's 3rd Belorussian Front to break through the German defence lines before the Inster Valley, then move on to take Königsberg. Rokossovsky's 2nd Belorussian Front was to destroy the German forces along the River Narew and push northwest to reach the mouth of the Vistula, taking Danzig and Elbing in the process. These attacks would isolate the German Fourth and Third Panzer Armies in East Prussia while destroying Weiss' Second Army in the Vistula Delta and in Pomerania. The group of German forces left in East Prussia would then be destroyed piecemeal. It was as clear in the winter of 1944 as it had been in the autumn that Chernyakhovsky's attack along the Königsberg axis would be difficult and costly. The Germans were well aware of Soviet intentions and had strengthened their already extensive defences to counter just such a blow. During the planning phase Rokossovsky had pressed that the main Soviet thrust towards Königsberg should be made from the south, from the Narew bridgeheads so that the strongest German defences were turned rather than battered through. This would have seen Chernyakhovsky's forces taking on a holding role as the Germans were destroyed by a thrust into their rear. Rokossovsky's suggestion was rejected by Stalin, who saw Chernyakhovsky taking on the main role against East Prussia. The attacks by the 2nd Belorussian Front therefore took the form of a deep thrust in order to isolate East Prussia as a whole and protect the flank of the 1st Belorussian Front as it moved forward towards the Oder. Chernyakhovsky was to batter his way through to Königsberg against what he, and many of his army and corps commanders knew, would be determined German resistance. To carry out this plan, a number of redeployments had taken place over the winter months, so that the bulk of the 3rd Belorussian Front could be grouped into as strong an assault grouping as was possible.

To the north, the main part of Bagramyan's 1st Baltic Front continued to face the defenders of Memel and the forces in Courland. Of the Front's forces, only Beloborodov's 43rd Army now faced south, along the northern bank of the River Niemen opposite Wuthmann's IX Corps. Chanchibadze's 2nd Guards Army, which had previously held this position, had been taken out of the line and moved south to join the left wing of the 3rd Belorussian Front. Bagramyan was to launch an attack along the Niemen with the 43rd Army after the 3rd Belorussian Front attack had succeeded in pushing through the German defence lines. He would also move to eliminate the defenders of Memel, before bringing his forces south to assist in the destruction of the Germans in Samland.

Chernyakhovsky's 3rd Belorussian Front, with over 700,000 troops, 800 tanks and Su's[1] and 3,000 artillery pieces, would strike along the axis that had held them up in October. His forces were deployed opposite the right wing of the Third Panzer Army and against the northern wing of the Fourth Army. The initial attacks were to destroy the Germans between Tilsit and Insterburg within the first ten days of the offensive. With the Tilsit-Insterburg defences breached, the 3rd Belorussian Front would then advance on Wehlau and Königsberg.

Chernyakhovsky deployed Lyudnikov's 39th Army on his northern wing between Sudargas and Schlossberg, with Provalov's 113th, Bezugly's 5th Guards and Prokofiev's 94th Rifle Corps, each of which had three rifle divisions. Lyudnikov had massed the bulk of his army on the left wing, with 5th Guards Rifle Corps northeast of Schlossberg and 94th Rifle Corps to the southeast. The 113th Rifle Corps held the remainder of the line with a thin screen of infantry, the majority of its men also being massed alongside the flank of the 5th Guards Rifle Corps. This left wing group was to break through the German line at Schlossberg and then push northwest into the rear of the German IX Corps, linking up with the 43rd Army on the River Niemen at Tilsit to encircle the right wing of the IX Corps and left wing of the XXVI Corps.

Deployed in the centre were the main breakthrough forces of the 3rd Belorussian Front. Between Schlossberg and Ebenrode was Colonel-General Nikolai Krylov's 5th Army with Kazariev's 72nd Rifle Corps on the right wing, Gorokhov's 45th in the centre and Perekrestov's 65th Rifle Corps on the left. The 5th Army was to crush the 349th Volksgrenadier Division and push forwards to the River Inster before moving on to skirt the southern defences of Königsberg. Once the rifle divisions had breached the German front Krylov would introduce the 2nd Guards Tank Corps into the battle to lead the exploitation phase through the Inster Valley. Part of the second echelon, the 2nd Guards Tank Corps under Lieutenant-General Burdeinyi[2], had been reinforced after its blooding at Nemmersdorf and was keen to exact its revenge on the Germans. Immediately south of the 5th Army was Luchinsky's 28th Army, positioned roughly between Ebenrode and Gross Trakehnen. It deployed Perkhorovich's 3rd Guards Rifle Corps on the right, Batitsky's 128th Rifle Corps in the centre and Shvarev's 20th Rifle Corps on the left. Luchinsky would strike directly east at first before wheeling to the southwest to take Gumbinnen and then Insterburg. His initial attacks would smash through the 549th Volksgrenadier Division and, after the Inster had been reached, would introduce the 11th Guards Army into its area of operations. From Insterburg, the 28th would move to the south bank of the Pregel and continue the drive into the Natangen region of East Prussia.

Held in the second echelon were the three Guards rifle corps of Colonel-General Galitsky's 11th Guards Army, a total of nine guards rifle divisions. Also grouped with them were the tanks of Butkov's 1st Tank Corps. The 11th Guards Army and 1st Tank Corps were to enter the battle after the German front lines had been broken through. They would enter the Inster Valley and make a thrust towards Wehlau. Galitsky was then to move his army directly along the Pregel with Königsberg as the target.

To the left of the 28th Army, in the area between Gross Trakehnen and Goldap, were the nine divisions of Chanchibadze's 2nd Guards Army split between the 13th Guards, 11th Guards and 60th Rifle Corps deployed from north to south. Their task was to break through Grossmann's VI Corps and push into the rear of the German forces in the Masurian Lakes area, driving on Nordenburg and Gerdauen in order to stop the Germans from transferring forces to the north. The left wing of the Front, from Goldap to the junction with the 2nd Belorussian Front at Augustow, was held by Lieutenant-General Glagolev's 31st Army with Oleshov's 36th and Koshevoy's 71st Rifle Corps. It would undertake a largely holding role, pinning the Fourth Army down to prevent the transfer of forces either to the Third Panzer or Second Armies.

Chernyakhovsky's attacks would again be supported by the aircraft of the 1st Air Army. Its fighter planes would keep the Luftwaffe from interfering in the course of operations while the bombers and ground attack aircraft added to the fire of the artillery, supported the ground forces and disrupted German command and communications network to the rear.

By mid January 1945 the Soviets had completed their preparations, moving artillery and armour up to their attack positions, repairing the road and rail network and stockpiling huge quantities of fuel and ammunition. Wherever possible the attacking units were brought up to strength with intakes of replacements. For the citizens and soldiers in

East Prussia the hour of reckoning had come, the Soviet hordes were about to descend on them with all the fury they could bring, exacting revenge for three and a half years of slaughter.

* * *

Across the front lines, the Chief of the German Army General Staff, Heinz Guderian, was a worried man. On December 24th, with the Ardennes offensive in full swing, he had driven to Hitler's western headquarters at Ziegenburg for the regular command conference. By this stage of the war the public, who were suffering under continual Allied bombing raids, and had enemy armies approaching their homes from both the East and West, never saw their Führer. To those who did see him, his appearance was markedly different from the early days of the war. As one German general wrote on seeing the Führer, he was a:

> ...stooped figure with a pale and puffy face, hunched in his chair, his hands trembling, his left arm subject to a violent twitching which he did his best to conceal. A sick man...When he walked he dragged one leg behind him.[3]

As the head of the OKH[4], Guderian was responsible for the operations of the armies on the Eastern Front. At the conference he outlined to Hitler and the others present the dispositions and strengths of the enemy forces in the East. General Gehlen, head of Fremde Heer Ost,[5] had provided Guderian with two extensive and extremely detailed reports on Soviet strengths. Gehlen estimated that the Soviet armies possessed a superiority of 11:1 in men, 7:1 in tanks and 20:1 in artillery, and predicted a new offensive would begin toward the middle of January 1945. Hitler, refusing to believe the Soviets could possibly be as strong as Gehlen claimed, angrily declared a fraud, accusing it of being based on an enemy bluff. "It's the greatest imposture since Genghis Khan" Hitler shouted "Who's responsible for producing all this rubbish."[6] He strongly asserted that Soviet rifle formations possessed 6-7,000 men at best instead of their regulation 10,000 (which was in actual fact about right), and that their tank formations had no tanks at all. On the latter point he was way off the mark. Jodl also opposed Guderian's arguments in order to protect his own area of responsibility. With the German counter attack in the Ardennes still in full swing[7], he wanted to keep Hitler's attention fixed on the Western Front, where he believed the Germans had regained the initiative.

Figure 25 - Heinz Guderian, Chief of the Army General Staff and head of the OKH

Undeterred, Guderian pressed on and requested that the forces trapped in Courland be evacuated. In this he also met with a flat refusal from Hitler. The suggestion that the divisions currently being evacuated from Finland into Norway be sent to the Eastern Front to build up some reserves was also ignored. The discussion then turned to the tactical deployment of the armies in the East. Guderian argued that the Main Combat Zone, where the Soviet offensive would be brought to a halt, should be sited several miles behind the Forward Combat Zone. This would ensure that the troops in that Main Zone, and the operational reserves deployed there, would not be affected by the opening barrage that was customary before a Soviet offensive. Despite clear evidence of the effectiveness of such a policy, Hitler again obstinately refused to agree to this sensible measure. He merely saw it as a way for the generals to give up territory without a fight. Instead of agreeing, Hitler made matters worse by issuing an ordered shortening the distance between the forward and main combat areas to just six miles. Guderian argued long and hard against this but on a day of defeats, this was yet another. Hitler's order placed the mobile reserves, and main line of resistance well within the range of the Soviet bombardment.

On New Years Eve 1944 Guderian again tried to convince Hitler of the need to strengthen the armies on the Eastern Front. This time, before going to the conference, Guderian visited Field Marshal Gerd von Rundstedt, the commander of the German Armies in the West, in order to get an understanding of his dispositions and to see if any forces could be released for transfer to the Eastern Front. Rundstedt told Guderian he could immediately release three divisions from the Western Front and also another from Italy. Armed with this information, Guderian then reported to Hitler. Another tempestuous meeting followed as Guderian again requested that reinforcements be sent to the Eastern Front. Jodl immediately stepped in and declared there were no forces available in the West that could be transferred. Guderian, armed with his information from Rundstedt, told Jodl which divisions could be released. Jodl had no reply to this and so this time Guderian secured the release of four divisions. Unfortunately, in what can only be seen as a deliberate attempt to undermine him, Hitler insisted that the divisions were deployed to Hungary rather than Poland.

While Hitler obstructed his own commanders, the concentration of Soviet forces in Poland and East Prussia had not gone unnoticed by the

Germans. To Guderian it was clear that the next offensive would strike at Army Groups Centre and A, but Hitler remained convinced that any new Soviet attack would strike the German forces in Hungary. Between January 5th and 8th Guderian toured the army group headquarters of the Eastern Front, meeting with or speaking to all of their commanders in order to build up a picture of what they believed the Soviets would do next, and what their own defensive capability was. The assessments made by General Harpe at Army Group A, which was deployed in Poland, and Reinhardt at Army Group Centre in East Prussia were the same, a Soviet offensive was expected by the middle of January. Both General Harpe at Army Group A, and Reinhardt at Army Group Centre, had come up with similar defensive plans. They each proposed that a strip of land twelve miles deep be abandoned in order to establish stronger defences along a shorter line. This would have the dual effect of creating an operational reserve while also disrupting Soviet preparations, as they would have had to move their entire line forward.

Infuriated by his seemingly unending struggle with Hitler and the apparent futility of his efforts, on January 9th 1945 Guderian nevertheless again tried to persuade him of the danger to Poland and East Prussia. For a third time he made the long journey to the western headquarters, this time accompanied by Gehlen. Armed with an updated intelligence report, Guderian urged that reinforcements be sent to the Eastern Front. Once more Guderian aimed to hammer home his argument with reference to the intelligence Gehlen had brought together. Presented with Gehlen's assessment Hitler:

> *...completely lost his temper when these were shown to him, declaring them to be 'completely idiotic' and ordering that I* [Guderian] *have the man who had made then shut up in a lunatic asylum. I then lost my temper and said to Hitler: "The man who made these is General Gehlen, one of my very best general staff officers. I should not have shown them to you were I in*

disagreement with them. If you want General Gehlen sent to a lunatic asylum then you had better have me certified as well.[8]

Hitler, never easily cowed when dealing with the General Staff, demanded that Guderian relieve Gehlen of his post. Guderian pointedly refused. Guderian then moved on to the suggestion made by Generals Harpe and Reinhardt that the front line be shorted by a short tactical withdrawal. Predictably, Hitler rejected these suggestions out of hand. His arbitrary decision condemned the armies in the East to stand on their existing positions. Despite the turbulent nature of this latest clash, Hitler closed his meeting with Guderian with words of encouragement:

'The Eastern Front has never possessed such a strong reserve as now. That is your doing. I thank you for it.' I [Guderian] *replied 'The Eastern Front is like a house of cards. If the front is broken through at one point all the rest will collapse, for twelve and a half divisions are far too small a reserve for so extended a front.'...With Hitler's parting remark 'The Eastern Front must help itself and make do with what it's got.' I returned, in a very grave frame of mind, to my headquarters at Zossen.*[9]

And so the Eastern Front made do with what it had. On the eve of the Soviet attack Reinhardt's Army Group Centre consisted of 580,000 men, 700 tanks and assault guns and 515 planes[10] across East Prussia. These forces were deployed between Raus' Third Panzer Army, Hossbach's Fourth Army and Weiss' Second Army, a total of thirty-four infantry, four panzergrenadier and three panzer divisions. Reinhardt's main armoured reserve was Panzer Corps *Grossdeutschland*, which was deployed behind the Second Army. Unfortunately, at the very moment Koniev attacked in southern Poland, Hitler transferred this unit to Kielce to meet the Soviet attack, meaning it took no part in the ensuing battles in East Prussia, while also arriving too late to influence events in Poland. The *Grossdeutschland* Panzergrenadier Division would remain in East Prussia during the latter stages of the battle, but crucially was absent in the critical first days.

Raus' Third Panzer Army had been restructured after the difficult battles of October 1944. At the beginning of the New Year, Raus' army comprised 120,000 troops in eleven divisions with around 100 tanks and 400 artillery pieces. The forces in the main combat line were distributed between three corps'. Wuthmann's IX Corps held the left wing along the south bank of the River Niemen with the remnants of Lieutenant-General Friedrich-Georg Eberhardt's 286th Security Division deployed close to the mouth of the Niemen, Major-General Siegfried Verhein's 551st Volksgrenadier Division west of Tilsit and Major-General Erich Sudau's 548th Volksgrenadier Division between Tilsit to Trappen. South of the river, protecting the extended right flank of the corps, were Major-General Walter Gorn's 561st Volksgrenadier Division and Major-General Edmund Blaurock's 56th Infantry Division, the latter situated north of Schillfelde. Running south from Schillfelde was General Matzky's XXVI Corps. In November the XXVI Corps had been transferred over to Third Panzer Army command from that of the Fourth Army. It comprised Lieutenant-General Siegfried Rein's 69th Infantry Division to the south of Schillfelde and Lieutenant-General Hans Schittnig's 1st Infantry Division to the north and east of Schlossberg. Facing the Soviet 5th and 28th Armies in the main assault sector before Kattenau were Major-General Karl Kötz's 349th and Major-General Karl Jank's 549th Volksgrenadier Divisions. To the rear, situated in the Inster Valley north and east of Breitenstein, was the reserve division of the Third Panzer Army, Major-General Rolf Lippert's 5th Panzer. The 5th had recovered some of its strength since the October battles and now deployed around seventy operational tanks plus thirty Jagdpanzer IV's. Another twenty tanks were also in the workshops undergoing repair. Also in reserve was Major Senff von Pilsach's Heavy Panzer Battalion 505 with a complement of Tiger II tanks. Separated from, but still part of, the Third Panzer Army was Gollnick's XXVIII Corps in the Memel bridgehead with its 58th and 95th Infantry Divisions.

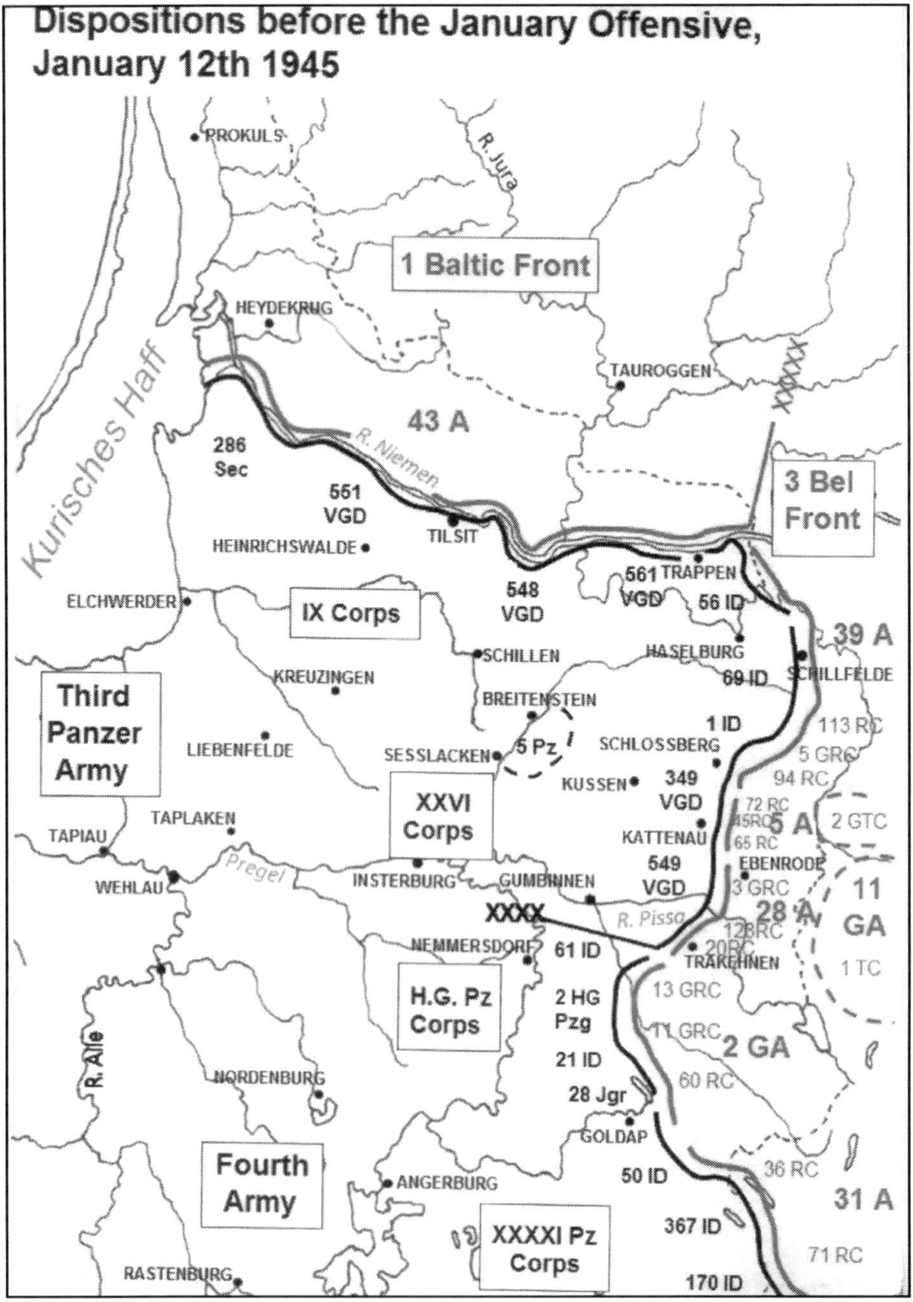
Dispositions before the January Offensive, January 12th 1945
PROKULS
R. Jura
1 Baltic Front
HEYDEKRUG
Kurisches Haff
TAUROGGEN
43 A
286 Sec
R. Niemen
551 VGD
3 Bel Front
TILSIT
HEINRICHSWALDE
561 VGD
TRAPPEN
548 VGD
56 ID
ELCHWERDER
IX Corps
39 A
SCHILLEN
HASELBURG
SCHILLFELDE
69 ID
KREUZINGEN
Third Panzer Army
BREITENSTEIN
1 ID
113 RC
5 Pz
SCHLOSSBERG
5 GRC
LIEBENFELDE
SESSLACKEN
94 RC
KUSSEN
349 VGD
XXVI Corps
72 RC
2 GTC
5 A
TAPLAKEN
65 RC
KATTENAU
TAPIAU
549 VGD
EBENRODE
WEHLAU
Pregel
INSTERBURG
GUMBINNEN
VGD
3 GRC
11 GA
XXXX
28 A
R. Pissa
NEMMERSDORF
61 ID
TRAKEHNEN
1 TC
13 GRC
H.G. Pz Corps
2 HG Pzg
11 GRC
2 GA
R. Alle
21 ID
60 RC
NORDENBURG
28 Jgr
GOLDAP
36 RC
Fourth Army
50 ID
ANGERBURG
31 A
367 ID
XXXXI Pz Corps
71 RC
RASTENBURG
170 ID

THE BATTLE OF KÖNIGSBERG

On the northern wing of Hossbach's Fourth Army, securing the junction with the Third Panzer Army was the Parachute-Panzer Corps *Herman Göring*. It comprised Colonel Wilhelm Söth's 2nd Parachute-Panzer Division *Herman Göring*, General Günther Krappe's 61st Infantry Division and a flak regiment and tank hunting battalion detached from the 1st Parachute-Panzer Division *Herman Göring*. The 61st Infantry Division, elements of which would fight in the final battle for Königsberg, was a veteran East Prussian unit which originated from Wehrkreis I. It had its peacetime headquarters at Königsberg and was raised from East Prussian reservists and other drafts. It began the conflict in Poland in 1939, being involved in the invasion as part of the Third Army. In 1940 it fought in its way through Belgium and harried the British and French forces back to Dunkirk before leaving France in the spring of 1941 to join the German Eighteenth Army for the invasion of the Soviet Union. The division then spent the remainder of the war on the Eastern Front, being heavily involved in the fighting around Leningrad and in the Valdai Hills in 1941 and 1942. It suffered very heavy casualties during these battles and in mid-1942 a battalion from each infantry regiment was disbanded so as to reinforce the remaining six battalions. In the winter of 1942/43 the division was involved in further bitter fighting around Lake Ladoga and remained in action near the city through 1943. After the disaster overtook Army Group Centre in mid-1944 it was brought down from the north as reinforcement, only to become embroiled in the retreat into Poland. After further heavy losses the division was reconstituted in October 1944, but remained with Army Group Centre. It included under its command the 151st, 162nd and 176th Grenadier Regiments. The Parachute-Panzer Corps *Herman Göring* was deployed south west of Gumbinnen. To the south, between Goldap and Treuburg, was the XXXXI Panzer Corps under General Weidling with its 21st Infantry, 28th Jäger, 50th, 367th and 170th Infantry Divisions.

Raus and Hossbach had spent much of December 1944 reinforcing the defence lines which stretched to a depth of fifty miles behind the forward lines. To all intents and purposes much of East Prussia became a fortified area. From the Forward Defence Zone to the

Reserve Position there were six successive lines of defence, two light defence lines in the forward zone, and four more in the main and reserve defence zones. The Germans had undertaken considerable training through the winter months and the men of the Third Panzer and Fourth Armies were confident that their newly built defence lines would blunt the Soviet offensive when it inevitably came. Despite the confidence the troops held in their defences, their shortage of anti-tank guns and artillery pieces could not be hidden. This left a great reliance on minefields and other obstacles to slow the initial Soviet offensive.

Despite it being obvious to any rational observer that a Soviet offensive was imminent, East Prussia was full of increasingly worried and nervous civilians. The repeated urging of General Reinhardt for the evacuation of the populace was ignored by the Party leaders. Koch and his deputy, Paul Dargel, made repeated exhortations that East Prussia would be held, and that any evacuation of the populace was out of the question. They even went so far as to declare that any attempt to prepare for an evacuation would be met with severe punishment. Only those areas under the direct control of the army were evacuated, and as the offensive progressed the Party acted far too slowly to enable the civilians to leave before the enemy were on their doorstep.

The German commanders were careful to observe the Soviet preparations, using all the intelligence measures they had at their disposal. Heavy enemy activity behind the front line on the nights of 9th and 10th January was followed by two days of unexpected quiet. Along the battle lines the Soviets undertook increasingly strong reconnaissance attacks. Particular attention seemed to be focussed on the Schlossberg and Ebenrode sectors, where the German defences were tested repeatedly. The capture of prisoners during January 12th enabled Raus to identify that the Soviet offensive would probably begin on the 13th and so, at 2200 hours on January 12th, he ordered the evacuation of the forward defence lines, and the movement of German artillery to their secondary positions. During the night the German troops pulled back carefully, to await the onslaught the next day.

THE BATTLE OF KÖNIGSBERG

* * *

On January 13th 1945 the great Soviet offensive against East Prussia, which Guderian had feared, Gehlen predicted and both Raus and Hossbach had prepared for, finally began. Churchill's plea of January 6th, when he called on the Soviets to launch an attack in the East to aid the Allied forces in their battle against the Germans in the Ardennes, had been taken up with relish by Stalin. Stalin promised that Soviet troops would attack no later than the second half of January. The opening phase of the attack, the offensive by Koniev's 1st Ukrainian Front, was duly brought forward from January 20th to the 12th, while the attack on East Prussia would begin on the 13th.

At 0530 hours on the 13th, with a dense mist obscuring the battlefield, a German bombardment broke the quiet of the night. Flashes of light lit the East Prussian battlefield as artillery and rocket launchers sent their ordinance into the Soviet positions, battering the tightly packed units of the 3rd Belorussian Front in their jumping off areas. The German bombardment was meant to disrupt the attacking forces and unsettle their timetable. Unfortunately, the lack of sufficient stockpiles of artillery ammunition precluded any major success, but the barrage did sent a message to the Soviet troops that their attack would not be without resistance. At 0600 hours the Soviets responded in kind as their two-hour artillery barrage by more than 3,000 artillery pieces poured a huge quantity of fire on the German lines, with particularly heavy shelling against the XXVI Corps in the Schlossberg to Ebenrode sector. During their barrage the Soviets fired off around 120,000 artillery shells. The German positions, which Soviet reconnaissance attacks over the preceding days had identified, were torn to pieces. Telephone lines were severed, strong points flattened and soldiers killed or wounded. Unfortunately, as with Bagramyan's offensive in October 1944, the weather hindered the effectiveness of the opening barrage, the mist preventing effective artillery observation and the ability of the 1st Air

Army to providing close support to the artillery and attacking infantry. The withdrawal of German units from the forward positions also had an impact, as attested by the Germans:

> *The area fire, covering up to three miles in depth, was scattered and damaged only evacuated towns and former command posts, the obvious targets of the Russian artillery. The German reserves were hidden in the woods and remained unharmed by the preparation fire. By 0800, after pulverising the first position, the Russian fire concentrated on the second one, but with less intensity. Half an hour later the shells were scattered through the depth of the battle position, gradually diminishing to area or harassing fire without definite targets.*[11]

At 0800 hours the leading assault units, which had already begun to advance under the cover of the artillery fire, were well into the German Forward Defence Zone. The dense mist which had reduced the effectiveness of the Soviet artillery fire now screened the movement of the attacking infantry and armour. By 1000 hours Soviet tanks and infantry had penetrated as far as the first line of the main defence zone, but were then pinned down by concentrated enemy fire. The Germans put up a hard fight, launching repeated counter attacks against the Soviet assaults. In heavy fighting close to Schlossberg, Schittnig's 1st Infantry Division put up a fierce defence against wave after wave of attacks by the 5th Guards and 94th Rifle Corps' of Lyudnikov's 39th Army. In heavy fighting Lieutenant-Colonel Trautmann's 22nd Fusilier Regiment of the 1st Infantry Division was pushed back to the outskirts of Schlossberg, but ferocious counter attacks regained control of the ruined houses and expelled the Soviet troops.

To the south, Krylov's 5th and Luchinsky's 28th Armies battered Kötz's 349th and Jank's 549th Volksgrenadier Divisions on the Kattenau axis. Krylov's men managed to claw their way just a mile into the Germans positions, but at a very heavy cost. Kattenau was eventually taken by the 3rd Guards Rifle Corps of the 28th Army after heavy fighting with the 1099th and 1097th Grenadier Regiments of the 549th Volksgrenadier Division. This loss forced Matzky to commit his corps reserve, amounting to a wholly inadequate single infantry battalion, the 1st Fusilier Battalion under Captain Schröder which had been detached from the 1st Infantry Division. This single battalion was to restore the situation where an entire division had failed. As Schröder and his men marched up to the front to help the embattled grenadiers, they came under ferocious and repeated attack, the weather having improved slightly so that Soviet aircraft were aloft in considerable numbers. As they drew closer to the battlefield they were struck by heavy artillery fire. The anticipated counter attack come to nothing and the badly battered battalion was sucked into the inferno and forced to give ground. The capture of Kattenau and partial collapse of the 549th Volksgrenadier Division exposed the positions of the 176th Regiment on the northern flank of the 61st Infantry Division. The 61st was already under fierce attack from the 20th Rifle Corps of the 28th Army, its 151st and 162nd Regiments struggling to maintain their front. To the right of the 61st Infantry Division, the men of the 2nd *Herman Göring* Division were also fending off wave after wave of attacks by other elements of the 28th Army's 20th Rifle Corps.

With his reserve committed and negated by heavy Soviet fire, Matzky was left with no option but to ask for help from Army headquarters. Raus, with just a single division in reserve to support his entire army, therefore ordered Lippert's 5th Panzer Division to prepare to march from Breitenstein to help the infantry hold the line together. The panzers would enter the fray the following day.

For Chernyakhovsky the first day of the offensive had been a difficult one. Clearly the Germans had been expecting the attack, but the tenacity of their resistance had been much greater than expected. The furthest advance had been that achieved by the 28th Army but that was barely two to three miles into the German positions. The 5th and 39th Armies had been held up a mile or so from their start lines, and had suffered considerable losses both in men and armour. While Kattenau had been taken, the Soviets had been unable yet to exploit their gain. Until the breakthrough operation had succeeded, Chernyakhovsky could not release his second echelon forces. They had to wait for the Germans to buckle under the pressure the infantry would bring to bear over the days to come.

The second day of the offensive again dawned overcast and so it began with a fresh Soviet artillery barrage to soften up the German positions before more massed attacks were made against their defences. The aircraft of the 1st Air Army were unable to get off the ground to provide support to the land forces until the afternoon, when the weather had cleared a little. At and north of Schlossberg, the 69th and 1st Infantry Divisions continued to struggle on against the attacks of the 5th Guards and 94th Rifle Corps. The 94th Rifle Corps managed to secure control of the small village of Blumenfeld, situated to the south west of Schlossberg, but a counter attack by the I and III Battalions of the 22nd Fusilier Regiment (1st Infantry Division) successfully regained control of the village that evening, albeit at the cost of heavy casualties to Captain Malotka's I and Captain Stelter's III Battalions.[12]

To the south, Lippert's 5th Panzer Division moved to support Schroeder's 1st Fusilier Battalion, and together they launched a determined counter attack to try to regain control of Kattenau. Lippert deployed his division in two battle groups, one to retake Kattenau and the other to move south of the town to secure the junction with the 549th Volksgrenadier Division. Bitter fighting erupted with the 65th Rifle Corps of the 5th Army as the Germans ran into a strong Soviet anti-tank position. Despite heavy losses the Germans pressed their attacks home and were able to regain control of Kattenau. The second battle group was less successful, being attacked in its flank which brought its advance to a halt. With his division quickly becoming embroiled in holding its own against increasingly strong enemy attacks, Lippert detached a third battle group, comprising the tank hunting battalion of the division, and sent it to support the 349th Volksgrenadier Division, which was also under heavy attack. While these battles raged, the

128th and 20th Rifle Corps of the 28th Army continued to develop their attacks to the east of Gumbinnen and slowly began to force the 61st Infantry Division back towards the town. With their defence lines established in depth though, the Germans foiled any Soviet attempt to achieve a breakthrough.

While Chernyakhovsky continued to develop his attacks on both the Gumbinnen axis and toward the valley of the Inster, to the south Rokossovsky opened the offensive of the 2nd Belorussian Front. The German Second Army, commanded by Colonel-General Weiss, came under heavy attack from the two Soviet bridgeheads on the north bank of the River Narew. Severe snowstorms here also prevented the Soviets from utilising their overwhelming air support and German resistance stiffened considerably in the opening hours of the assault. On the second day of their offensive Rokossovsky's men did succeed in smashing open the Second Army, although their success came at a heavy price. Fortunately for the attacking infantry and armour, the weather cleared later in the day and the Soviet air armies began to work over the German divisions with a vengeance. The attack from the Narew would develop rapidly over the coming days and result in the isolation of the German armies in East Prussia when Rokossovsky's tanks reached the Baltic coast near Elbing.

While Rokossovsky unleashed his attack from the Narew, the 3rd Belorussian Front offensive entered its third day. January 15th began with the now customary barrage of the German positions followed by massed infantry and armour attacks. An improvement in the weather during the afternoon brought Soviet aircraft over the battlefield in great numbers, adding to the German woes. The Luftwaffe was also able to put up a number of sorties, although it failed to influence the course of operations. After yet another day of bitter fighting the men of the 1st Infantry Division, almost dead on their feet from exhaustion after three days of constant fighting and marching, were compelled to pull out of Schlossberg that night. A dangerous Soviet penetration south of the town made further resistance untenable, the Germans being in increasing danger of isolation. Further south, Kattenau was also retaken by the Soviets as the men of the 3rd Guards Rifle Corps forced back the weary 549th Volksgrenadier Division, which struggled to establish a shortened defence line to the rear. The 549th was by this stage of the battle close to breaking apart. This prompted the 5th Panzer Division, which was already hard pressed, to take over part of its combat sector to prevent a total collapse. Frustratingly for Chernyakhovsky, the German line, although it was being shoved back relentlessly and coming perilously close to cracking, still remained essentially intact. Losses were mounting though, and the combat strength of the German divisions was rapidly melting away. So heavy had been the losses in manpower that Matzky was forced to maintain portions of his front line by manning strong points only, with just a light screen of men between each of them. A break through was clearly just a matter of time, and both the Germans and Soviets knew it. Recognising this danger, Reinhardt began to pull forces away from the hitherto lightly attacked units of the Fourth Army in order to reinforce those on the Gumbinnen-Kattenau-Schlossberg sector. With the centre of his army in imminent danger, Raus in his turn requested permission to pull back the increasingly exposed divisions on the right wing of the IX Corps, both to shorten the combat line and to create a small reserve. Hitler refused to sanction any withdrawal but an undeterred Raus nevertheless began to withdraw his forces, doing so battalion by battalion so as not to attract the attention of the High Command.

January 16th brought no respite for the Germans as the Chernyakhovsky threw in yet more attacks. Clear frosty weather allowed the Soviet air armies to come up in force and their incessant attacks exacted a heavy toll on the defenders. In the early hours Schlossberg was occupied by the 39th Army's 94th Rifle Corps. Schittnig's 1st Infantry Division continued a dogged resistance to the west of the town. Their stubborn defence slowed the Soviet advance to a crawl. To reinforce the left wing of the 39th Army, Chernyakhovsky moved Butkov's 1st Tank Corps up behind the 94th Corps. Butkov's armour was to get behind the 1st Infantry Division and push northwest into the rear of the IX Corps. Further south, near Kattenau, Burdeinyi's

2nd Guards Tank Corps finally entered the battle in the centre of the 5th Army, in the 45th Rifle Corps' sector. Hoping to blast their way through the German lines, more than 200 tanks smashed into the exhausted 349th Volksgrenadier Division. The tanks were making for Kussen, but again, with the support of elements of Lippert's 5th Panzer Division, the Germans were able to beat off the initial attack, inflicting heavy losses on the Soviet armour with their anti-tank guns and Panzerfaust. The fighting was desperate and without quarter by both sides:

> *Pinned down by the fire of all German guns and the ladder fire of the rocket projector brigade, their* [the Soviet] *advance came to a sudden halt. The Russian infantry sent out distress signals for immediate tank support. Poor visibility prevented the enemy from taking advantage of his superiority in fire power and in the air. Nevertheless, the Russian infantry succeeded in penetrating between individual strong points. When the fog lifted, these spearheads were cut off and annihilated....*
>
> [The Soviet] *infantry, attempting to follow the tanks, was repelled with heavy casualties along the forward line of the main battle position. The Russian armoured units, however, continued their thrust...because the German antitank guns were unable to cope with such masses of tanks. This threat was all the more serious since enemy planes appeared in great numbers and were initially unopposed.*[13]

Repeated attacks by Burdeinyi's tanks eventually carried the Soviets into Kussen. Meanwhile, the 549th Volksgrenadier Division was also being pushed back. The 5th Army and 28th Army were both now making steady progress to the east and northeast of Gumbinnen, which prompted a battle group of the 5th Panzer Division to move to help halt the Soviet attacks. Eventually a thrust by the 65th Rifle Corps of the 5th Army penetrated between Jank's 549th Volksgrenadier Division and

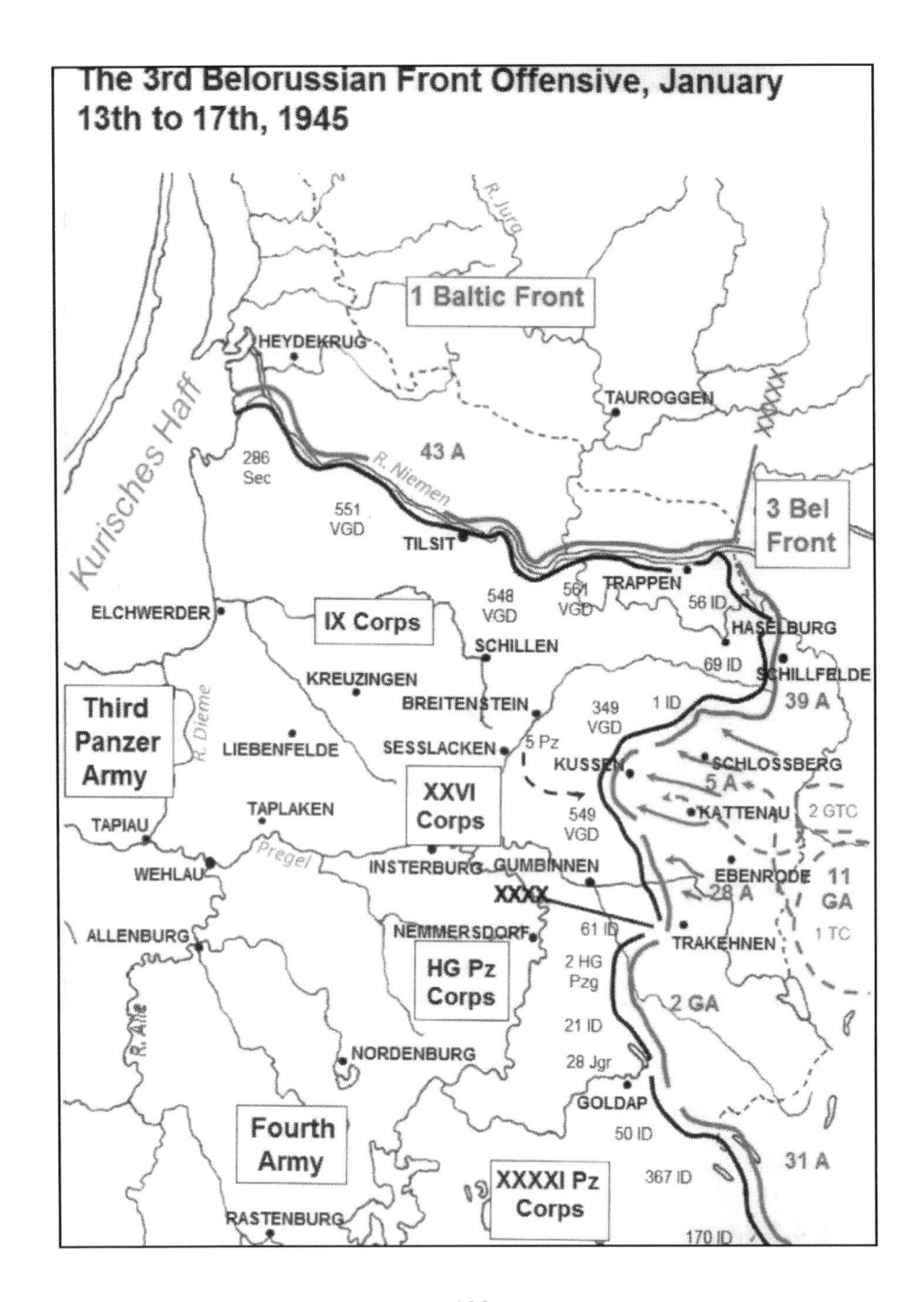

The 3rd Belorussian Front Offensive, January 13th to 17th, 1945

Kötz's neighbouring 349th Volksgrenadier Division, threatening to peel open the German front.

On January 17th, Chernyakhovsky decided to outflank the stubborn defenders of Gumbinnen by turning their northern flank. He duly shifted the axis of the attack by the 11th Guards Army from behind the 28th Army to between the junction of 39th Army and 5th Army. The 11th Guards, with the support of the 1st Tank Corps, was to push to the northwest to reach the River Inster. This movement would both threaten the German IX Corps with encirclement east of Tilsit while also preparing for the exploitation phase in the direction of Insterburg and Königsberg. The 2nd Guards Tank Corps was also to pull out of its positions near Kussen, where it was attacking the 349th Volksgrenadier Division, and move north to join the attack alongside Galitsky's army.

While the Soviets set in motion the redeployment of Galitsky's army and the two tank corps that would support it, the forces at the front continued their bludgeoning assault against the German defences. The 549th and 349th Volksgrenadier Divisions again came under ferocious attack from the 5th and 28th Armies. The 5th Panzer Division counter attacked and was able to restore the badly shaken junction of the 349th and the 1st Infantry Divisions, which had been in danger of disintegration. Again the Germans suffered heavy losses. The Volksgrenadiers, exhausted after days of relentless battle, were almost spent.

Reinhardt and his army commanders recognised that although the troops were fighting hard, it was inevitable that the front would be breached somewhere and the collapse of Guderian's house of cards would begin in earnest. A controlled withdrawal would disrupt the Soviet attacks and give the front line infantry a chance to regroup before the situation ran out of control. Reinhardt, who had already requested permission on the 16th to pull back the Fourth Army, made another call on 17th to discuss the situation. He was forced to speak to Hitler through General Burgdorf but without success. Reinhardt requested that the increasingly exposed salient occupied by the Fourth Army be evacuated so that the Second Army, which was now in a critical situation, could be reinforced. Hitler refused to allow any withdrawal and instead suggested the Second Army obtain its reinforcements by making use of the Volkssturm. He did give permission for Raus to pull back his 561st Volksgrenadier and 56th Infantry Divisions, which he had refused to allow previously.

On January 18th, Beloborodov's 43rd Army opened its attacks on Verhein's 551st and Sudau's 548th Volksgrenadier Divisions around Tilsit. With his front line aflame from end to end, Raus accelerated the withdrawal of the 561st Volksgrenadier and 56th Infantry Divisions. Renewed attacks by 39th and 11th Guards Armies also crashed into Rein's 69th Infantry Division as it tried to pull back. The 39th broke through the 69th as it withdrew and overran its headquarters, Lieutenant General Rein being killed in the fighting. The leaderless division was cut to pieces by the Soviet thrusts, shattering it as an effective force. The remnants streamed back towards the Inster. A little further south the 11th Guards Army and 1st Tank Corps reached the River Inster either side of Breitenstein, taking the town and securing a bridgehead over the river. They then prepared to turn southwest to push down the Inster Valley and on to Insterburg. To counter this threat the 5th Panzer Division was hastily pulled out of the line near Kattenau and ordered back to the Inster Valley. The panzers though were struck by fierce air attacks as they tried to redeploy and lost yet more men and vehicles. As the 5th Panzer Division pulled back from Kattenau the 5th and 28th Armies increased their attacks, pushing the Germans back west of Kussen.

Around Tilsit there was fierce fighting throughout the 19th, the 43rd Army pushing across the Niemen in force. Ragnit, just east of Tilsit, was taken amid heavy fighting. Beloborodov's army was now transferred over to Chernyakhovsky's 3rd Belorussian Front in order to ease the co-ordination of the forces on the northern wing of the attack. As the 43rd pushed southwest, the 39th Army funnelled its attacks between the Niemen and Inster rivers. Schillen, on the banks of the River Ange, was overrun as the 56th Infantry Division and the remnants

The Battle of Königsberg

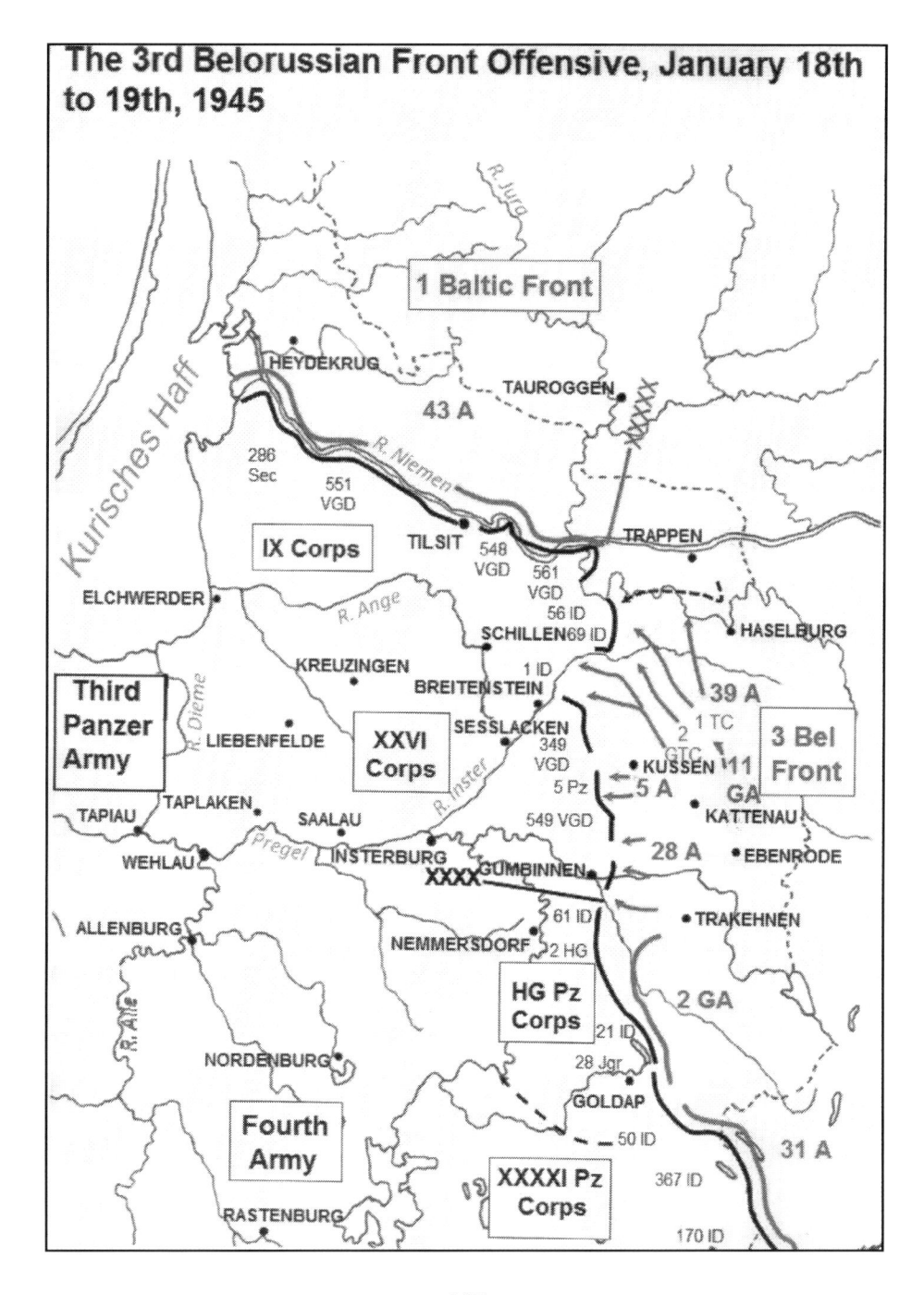

The 3rd Belorussian Front Offensive, January 18th to 19th, 1945

of the 69th Infantry Division fell back. A short distance to the south east, in the Breitenstein area, the 5th Panzer Division tried and failed to halt the onrush of the 11th Guards Army. The German panzers and their supporting infantry were held at bay by strong anti-tank fire. The 5th Panzer was joined by the 1st Infantry and 349th Volksgrenadier Divisions, who had fallen back toward the Inster after their front had finally collapsed.

To the south the situation at Gumbinnen had also become critical as the 28th Army fought its way into the outskirts. The 549th Volksgrenadier Division to the north and 61st Infantry Division to the east had suffered extremely heavy losses in their protracted battles to keep the Soviets out of the town.

On January 20th the fighting on the Tilsit axis reached a crescendo as the Soviets surged forwards, the 43rd Army taking Tilsit and Heinrichswalde as the Germans tried desperately to form a new front line to the south and west. Beloborodov's 43rd Army poured out of its bridgehead, pushing back the 551st and 548th Volksgrenadier Divisions as it made for Labiau. Beloborodov's advance reached the mouth of the River Ange later in the day. The 286th Security Division, which tried to hold up the right wing of the 43rd Army, virtually ceased to exist during the ensuing retreat. Simultaneously, the flank of the German troops who were trying to pull back through the Inster Valley was coming under increasingly heavy attack from the 39th Army and 11th Guards Army. The 39th had thrown its leading elements as far forward as Kreuzingen and Liebenfelde, just eighteen miles east of Labiau. This movement threatened the left wing of the 56th Infantry Division which was trying to make a stand to the east. Behind the 39th Army, the 1st Tank Corps was moving into position to enter the fighting, aiming to push forward towards Wehlau. In the Inster Valley the Germans continued to be harried by the fast moving columns of Soviet tanks and infantry. The collapse of the 69th Infantry Division on January 18th had undermined the line that 5th Panzer, 1st Infantry and 349th Volksgrenadier Divisions were trying to hold against Galitsky's 11th Guards Army. The Germans had no option other than to pull back upon Insterburg and Wehlau to avoid isolation by the Soviet forces which were now pouring down the Valley. The 1st Infantry Division attempted to make a stand west of Sesslacken but was assaulted by the 36th Guards Rifle Corps of the 11th Guards Army. On the opposite bank, with its front facing eastward, the 349th Volksgrenadier Division also tried to establish a line of defence but attacks by the right wing of the 11th Guards Army and the 5th Army pushed the Germans back steadily. Around Gumbinnen, the 28th Army, which had approached the outskirts from the east the previous day, sent its 20th Rifle Corps into attacks from the southeast while the 128th Rifle Corps attacked from the east. The 3rd Guards Rifle Corps, on the northern wing of the army, was sweeping down to the north of Gumbinnen, pushing the 549th Volksgrenadier Division before it. The German forces east of the town were being pressed hard, the 61st Infantry Division being involved in fierce fighting which saw it forced out of the town later that day.

As his front line was rolled to the west, Raus pulled the headquarters of his Third Panzer Army back to Königsberg to avoid the danger of being overrun. The collapse of the Third Panzer Army, and of Second Army, left Hossbach's Fourth Army increasingly exposed in its salient in the Masurian Lakes. Weiss' Second Army, shattered by the drive of the 2nd Belorussian Front, had failed to prevent enemy tanks pushing towards Elbing. Reinhardt was well aware of the danger posed by the Soviet advances on either flank and put in yet another request to Hitler that the Fourth Army be pulled back in order to send forces to strengthen both the Third Panzer Army's position on the Pregel, and the Second Army's near Osterode. Despite the obvious danger of encirclement, which could be seen by just a glance at the situation map, Hitler obstinately refused to allow Reinhardt to give up the Fourth Army's positions. Guderian, at the evening command conference at Hitler's headquarters, pressed for the withdrawal of the Fourth Army but Hitler obstinately refused to allow it. He did finally agree to transfer forces from Courland and Denmark to East Prussia. It was of course far too late for this order to have any effect on the battle that was now raging.

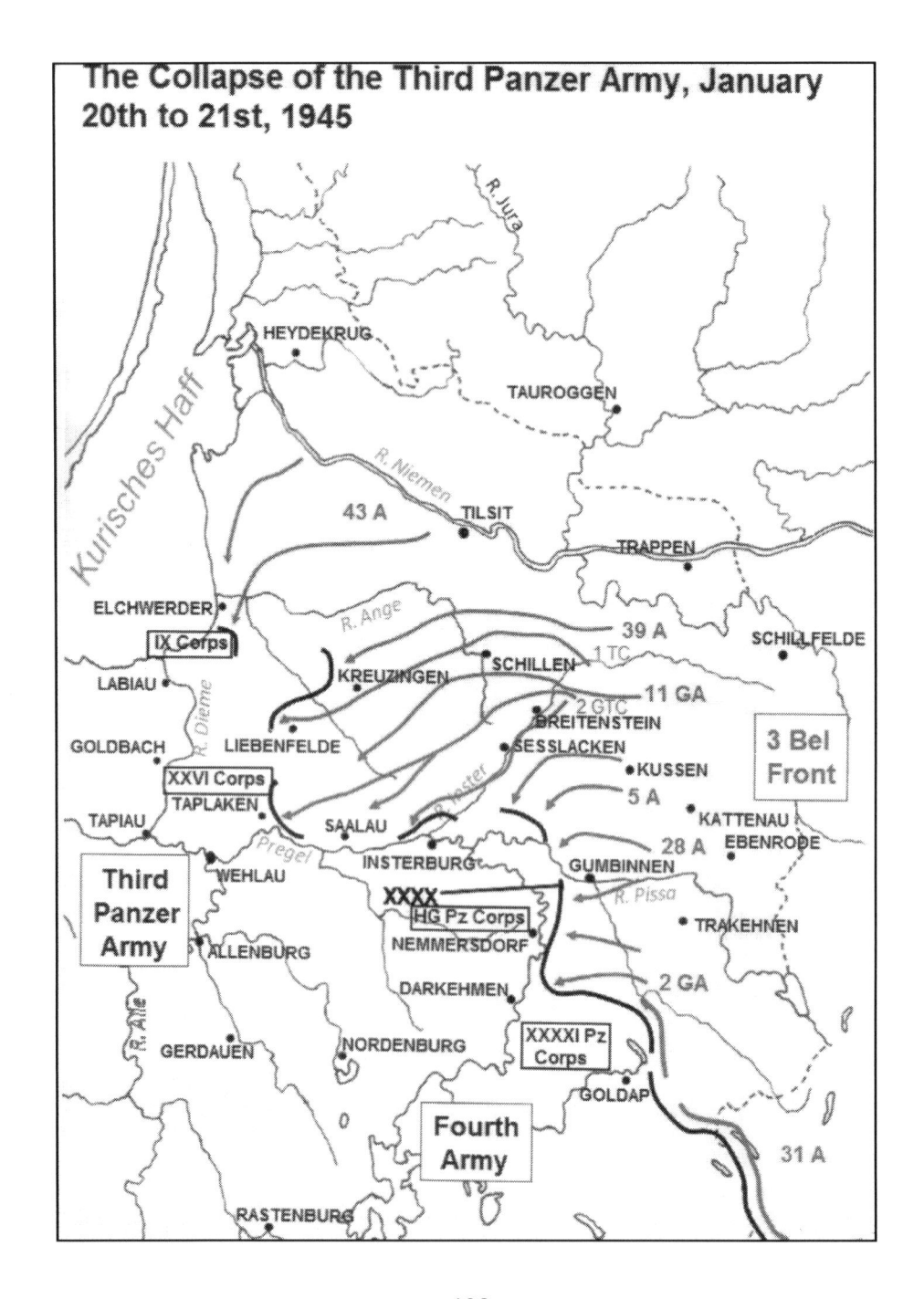

THE BATTLE OF KÖNIGSBERG

THE BATTLE OF KÖNIGSBERG

On January 21st the situation at the front continued to deteriorate as the Soviets pushed forwards aggressively across the whole of the Third Panzer Army's disintegrating lines. The 1st Tank Corps entered the fighting and quickly punched through the 56th Infantry Division, surging ahead to skirt the defenders of Gross Ponnau which was then captured by the infantry of the 8th Guards Rifle Corps. The 1st Tank Corps then swung west to head for Tapiau. To the north, the 39th Army pushed forward from Kreuzingen on a broad front. While the 8th Guards Rifle Corps pushed out on the right wing of the army, the 16th and 36th Guards Rifle Corps of the 11th Guards Army began to envelop the Germans north of Insterburg. The 5th Panzer Division tried unsuccessfully to hold up the right wing of the advancing Soviets forces but was pushed back remorselessly by the 2nd Guards Tank Corps, which was operating between the 8th and 16th Guards Rifle Corps. They herded the remnants of the 69th Infantry Division, and elements of the 61st Infantry Division which had been transferred from the Gumbinnen area, back towards the Pregel at Norkitten, Saalau and Plibischken. The 36th Guards Corps attacked Insterburg from the north, roughly handling the 349th Volksgrenadier Division in the process. The 72nd Rifle Corps of the 5th Army also attacked from the east, forcing back elements of the 549th Volksgrenadier Division. The town fell in the late hours of the 21st, a mass of flaming ruins, its streets strewn with wrecked vehicles and the bodies of fallen soldiers and civilians. The 349th Volksgrenadier abandoned its defences and pulled back along the northern bank of the Pregel, heading for Plibischken while the 549th tried to make a stand to the southwest. To the south of Gumbinnen the advance of the 28th Army continued as Soviet forces reached the Angerapp, capturing Nemmersdorf and securing a bridgehead across the river. The troops of the 28th and 2nd Guards Armies were also relentlessly forcing the 2nd *Herman Göring* and 21st Infantry Divisions back before them, deepening the considerable bulge occupied by the German Fourth Army to the south.

Reinhardt again tried to save the Fourth Army and at Guderian's suggestion, put in a call to Hitler. Reinhardt explained the extremely dangerous situation the army found itself in, with its flank armies in tatters and no new forces available to restore the lines. After protracted argument, Hitler finally sanctioned a limited withdrawal of the Fourth Army from the Masurian Lakes in order to release forces to cover the now open right flank at Wormditt. During the night of 21st–22nd January, without any authorisation for such a large scale movement of forces, General Hossbach began to withdraw major elements of the Fourth Army away from the heavily fortified Lötzen position to create a strike force closer to the sea. His plan, rather than just being to rebuild the broken right wing of the Fourth Army, was for northing less than the evacuation of East Prussia. Rather than let his army be isolated and destroyed, he planned to take it west, to fight a way through to the Second Army and then resume the battle in Pomerania as part of the main combat front. Raus and his Third Panzer Army were not informed, and would either have to pull back into isolation to Königsberg, or try to join the break out as it developed. Hossbach's actions were clearly treasonous and accepted that East Prussia would be given up entirely. In acting without approval, and abandoning such a large tract of German territory to the enemy, he could face a summary court martial and probably a firing squad.

In the Third Panzer Army sector, Hitler finally agreed to the evacuation of Memel. Gollnick's XXVIII Corps began its evacuation immediately. Over the next three nights the majority of the men were taken out by ship while the 58th Infantry Division acted as a rearguard. They would later march along the Nehrung to Cranz, where they rejoined the battle for Samland. Reinhardt also warned Hitler of the threat posed to Königsberg by the Soviet advance down the Inster and Pregel valley's, but Hitler refused to authorise the withdrawal of the Third Panzer Army, or the evacuation of the increasingly alarmed civilian population.

Gauleiter Erich Koch finally decided on January 20th that it was time to alert the populace of East Prussia to the approach of the Soviet troops. He gave the order that civilians were to be evacuated from the border districts but it was clearly far too late for this and the civil authorities were predictably overwhelmed by panicking civilians, who crowded trains and took to the roads in their thousands to escape. The movement of so many people was so great that Army had the greatest of difficulty in moving along the main communication routes. The Party authorities in Königsberg added to the confusion by sending trains loaded with refugees south to Allenstein, unaware that the town had already fallen to advancing Soviet troops. During the night of the 21st, Koch showed his true colours to the people of East Prussia as he fled from Königsberg aboard a specially equipped train. He only went a short distance, taking up residence at his Gross Friedrichsburg estate outside the city. He would not stay long though, fleeing to Berlin toward the end of the month. He eventually returned to the province, but only to his purpose built bunker at Neutief, near Pillau. While he condemned thousands to their deaths, he had kept a constant eye on his own escape route.

Inside Königsberg confusion reigned. Lasch's Wehrkreis I administration was now redundant as much of East Prussia fell into enemy hands. Himmler ordered the dissolution of Lasch's command on January 21st and Lasch suddenly found he was surplus to requirements. He was placed under Army Group Centre command but had no responsibilities. His Wehrkreis staff was broken up and many were pulled out of Königsberg. The troops inside the city were subordinated to the Army Group, who in turn placed them under the command of Raus' Third Panzer Army. Lasch left the city for Moditten, a short distance west of Königsberg, to await further orders. The abolition of his command, Koch's desertion, and the paucity of Third Panzer Army commanders in the city left a power vacuum. There was no-one in charge any more, just at the moment the city started to fill up with refugees.

After nine days of bitter fighting General Chernyakhovsky had finally managed to break the back of the German forces on the Königsberg axis. The difficult and costly battles at the frontier had sapped the strength of both the German and Soviet forces. Unfortunately for the Germans, Chernyakhovsky had kept his reserves uncommitted, and as the German defences began to crack, the Soviets were able to commit their tank forces, and Galitsky's still fresh 11th Guards Army. The advance on Königsberg could now begin.

[1] The Su was the Soviet version of the German assault or self propelled gun, Su standing for Samokhodnaya Ustanovka (self propelled). The Su 85 and Su 122 were armed with an 85mm or 122mm main gun on a T-34 chassis but served very different purposes. The Su-85 was introduced into service in late 1943 in as a mobile anti tank vehicle in response to the entry into service of the German Panther. The Su-85 was considered obsolete by late 1944. The Su-122 was a self propelled artillery vehicle, being armed with a 122mm howitzer, and was used in an infantry support role.

[2] Burdeinyi had been promoted to Lieutenant General on November 2nd, 1944.

[3] Shirer, *The Rise and Fall of the Third Reich*, p1091

[4] OKH – The OKH (Oberkommando des Heeres) was the High Command of the Army. The OKW (Oberkommando der Wehrmacht) was the High Command of the Armed Forces and had control of military operations in the West, Mediterranean, Scandinavia and the southern Balkans. The OKW was headed up by Field Marshal Keitel, while Colonel General Alfred Jodl was the Chief of the Operations Staff. They jealously protected their area of responsibilities against any interference from OKH.

[5] Foreign Armies East, the intelligence section of the OKH responsible for the Eastern Front.

[6] Guderian, *Panzer Leader*, p383

[7] Hitler had gambled his last strategic reserve on a blow against the Allies in the West. The German armies had launched their counter attack on December 16th but by the end of the month it was clear the attack had failed. Guderian was keen to draw these forces east to reinforce the hard pressed Eastern Front.

[8] Guderian, *Panzer Leader*, p387

[9] Guderian, *Panzer Leader*, pp387-8

[10] Erickson, *The Road to Berlin*, p449

[11] Raus in Tsouras (ed), *The Anvil the War*, pp166-7

[12] Dieckert & Grossmann, *Der Kampf um Ostpreussen*, p98

[13] Tsouras, *The Anvil of War*, p167

Chapter Five - The First Battle for Königsberg

Having broken through the German defence lines, Chernyakhovsky offensive entered its exploitation phase. His aim was to take Königsberg and destroy the Third Panzer Army. For Generals Raus and Reinhardt the situation in East Prussia was running out of control. Repeated refusals by Hitler to allow operational freedom hampered the German efforts to rebuild their shattered front, a situation which was exacerbated in the days to come. As the 5th and 28th Armies advanced, pushing towards the Brandenburg coast, they would separate the Fourth Army from the Third Panzer Army, enabling the remainder of the 3rd Belorussian Front to concentrate on Königsberg and Samland. It is to the battle for the city that we will now turn.

On January 22nd the 39th Army continued its drive towards Samland, striving to reach the line of the River Deime from Labiau to Tapiau. Elements of the 561st and 548th Volksgrenadier Divisions were pushed back as the Germans desperately tried to hold up the Soviet advance along the line of the River Deime and to the south, along the Pregel and Angerapp. The Deime Line was supposed to form a cornerstone of the German defences protecting Samland and Königsberg, but without sufficient forces to man it was simply a defence line on paper only. Raus' intention had been to try to establish a line of defence along the Deime, Pregel and Alle rivers. It seemed unlikely that these lines could be held, given the fact that Soviet forces were already attacking this line and the forces required for the defence were in considerable disarray. Volkssturm units were also rushed into battle to try to fill the gaps torn in the lines of the Third Panzer Army but their lack of heavy weapons and effective training meant that, despite bitter resistance, these civilian soldiers were often swept away after suffering crippling losses.

The 11th Guards Army continued its approach to the Pregel on a broad front. On the right wing of the army the 8th Guards Rifle Corps thrust forward and captured Taplacken then fought their way into the outskirts of Wehlau. The Germans pulled elements of the 56th Infantry Division back to support the remnants of the 69th Infantry Division that were around the town but they failed to hold the Soviets back. Battlegroup Jaedtke of the 5th Panzer Division was ordered to eliminate the Soviet forces at Wehlau but it lacked the strength to alter the course of the battle. A little to the east, during the afternoon the 2nd Guards Tank Corps and part of the 36th Guards Rifle Corps pushed their forward detachments close to Norkitten, where other battle groups of the 5th Panzer and 349th Volksgrenadier Divisions tried in vain to hold the Soviet forces at bay. Detachments from the 1st Infantry Division were also hurriedly rushed to the south bank of the Pregel to try to reinforce the defence. Meanwhile, further east Krylov's 5th Army pushed the 549th Volksgrenadier Division back along the railway line running out of Insterburg, aiming to reach the Angerapp, which the 28th Army was already against in force to the south.

January 23rd brought Soviet forces closer to Königsberg as the 39th Army reached Goldbach, having crossed the River Deime to penetrate the German defence line. The 561st Volksgrenadier Division had thrown out a thin screen of troops along the river line but was unable to prevent the Soviet forces from crossing. South of the Pregel, Galitsky continued his advance. Elements of the 8th Guards Rifle Corps, with the 1st Tank Corps supporting, attacked Tapiau. The 1st Tank Corps skirted around the town and continued to push west against the German defences on the north bank of the Pregel. The 8th Guards Rifle Corps crossed the Pregel a short distance east of Tapiau and established a bridgehead on the southern bank. Elements of the 549th Volksgrenadier Division had been pulled back to try to reinforce the collapsing line on the south bank but they failed to prevent the Soviets from using a still intact bridge over the Pregel to establish their bridgehead. Unfortunately for the Germans the demolition of the bridge had taken place, easing the Soviet crossing considerably. Battlegroup Jaedtke was duly ordered back to Tapiau to halt the Soviet forces. A little to the east, a short distance west of Wehlau, the remnants of the

69th and 56th Infantry Divisions, and elements of the 549th Volksgrenadier, continued to try to hold up the 2nd Guards Tank Corps and 11th Guards Army as they tried to punch their way across the Alle south of Wehlau. The 69th Infantry Division was pushed back across the river while the 1st Infantry and 349th Volksgrenadier Divisions fought in a pocket on the eastern bank, trying to hold the 36th Guards Rifle Corps back. To their south the Soviet 5th and 28th Armies continued to push hard against the northern wing of the Fourth Army.

While Chernyakhovsky's forces ripped the Third Panzer Army apart, to the west the men of the 2nd Belorussian Front continued their devastating advance. Elements of the 5th Guards Tank Army approached the outskirts of Elbing and had almost severed the westward land routes out of East Prussia. A single corps of the tank army did manage to thrust into Elbing from the east but met fierce resistance from mixed alarm units that Hossbach had pulled back into the town. This latest penetration prompted him to accelerate the withdrawal of the Fourth Army from the Masurian Lakes in order to amass his forces in the Vistula Delta. Reinhardt was well aware of Hossbach's intentions but neither he nor Hossbach had sought authorisation from Hitler or the High Command for such a movement. It was clear to them that Hitler would never authorise such a drastic redeployment or the abandonment of such large tracts of East Prussian territory. The next day (the 24th) the 5th Guards Tank Army captured Mulhausen and moved into Elbing itself. Soviet tanks advanced steadily through the town and reached the coast by midnight, isolating the Third Panzer Army and Fourth Army in East Prussia. With Hitler's usual stand fast orders, the greater part of Army Group Centre was condemned to inevitable destruction.

Meanwhile, the battle on the approaches to Königsberg continued to intensify during the 24th. The Third Panzer Army's combat line between Labiau and Allenburg was pulled apart as the 43rd Army took Labiau. Nautzken fell to the left wing of Beloborodov's army while the 39th Army and 1st Tank Corps continued their advance along the northern bank of the Pregel in the direction of Königsberg, despite facing determined

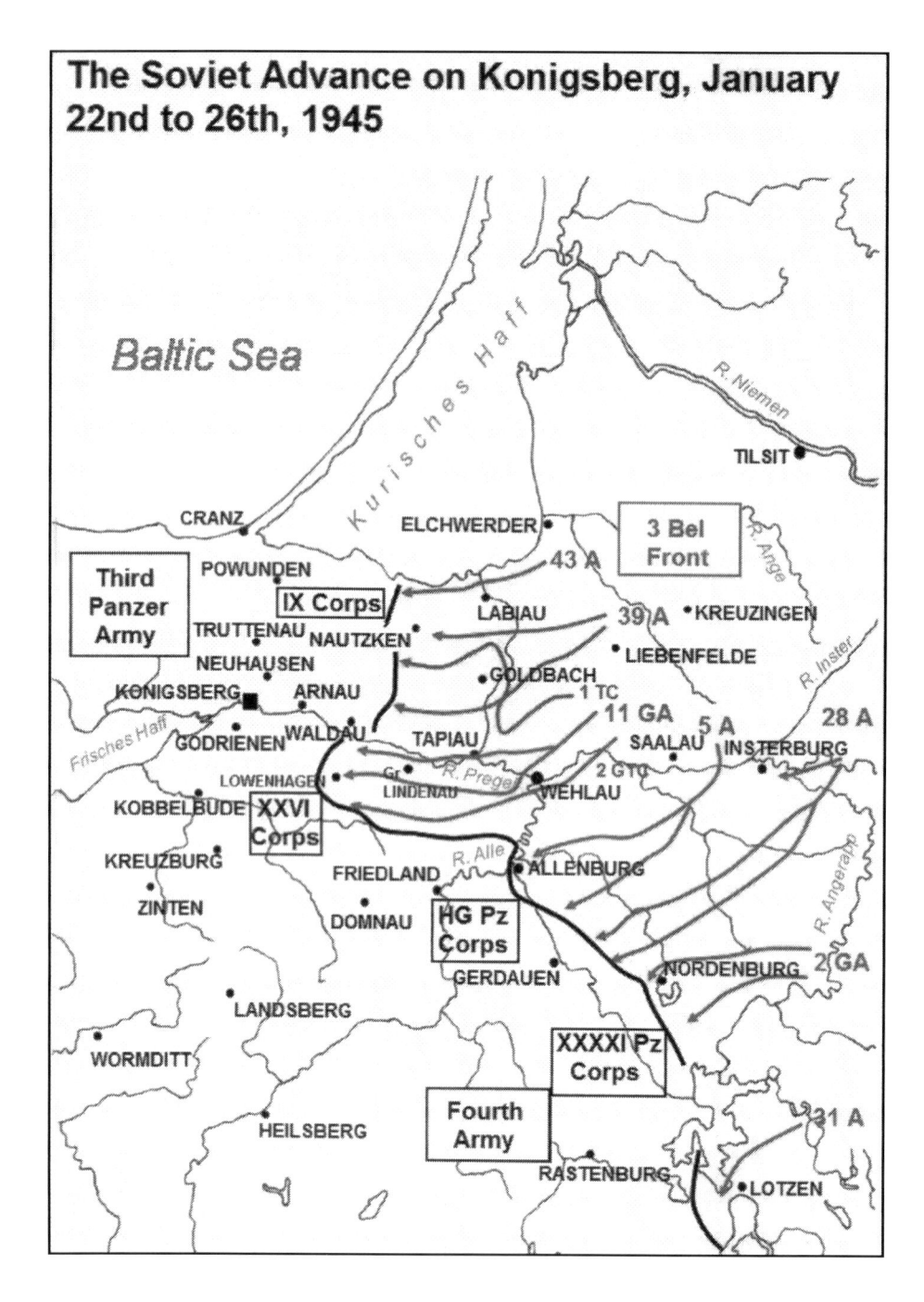

The Soviet Advance on Konigsberg, January 22nd to 26th, 1945

resistance and repeated counter attacks from the 561st Volksgrenadier Division.

On the southern bank of the Pregel the 11th Guards Army secured control of both Tapiau and Wehlau as the German line was rolled back between the Pregel and the Alle. Repeated counter attacks by the 5th Panzer Division and supporting infantry forces slowed the Soviet advance but could not halt it entirely. Galitsky's 11th Guards Army and 2nd Guards Tank Corps now began their advance to isolate Königsberg by reaching the Brandenburg coast between the city and Heiligenbeil. On the River Alle, Allenburg fell to the 5th Army. The defence line on the River Alle had been sundered, despite desperate counter attacks by the Germans.

As fighting continued at the front, the German High Command undertook a number of command redesignations on January 25th. Army Group Centre was renamed Army Group North while Army Group North, still isolated in Courland, became Army Group Kurland. Army Group A, fighting in Poland, was named Army Group Centre. The headquarters of the Third Panzer Army, which had only been in Königsberg for a short time, left the city for Fischhausen, near the tip of the Samland Peninsula, as the fighting closed in. Lasch, still unsure as to his position but concerned at the plight of the civilians who were crowding into the city, took the opportunity to travel to Pillau to discuss the evacuation of the civilian populace with the naval authorities there. While Lasch carried out this mission, the Third Panzer Army began to move Schittnig's 1st Infantry Division and Lieutenant General Hermann Hähnle's 367th Infantry Division into Königsberg to reinforce the units trying to establish a defensive perimeter around the city. The 367th had been released from its positions in the Masurian Lakes following Hossbach's withdrawal and was able to move north to reinforce the Third Panzer Army. Hähnle had commanded the division since August 1944, having previously commanded artillery formations during the earlier years of the conflict. The 367th had been raised in the Balkans in late 1943 and deployed to Croatia at the end of that year. During 1944 it was committed to the fighting on the Eastern Front and was heavily involved in the bitter battles around Kamenets-Podolsky in the Ukraine, where it supported the II SS Panzer Corps in the battle to free Hube's First Panzer Army. The division was then involved in the fighting around Brody, where Otto Lasch led the remnants of his 349th Infantry Division to safety. The 367th was then redeployed to the Bialystok sector. From the beginning of the Soviet offensive upon East Prussia the division had been in action near Lötzen and Rastenburg.

While the Germans tried to pull together their forces to defend Königsberg, Burdeinyi's 2nd Guards Tank Corps launched new attacks which forced the 548th Volksgrenadier Division back along the southern bank of the Pregel. Soviet troops were able to secure control of Gross Lindenau. Battlegroup Jaedtke launched a counter attack to try to recover the town but the Soviets were able to bring up anti-tank guns and halted the Germans in their tracks. South and east of Gross Lindenau the 69th and 56th Infantry Divisions also tried to hold back attacks by the infantry of the 11th Guards Army but the penetration of the tank troops at Gross Lindenau threatened their flank.

January 26th saw the arrival of the first elements of Schittnig's 1st Infantry Division and Hähnle's 367th Infantry Division in Königsberg, but also the departure of Colonel General Reinhardt, who was dismissed from his post as commander of Army Group North. Reinhardt, who had done so much to try to maintain an effective defence in East Prussia, suffered for the loss of territory in the Fourth Army sector. Hitler had finally found out about the unauthorised withdrawal of Hossbach's army after the shocking loss of the Lötzen Fortified Position. Reinhardt had continued to press for the Fourth Army to be allowed to withdraw, his last signal to High Command being to request permission to pull the Fourth back from the line of the Alle, which had become untenable. He vainly waited for a reply, and finally, late in the day, sent a signal that in the absence of any orders he would pull the army back. Just two hours later a message arrived bearing news of his dismissal. Hitler held Reinhardt directly responsible for disobeying his orders to stand fast. Reinhardt, who had worked so well with his subordinate commanders, was replaced with Colonel General Lothar Rendulic, an ardent Nazi who was noted for rigorously enforcing discipline in the rear areas by flying courts martial. They would summarily try and execute any hapless soldier found in the rear areas without a good reason. Rendulic was given the strict instruction that Königsberg was to be held at all costs.

To the north east of the city, as the 43rd and 39th Armies pushed west from Labiau the Germans threw together a defence force consisting of elements of the 58th Infantry Division, part of Tiger Detachment Förster and a number of Volkssturm troops to secure the front line east of Cranz. Heavy fighting erupted around Neuhausen, just three miles from the outskirts of Königsberg as the 94th Rifle Corps of the 39th Army tried to rush into the city. The Soviet troops were repulsed in their attacks as the 367th Infantry Division rushed to deploy. The fighting all around the city began to intensify as the Germans brought up additional forces. The 561st Volksgrenadier Division, together with elements of Colonel Grimme's battered 69th Infantry Division and the 95th Infantry Division, which had been evacuated from Memel, fought to slow the Soviet onrush. The 5th Panzer Division, which had pulled its scattered units back to take up positions to the east and south of Königsberg, was also ordered onto the defensive. In its efforts to reach the coast, the 2nd Guards Tank Corps and 11th Guards Army launched strong attacks against the 5th Panzer Division, the 2nd *Herman Göring* Division and the 56th and 61st Infantry Division which were south of the city. The Germans were gradually forced back to a line Löwenhagen-Üderwangen, but their ferocious resistance sapped at the strength of the attacking forces. The Germans suffered badly themselves though, the 5th Panzer being reduced to just twenty-five running tanks.

The mood inside the city during the 26th was one of despair. This became worse when Soviet artillery fire began to land in the streets. Civilians took to their cellars to hide from the shells that spread death and destruction far and wide. Even for the military these days were confusing, as one soldier later recorded:

THE BATTLE OF KÖNIGSBERG

The first few days gave the impression of chaotic conditions inside the fortress. No one knew anything; the command structure was entirely confused. Some units fought where they could, while others retreated into the city. No one knew what was happening to his right or left, the troops had come to the end their strength.[1]

As chaos reigned inside and around the city, from the safety of his estate at Gross Friedrichsburg Gauleiter Koch sent one of his deputies, Kreisleiter Ernst Wagner, back into Königsberg during the night of 26-27th January to take control of the Party personnel who remained inside the city. Wagner, known as Hoarder Wagner to the people of East Prussia following his hoarding of food stocks earlier in the war, was of a different temperament to his boss. He was able to work well with the army and co-operated fully with the military authorities. Unlike Koch, he was no coward and took direct command of Volkssturm units fighting on the north eastern outskirts, seeing action himself.

Repeated Soviet air attacks struck the German forces around Königsberg and in the Pregel valley throughout January 27th, inflicting heavy losses and preventing the Germans from moving their forces easily. To the north and north east the advance of the 43rd and 39th Armies continued. Beloborodov's men took control of Powunden as they approached the base of the Spit from Memel. German resistance was considerable as the line of retreat of the XXVIII Corps had to be kept open by those units which had already reached Samland. A little to the south the 1st Tank Corps took Truttenau as it tried to outflank the defenders of Königsberg from the north.

During the afternoon the Soviet shelling of the city abruptly ceased but then aircraft began to launch waves of attacks, machine gunning and bombing any targets they found. Meanwhile, around the city perimeter the Germans east of the city tried to establish defences between Neuhausen and Arnau. The badly overstretched 561st Volksgrenadier Division was reinforced by Volkssturm troops and the 1st and 367th

Infantry Divisions in an effort to halt a Soviet drive directly into the city. New attacks by the 94th Rifle Corps of the 39th Army resulted in heavy fighting around Lauth, near Fort I, and on both sides of Reichsstrasse 1. The Volkssturm units here were involved in heavy fighting as Soviet forces east and north of the city reached the line Neuhausen, Uggehnen, Karmitten and Powunden. Kreisleiter Wagner had thrown himself into the action and with Volkssturm troops was involved in the bitter fighting. He and his men acquitted themselves well, Wagner being awarded the Iron Cross First Class for his actions. Koch would later censure him for accepting the honour from the Army rather than from the Party. As the Soviets continued their attacks, elements of the 976th Grenadier Regiment of the 367th Infantry Division were involved in the bitter fighting at Neuhausen, north of Malden and on the Bäckerberg Mount. The 974th Grenadier Regiment of the 367th was also heavily attacked along the Königsberg to Cranz road. Both of these regiments were able to beat off the Soviet attacks with the support of some anti-tank guns and the use of their Panzerfaust.

Königsberg was now overflowing with frightened refugees as thousands passed through the city in their effort to reach Pillau and a ship to the West. The Nazi authorities made a difficult situation even worse by broadcasting over loudspeakers that civilians should evacuate the city immediately as Soviet forces were advancing from Tapiau. The roads rapidly became choked with men, women and children trying to reach safety, hoping for evacuation but hindering the movement of military forces. The Army also ordered its female medical personnel to leave the city during the night. Lasch, who was returning from Pillau to his headquarters at Moditten and was held up by the onrush of refugees. The short journey back took all day due to the congestion on the roads. As he later recalled:

On my way back from Pillau to Königsberg it was almost impossible to move the car. As a result of the thoughtlessness of the Party officials there were now huddled together on the roads unimaginable crowds...In Königsberg harbour a few ships were loaded with refugees but there was not nearly enough cabin space. Thousands of people were piling into the port.[2]

Once back at Moditten he was told by his aide that he was to go at once to Gauleiter Koch, who was still at his estate at Gross Friedrichsburg. Lasch reluctantly set out once more onto the crowded roads. After reaching Gross Friedrichsburg, Koch informed Lasch that he had taken a call from Hitler earlier in the day. Hitler had enquired, Koch explained, as to Lasch's suitability as commander for the defence of Königsberg. After a brief discussion Lasch left Koch's estate a worried man. His worst fears were realised later in the night when a telex arrived stating that with immediate effect he had been appointed commander of Fortress Königsberg. The new command, which was a fortress in name only, was subordinated to the Third Panzer Army. During the night Lasch contacted Guderian with the news that the Soviets had pushed into Samland and were threatening Königsberg. He also pointed out that his appointment as Fortress Königsberg commander overlapped with the responsibilities the Third Panzer Army had on the city. Guderian fully understood the situation and reassured Lasch that he would take his concerns to Hitler. Lasch then tried to contact Army Group headquarters in order to speak with Reinhardt. He found to his surprise and regret that Reinhardt had been dismissed the previous day and that the new commander, Colonel-General Rendulic, would contact him later that day. Rendulic, being an ardent Nazi, would be unlikely to be sympathetic to Lasch's concerns, his appointment having come direct from Hitler.

While Lasch struggled to clarify his position, to the south of the Pregel the German forces continued to pull back. The 11th Guards Army pushed ever closer to the southern edge of Königsberg, threatening to separate the city from the forces fighting to the southwest. The 548th Volksgrenadier Division tried to hold up the right wing corps of the 11th Guards Army before Gutenfeld while to the south the 2nd Guards Tank

THE BATTLE OF KÖNIGSBERG

Corps and the other two corps of the Guards Army continued their attacks on the 549th Volksgrenadier, 56th Infantry and 2nd *Herman Göring* Divisions.

During the morning of the 28th Colonel-General Lothar Rendulic arrived at Lasch's headquarters in Moditten for a fleeting visit. He duly confirmed Lasch's appointment as commander of Fortress Königsberg. Lieutenant-General Schittnig of the 1st Infantry Division, who had tried to calm the situation in the city when his troops had arrived a few days earlier, was to join Lasch's staff. Lasch spent the remainder of the day with Schittnig, being apprised of the situation in and around the city. One of Lasch's first moves was to relocate his headquarters inside the city, into the basement of the Main Post Office building in the city centre. He would again relocate his headquarters to a specially built seventeen room bunker underneath the Paradeplatz on March 7th. Lasch established what forces were currently available to him to defend the city but was worried that the Soviets would launch a strong drive into the city given the perilous nature of the German defences. The eastern face of the perimeter was being held by the 548th Volksgrenadier Division, which had troops both north and south of the Pregel. To the north were the 1st Infantry Division and 367th Infantry Division, facing the 94th Rifle Corps of the 39th Army. The northern face of the city perimeter was held by the 561st Volksgrenadier Division. South of the Pregel was the 5th Panzer Division, situated close to the coast, the 69th and 56th Infantry Divisions and elements of the 549th Volksgrenadier Division.

While Lasch tried to get a grip on the situation the 39th Army pushed across Reichsstrasse 128 between Königsberg and Cranz as the 551st Volksgrenadier Division crumbled. The 1st Tank Corps also moved west with the aim of reaching the Haff coast to the west of Königsberg. Fuchsberg and Tannenwalde were taken and there were strong Soviet attacks on Charlottenburg in the area between Forts V and IV. The infantry of the 5th and 13th Guards and 113th Rifle Corps of the 39th Army moved up to support the armour[3]. As the northern wing was turned, the threat northeast of Königsberg intensified as Neuhausen

THE BATTLE OF KÖNIGSBERG

was lost to the 94th Rifle Corps. A hastily organised defence by the 976th Grenadier Regiment of the 367th Infantry Division and elements of Tiger Detachment Förster brought the Soviet advance to a halt. To the east of the city the 974th Grenadier Regiment was pushed back by repeated Soviet infantry and tank attacks. Major Schaper, with the 974th Grenadier Regiment recalled the fighting here:

On January 28th the focus of the fighting shifted to Neuhausen. By late afternoon, despite my warnings, the poor deployment of II Battalion, Artillery Regiment 367 left a gap behind the left wing of the Division Fusilier Battalion. The latter was broken up by the attacking Russians while trying to defend their exposed positions. There were no reserves for miles around. Attacked from the flank and the rear, the Division Fusilier Battalion fell back...About 150 meters west of the Königsberg to Cranz road they set up a front facing north, but again their left wing was open... The situation during the evening of January 28th remained very tense; the noise of tanks indicated an enemy attack. At my request, the division finally released to me the assault gun detachment. However, they would only arrive later that night...

Between 2300 and 2400 hours enemy tanks advanced on both sides of the Cranz road. Dense masses of tanks and infantry attacked and were within 200 meters of our positions. The crisis had come not only for us but for Königsberg. We fired with all of our weapons. When no help came, the situation became untenable.

Then - as though sent from heaven –here come our assault guns, driving up the Cranz road. They identified the Russian tanks under the light of flares. The five or six assault guns made a great impact on the battle, and shot up six-eight Russian tanks, including some 'Stalin' types. The whole area was lit as bright as day by the exploding shells and flames of burning tanks.

That was the turning point... With assault rifles, machine guns and anti-tank guns, the 14th Company slammed into the Russian infantry, who had accompanied their tanks in tight packs. They retreated in the face of our fire. It was a great success. That night, with a few assault guns of the 367th Infantry Division, Königsberg was saved, as behind our regiment there were no more reserves. The Russians were evidently unaware of their actual superiority.[4]

The attacking force had lost around thirty tanks knocked out in this dramatic night action and the stubborn resistance of the 367th Infantry Division had prevented the early capture of Fort IIA near Quednau.

The German divisions defending the southern approaches were also involved in heavy fighting against the repeated attacks of the 11th Guards Army. Galitsky was pushing the 8th Guards Rifle Corps hard against the south eastern approaches to Königsberg, striking the 548th and 549th Volksgrenadier Divisions, while the 16th Guards projected a front to the west, facing the southern suburbs. The Soviet penetration south of Königsberg was rolling the 56th and 69th Infantry Division back into the southern suburbs of the capital. Meanwhile, the 5th Panzer Division and 2nd *Herman Göring* fought to halt the advance of the 2nd Guards Tank Corps and 36th Guards Rifle Corps at the tip of the salient. Later in the day Ludwigswalde and Gutenfeld were lost to Soviet troops.

As the 29th dawned, the 39th Army continued its efforts to envelop Königsberg from the northwest. Trankwitz and Wargen were captured as the 1st Tank Corps and supporting infantry began to push south toward the coast. The 548th Volksgrenadier Division, which had been fighting east of the city, was now pulled back to the western suburbs during the night, just as the leading elements of the Soviet spearhead occupied Metgethen and Seerappen. To the south of the city, the tanks of the 2nd Guards Tank Corps broke through the positions of the 13th Panzergrenadier Regiment of the 5th Panzer Division and reached the Frisches Haff at the small village of Heide Maulen. While the tank

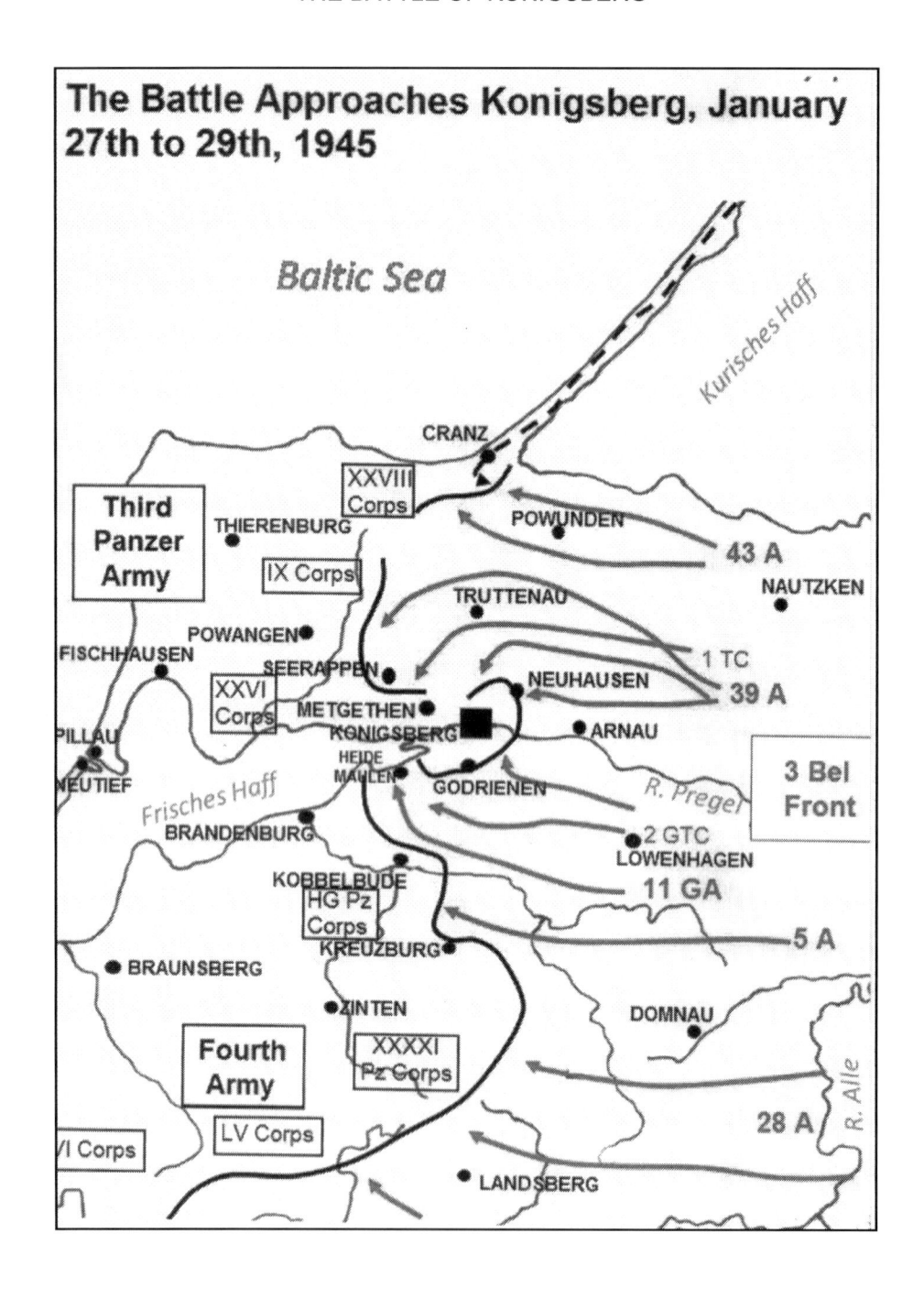

THE BATTLE OF KÖNIGSBERG

The Battle Approaches Konigsberg, January 27th to 29th, 1945

troops succeeded in pushing their way to the coast, elements of the 16th Guards Rifle Corps wheeled north to attack the southern defences of Königsberg, taking the defenders of Fort IX *'Dohna'*, by surprise. Despite a brave defence, the Soviets were able to bring up tanks to pound the defence works. Bitter fighting followed as the troops and engineers stormed the fort and eventually the German garrison was wiped out by an overwhelming explosion within the fortress. The loss of Fort IX was followed by the capture of the connecting defensive works around Altenberg. Hard fighting also broken out around Forts X, XI and XII but these remained firmly in German hands.

In response to the Soviet successes south of the city the *Grossdeutschland* Panzergrenadier Division was brought back to the coast. The division had spent many days fighting further inland with Fourth Army and had suffered heavy casualties. The survivors, with their remaining tanks and heavy weapons, assembled around Kreuzburg, southwest of Königsberg along the Haff coast. The divisional commander, Major-General Karl Lorenz planned to launch a counter attack that would re-establish the connection between the Fourth Army and Königsberg. The Panzer Regiment of the division had around twenty five tanks left, but luckily many of them were the powerful Tiger and highly effective Panther tanks.

Throughout January 30th the men of the 1st Tank Corps, supported by the 13th Guards Rifle Corps, pushed slowly forward through the Kobbelbuder Forest, between Metgethen and the coast. The citizens of Metgethen had been told the previous day to prepare to evacuate, and a train bound for Pillau had been stopped at the station there for the civilians to board. Unfortunately the train's departure was delayed and it did not leave until the 30th. By then it was too late.

Before Seerappen a Russian tank blocked the track and fired on the train. The passengers were driven out and were robbed and the women raped. Those refugee's who managed to escape brought gruesome tales to the people of Königsberg.[5]

The 113th Rifle Corps of the 39th Army also launched strong attacks around Metgethen and threatened to penetrate into Königsberg from the west. As darkness fell the leading tanks of the 1st Tank Corps reached the Haff coast, completely severing the route to Pillau. Königsberg was now isolated both from the Fourth Army to the south, and from the XXVIII Corps in Samland. With the danger of the 113th Rifle Corps driving straight into the city from the west, the Germans had to try to build a new defence line west. Lasch ordered Lieutenant-General Hans Mikosch to form an emergency battle group, which later became known as z.b.V.[6] Division Mikosch. His prompt and energetic action secured the defence of the western perimeter, and stabilised the new front on the line Gross Friedrichsburg, Moditten and Holstein. As Major Dieckert, who was despatched by Mikosch relates, action was needed urgently:

> *During the night of 29th to 30th January 1945 I received...a call from the staff of the fortress commander and was told I should make myself ready for employment by Lieutenant-General Mikosch. A car took me to his command post. An hour later I presented myself... before General Mikosch in Fort 'Queen Luise'. He was sitting in a dimly lit basement room at a table which was covered with a large map. He addressed me with just a few words: "The Russians are advancing north-west of Königsberg. The exact location of the current front line is unknown and only scattered units are in the area. At Seerappen airfield there are Luftwaffe ground staff, set up an alarm unit and take command. Report back to me on the success of your mission."*[7]

Dieckert left but did not make it to Seerappen, the town and its airfield having already fallen to the Soviets. He found the roads, deep with snow, difficult to traverse and crowded with refugees and, mixed in among them, retreating soldiers. News quickly reached Dieckert that the Soviets were already between his current position and Seerappen, and the Luftwaffe personnel at the airbase had already been evacuated. Dieckert reported the failure of his mission to an annoyed Mikosch and suggested that he gather what forces he could to build a defence line, which he succeeded in achieving. Mikosch had initially set up the command post of his z.b.V. Division in the basement of Fort VI, where Dieckert had seen him, but like Lasch he soon moved it inside the city. His was a division in name only, being well below strength and comprising stragglers, construction crews and Luftwaffe personnel. Mikosch himself was an experienced pioneer officer and used to dealing with crisis situations. After commanding troops in the Polish and French campaigns and on the Eastern Front, he had led a z.b.V. unit near Stalingrad in the bleak early days of 1943. He took command of the 10th Panzergrenadier Division in late 1943 and in early 1944 was in command of the 13th Panzer Division. He then took command of the defences of Boulogne in June 1944 before finding his way to the East once again in September 1944, as commander of the Pioneer forces and the fortifications in East Prussia. His final promotion to Lieutenant-General followed in March 1945.

While Mikosch tried to construct a defence line in the west, to the east of the city the great concrete Palmburger Bridge, which spanned the Pregel south of the village of Lauth, was blown up. The central span of the bridge was destroyed, leaving the remaining portions at each shore pointing like accusing fingers at the sky. The bridge had been blown as Soviet troops had been on the verge of capturing it. Its loss would have eased the transit of Soviet forces from the northern to southern bank of the river. The pressure against the eastern perimeter, which had been intense thus far, now began to ease as the 39th Army was increasingly stretched. Galitsky's attacks south of the city were also facing determined German resistance and despite their best efforts, the Soviet troops were unable to break through into the urban area.

THE BATTLE OF KÖNIGSBERG

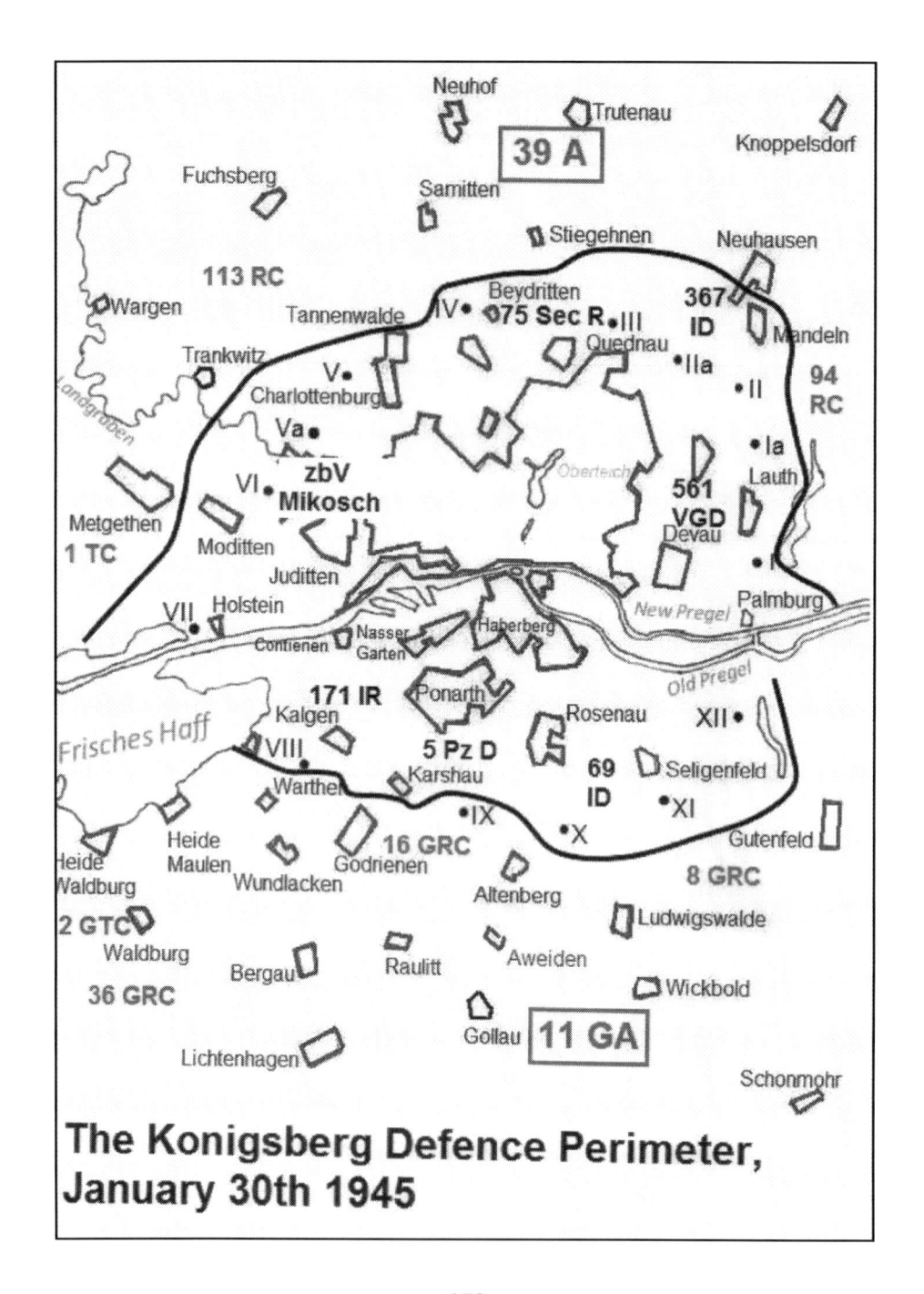

The Konigsberg Defence Perimeter, January 30th 1945

Increasing pressure on the flanks of the salient, where the Germans had begun to counter attack, were sapping the offensive strength of the Soviet corps.

Outside the pocket the *Grossdeutschland* Division had begun its counter attack. As Lorenz's men moved forward from outside, within the pocket Lieutenant-Colonel Rieger of the 171st Grenadier Regiment (part of the 56th Infantry Division) launched an attack from Karschau and Kalgan. The 171st had been reduced to just a few hundred men in the bitter fighting of the last few days and was nowhere near regimental strength. Nevertheless, in a day of difficult fighting the *Grossdeutschland* Division managed to push on and take Maulen but then came under severe anti-tank fire between Wundlaken and Warthen and was forced to halt.

The fighting continued the next day, January 31st, as Soviet troops on the outward facing perimeter in Samland attacked toward Nautzwinkel and Gross Heydekrug. North and south of Königsberg the Germans still had relatively weak forces. Lasch was surprised that the Soviets had not made a more determined effort to push into Königsberg and used the unexpected breathing space he had been given to try to organise a more effective defence of the city. He built up the defensive positions around the city perimeter, particularly the almost non-existent lines to the west. Inside the city there was still a feeling of chaos as the thousands of refugees who had been trying to reach Pillau now found their road west cut. The city had filled to capacity with this miserable mass of humanity, cold and hungry and suffering terrible privations in the bitter winter conditions. Among these civilians were German soldiers who had been swept along in their retreat. Over the next two weeks Lasch sent officers among them to round them up and put them back into the front line. Notices were also posted around the city which called on all men from the age of sixteen and up to register for service in the Volkssturm, SS or Army by February 3rd. Lieutenant-Colonel Dr Würdig, serving under Lasch, was able to pull together a force totalling eight infantry battalions which were sent into the battle to reinforce the hard pressed units at the front.

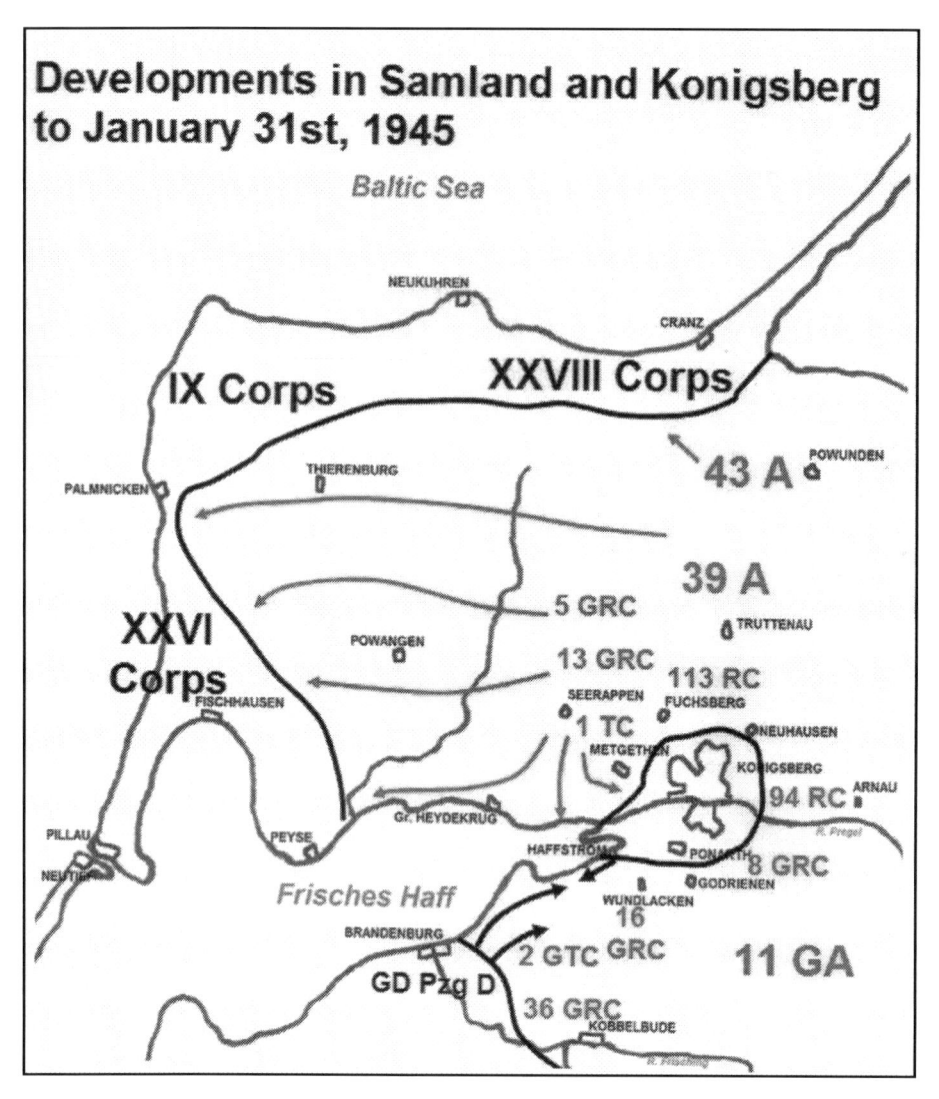

Developments in Samland and Konigsberg to January 31st, 1945

While Lasch continued with his efforts to impose order inside Königsberg, the *Grossdeutschland* Division pursued its attack along the Haff coast. After another day of fierce fighting with the 36th Guards Rifle Corps it managed, during February 1st, to reach the positions of Battlegroup Rieger, which had been held up by stubborn Soviet defences. Königsberg was no longer isolated, but the corridor which was opened was extremely narrow and immediately came under intense and continuous Soviet artillery fire. Although Lasch's command remained isolated from the forces in Samland, at least a line of communication to the south, to the Fourth Army, was now open. Unfortunately, the flood of wounded which followed, some 10,000 or more, merely added to Lasch's troubles. Soviet artillery fire on the city also resumed and spread destruction indiscriminately, inflicting casualties on both troops and civilians. Houses collapsed in ruins, blocking streets and making life in the packed city all the more difficult.

The Soviet forces would shortly turn their fire on the Fourth Army before dealing with the Königsberg pocket. Hossbach had been dismissed on January 30th following his continued efforts to break through to the west in spite of Hitler's stand fast orders. His replacement was General Friedrich-Wilhelm Müller, known to the Western Allies as 'The Butcher of Crete'. Müller was a mediocre general, a man who openly admitted he simply followed the orders he was given, and did nothing to inspire his men. He had seen action on the Eastern Front from 1941 and was promoted to Colonel in April 1942 and Major-General in August of the same year, when he was also appointed commander of the 22nd Air Landing Division which was in the process of redeploying from the Eastern Front to Crete. He remained in command of this unit until August 1944, when he was made Commandant of Fortress Crete, replacing Luftwaffe-General Bruno Brauer. His period in command of 22nd Air Landing Division and the Crete garrison were marked by a series of atrocities against the civilian populace, with whole villages being punished for the actions of partisans and civilians murdered en masse in reprisal for the killing of German soldiers by the Greek resistance. He would eventually pay with his life for these acts of revenge. After leaving Crete, Müller had commanded the XXXIV Corps and LXVIII Corps before finally being appointed commanding officer of the Fourth Army. His tenure in command of the Fourth Army, and his impact on the defence of Königsberg was, as we shall see, to be disastrous.

Figure 26 - Friedrich-Wilhelm Müller

Following the successes of the East Prussia Offensive thus far, the Soviet High Command turned its attention to the systematic elimination of the Fourth Army in the Heiligenbeil pocket, of those units around Königsberg and the remnants of the Third Panzer Army in Samland. To this end the Stavka began to reorganise its forces both in the Baltic and in East Prussia. On February 6th the 2nd Baltic Front, facing the German forces trapped in Courland, was instructed to take command of those elements of the 1st Baltic Front that were still in that sector. In return, the 1st Baltic Front gained Beloborodov's 43rd Army, Lyudnikov's 39th and Galitsky's 11th Guards Armies from the 3rd Belorussian Front, together with the 1st Tank Corps and 2nd Guards Breakthrough Artillery Division. Bagramyan and his staff arrived at their new command post in East Prussia during the evening of February 9th and were greeted by Chernyakhovsky, who summed up the situation succinctly:.

> *The remnants of Army Group Centre, now North, are locked up in the Samland Peninsula, pinned against the sea in the vicinity of Königsberg and to the south west. Thus the whole army group is split into three isolated pockets, in Samland, Königsberg and to the south west, in the Heilsberg fortified area...As a result of the breakthrough by the forces of Rokossovsky to the Frisches Haff the escape route of Army Group North is closed. Our task is to destroy this force. Your men must tackle those at Königsberg and in Samland while the 3rd Belorussian Front takes on the Fourth Army at Heilsberg.*[8]

Bagramyan's forces were stretched across a long front line and were weary after a month of costly fighting. Beloborodov's 43rd Army was deployed in Samland with the 54th, 90th and 103rd Rifle Corps, a total of just 27,000 men and 350 artillery pieces. Lyudnikov's 39th Army held a very long front. Part of it faced west into Samland while the remainder covered the perimeter to the west of Königsberg, right around the north and on to the banks of the Pregel on the eastern side of the city. These long lines were held by the 5th, 11th and 13th Guards Rifle Corps and 94th and 113th Rifle Corps, a total force of 52,000 men with 550 artillery pieces.[9] To the south of the river was Galitsky's 11th Guards Army, which faced the southern approaches to the city but also had an eye to the southwest, where the *Grossdeutschland* Division kept hammering away. Galitsky's army numbered 57,000 infantry with 600 artillery pieces and 167 anti-tank guns.[10] Bagramyan's only armoured asset, Butkov's 1st Tank Corps was considerably under strength, having just thirty-three operational tanks left.

Chernyakhovsky's own Front received three armies and a tank corps from 2nd Belorussian Front, including Ozerov's 50th Army which would later redeploy onto the eastern face of the Königsberg perimeter. To support his offensive against the Fourth Army Chernyakhovsky was provided with the 3rd Air Army, which deployed to Insterburg to assist in the destruction of the Heiligenbeil Pocket.

The rationale behind these moves was to free up Rokossovsky to destroy the German forces in Pomerania and around Danzig so that he could ultimately redeploy along the River Oder to take part in the Berlin Offensive. Meanwhile, Chernyakhovsky and Bagramyan would clear the Germans from Heiligenbeil and Königsberg-Samland respectively. The Stavka was growing increasingly impatient that the Germans in East Prussia should be destroyed so that as many units as possible could be released for the Berlin Offensive. Chernyakhovsky was therefore ordered to complete the destruction of the German Fourth Army by 20-25th February, but he had to give the reply that this would not be possible, as the encircled German forces proved a tougher nut to crack than originally thought.

While the Soviets made their new arrangements, the Germans resumed the battle to reconnect the pockets of resistance in East Prussia into one single entity. On February 3rd a counter-attack by the XXVIII and IX Corps from Samland began, their objective being to reach Königsberg. Despite bitter fighting, the German forces lacked the strength to punch their way through the formidable defences put up by the 39th and 43rd Armies. The following day the fighting southwest of Königsberg, on the Haff coast, erupted again as the Soviets launched a new attack. The Germans had established strong defensive positions along a line from Neucolbnicken, Maulen and Warthen, and had planned to deepen the corridor with a new attack beginning on the 5th. Unfortunately for them, the 11th Guards Army launched its own attack just hours before, pushing its 16th and 36th Guards Rifle Corps across the Königsberg-Kobbelbude railway line. The Soviet forces aimed to cut the German corridor once again, severing communications between Lasch and the Fourth Army. Having disrupted the German counter attack, the 11th Guards Army resumed its attacks on the 6th. The *Grossdeutschland* Division and Colonel Kassner's 975th Grenadier Regiment (part of the 367th Infantry Division which had been brought out of Königsberg) were put under intense pressure as the Soviets very nearly reached the coast again. The villages of Wundlacken, Warthen and Maulen were retaken by the 11th Guards Army and, despite their repeated counter attacks, could not be recovered by the Germans. The corridor that connected Königsberg to the Fourth Army was now just 600 meters wide. The *Grossdeutschland* Division immediately made preparations to launch yet another attack, the 975th Grenadier Regiment being brought up again to support them. The attack began during the night of February 6-7th but started badly as German engineers mistakenly set off flares, illuminating the attacking force. The Soviets, seizing on this unexpected opportunity, opened fire on the brightly lit German formation and inflicted heavy losses, knocking out two Panther tanks and cutting down the infantry. The Germans nevertheless recovered and persevered with their attack. After such a bad start it was almost inevitable that the assault would fail, and they were forced to abandon their attack after having suffered heavy losses for no appreciable gains. The next day the German High Command changed the command set up in Königsberg and Samland. The newly formed Army Detachment Samland, created around the headquarters of Gollnick's XXVIII Corps, took command of the forces in Samland and also the Königsberg garrison. The reason behind this decision was the withdrawal of the headquarters of the Third Panzer Army, which was sent to Pomerania.

In Königsberg, Lasch had spent the first two weeks of February restoring the city defences and organizing his forces. Great efforts were made to try to build up a reserve of ammunition, which had been severely lacking during the fighting at the end of January. Shells were produced in the city although the detonators required to fire them had to be flown in from the Reich. Despite their best efforts, artillery ammunition remained in short supply, and Lasch and his commanders urged the collection and use of as much discarded equipment as they could. Lasch had also been busy planning to strengthen the junction both with the Fourth Army and the forces in Samland. By the middle of the month both he and Müller had laid plans to launch an attack to widen the corridor to the southwest of the city. Unfortunately by the time the Germans were ready the situation with the Fourth Army had deteriorated so much due to the continual Soviet pressure on the Heiligenbeil perimeter that the planned attack had to be abandoned. Lasch then turned his attention to the western perimeter, where he planned to launch a new attack in conjunction with General Gollnick's forces in Samland. On February 17th Gollnick had contacted him to advise him of the intention of the Samland Group to launch a relief attempt in just two days time, on February 19th Lasch was given orders to commit minor elements of the 5th Panzer and 1st Infantry Divisions to attack from the city, these forces linking up with infantry units from Samland. Lasch and his Chief of Staff, Lieutenant-Colonel Hugo von Süsskind-Schwendi, were worried that the attack from Samland, with just limited forces supporting them from Königsberg, would fail as the Soviets had built up strong defences in their path. Lasch therefore proposed using the whole of Schittnig's 1st Infantry Division together with all of the 5th Panzer Division as well as parts of 561st Volksgrenadier Division, for the attack from Königsberg. In order to do this Lasch would have to pull the 5th Panzer Division out of its positions south of the city and replace them with the 69th Infantry Division. The 561st Volksgrenadier Division, which held defensive positions on the eastern face of the fortress perimeter, was also pulled out of the lines, to be replaced by a mixture of Police and Volkssturm units. This was a considerable risk. If the Soviets became aware of the German redeployment they could well exploit the weakness of the perimeter to storm their way into the city. Indeed, the Soviets had suspected as early as the February 15th that the Germans would attempt a counter attack between Königsberg and Samland. It was obvious that the Soviet corridor centred on Seerappen was an easy target if the Germans sought to reunite the two forces. To deter just such an attack Bagramyan had ordered the construction of strong defences around

Metgethen and deployed three rifle divisions of the 113th Rifle Corps there. These units though had been involved in hard fighting and were considerably depleted. Discipline had also broken down to some degree as the effects of plundering and alcohol took their toll both on officers and their troops.

Lasch spoke with Gollnick again on the 18th and informed him of his plan to use the whole of the 5th Panzer and 1st Infantry Divisions in the attack, as well as the redeployment of the 561st Volksgrenadier Division for use as a second echelon. Gollnick was very worried by the weakening of other sections of the city defence lines; he felt the redeployment would leave Königsberg vulnerable to attack. Lasch nevertheless stood his ground and maintained that without such a concentration of force the counter attack would surely fail. Gollnick reluctantly agreed to Lasch's proposal, but added the clause that he took those actions of his own authority and at his own risk.

During the evening of the 18th the German units began to take up their attack positions, the commanders of the divisions concerned being given just a few hours notice to move their men and prepare for the assault. For the counter attack the 1st Infantry Division was formed into three battle groups, one under the command of Captain Singer, another from the Fusilier Battalion under Captain Schröder and a third from the 22nd Fusilier Regiment under Captain Malotka. The infantry, with a small armoured component in the lead, would attack along the road out of Juditten and follow it, and the railway line that ran alongside, as far as Metgethen. Once they reached the eastern edge of the Metgethen the 5th Panzer Division would then begin its attacks. This attack, which would be launched from Friedrichsburg, a little to the north of the infantry, was led by the reliable and battle-hardened Battlegroup Jaedtke, including elements of 13th Panzergrenadier Regiment and 31st Panzer Regiment. Further units from these two regiments formed a second supporting battle group whose task was to protect the right wing of Group Jaedtke. The 5th Panzer Division was now commanded by Lieutenant-Colonel Karl Herzog following the departure of Rolf Lippert in early February. Shortly before the battle began, Major-General

Hoffmann-Schönborn arrived to take command of the division, but he sensibly decided to assume command once the attack had been completed so as not to disrupt Herzog's preparations. The 5th Panzer had at this time around eighty operational tanks and assault guns. Fuel supplies were sufficient to see the division through the offensive but as with the other forces in and around Königsberg, ammunition supplies were tenuous at best. The attack by the armour was only to begin once the German infantry had secured control of Metgethen. The attack, codenamed Operation Westwind, was due to begin the next day. The offensive from Samland was to be conducted by three infantry divisions. The 548th Volksgrenadier Division was to attack along the Haff coast, the 58th Infantry Division in the centre and the 93rd Infantry Division on the northern flank. As the final few hours before the assault ticked away, the men moved into their attack positions and made their final preparations. A tense night followed as the clocks counted down the hours until the artillery signalled the start of the attack.

While the Germans had been making their preparations to counter attack the Soviets had been hard at work. Bagramyan had realised his forces lacked the strength to launch a storming attack on Königsberg and on February 14th issued orders for an assault group to assemble to the west of the city with the intention of pushing the Germans back through Samland to take Fischhausen and Pillau. This would leave Königsberg isolated far to the rear, whence the German garrison could then be destroyed by a renewed concentration of the Soviet armies. Bagramyan was worried in particular by the situation in the 39th Army sector. Lyudnikov's men were badly overstretched, having to man lines that faced both west and east, while also masking the northern and eastern perimeters. As it turned out, his worries were not unfounded.

Meanwhile, on February 18th Stalin spoke with Vasilevsky, who had returned to Moscow, about the situation in East Prussia. Stalin had suggested that given the continuing difficulty the 3rd Belorussian and 1st Baltic Fronts were having in eliminating the German forces,

Vasilevsky should travel to the front to give his assistance as Stavka representative to Chernyakhovsky and Bagramyan. Stalin also went on to explain that both Fronts would need to release forces to strengthen the attack on Berlin and in the Far East[11]. Vasilevsky was then told that he too would be going to the east to run operations against the Japanese in Manchuria once the campaign in East Prussia was wound up. Within hours of receiving this news Vasilevsky received an urgent summons to report to Stalin once more. Once in his presence he was given the grave news that General Chernyakhovsky, the talented commander of the 3rd Belorussian Front, who had struggled so long to destroy the German forces in East Prussia, had been killed earlier that day. Chernyakhovsky had been travelling in his jeep to the command post of the 3rd Army when artillery fire near Mehlsack had sent a splinter of shrapnel into his chest. He died less than an hour later. The loss of this exceptional commander was a hard blow for the Soviets, and prompted Stalin to make a number of command adjustments. During the evening of the 19th he appointed Vasilevsky commander of the 3rd Belorussian Front, and sent him on his way to East Prussia. While he was travelling, events in East Prussia took another turn for the worse.

* * *

At 0430 hours on February 19th, just hours before Vasilevsky was receiving the news of his new appointment from Stalin, the German counter attack from Samland and Königsberg began. The attack opened with a powerful artillery barrage which struck the positions of the 39th Army. From Königsberg the 1st Infantry Division, with Battlegroups Singer and Schröder in the lead, opened its attack from Juditten, hitting the 113th Rifle Corps hard. The attack by the 1st Infantry Division was led by a small force of tanks, with a captured T-34 in the lead to try to fool the Soviets. The ruse appeared to work as the infantry reported back surprisingly quickly that they had broken through the Soviet trenches and had already reached Metgethen. This information was immediately passed on to Herzog, who ordered the 5th Panzer Division to begin its attack. Jaedtke led his battle group forward; his line of advance being along an elevated dyke, with boggy ground on either side, meaning the armour had no room to manoeuvre in the event of enemy fire. After pushing forward a few hundred yards the leading Panther tank was suddenly knocked out by Soviet fire, blocking the road. The tanks following behind were now held up, and as the panzer grenadiers accompanying them took cover in the roadside ditches, they unexpectedly encountered infantrymen who had themselves been pinned down. Unfortunately it then transpired that the 1st Infantry Division had not in fact reached Metgethen, but were in Moditten, the village before Metgethen. They had mistakenly thought they had reached Metgethen. The infantry resumed their attacks along the road but Jaedtke, with some difficulty, turned his tanks around and they retraced their steps to Friedrichsburg, their intention being to follow the second wave in their diversionary attack on the right wing.

The second wave, now in fact the leading wave of the armoured assault, had moved forward from Friedrichsburg as planned and pushed on to Rablacken. They also managed to reach Moditten but then came under heavy fire from a well dug in Soviet anti-tank gun position. Avoiding a frontal confrontation the Germans tried to manoeuvre their tanks around the Soviet flank but then encountered a force of Soviet tanks. After a short fire fight the Soviets were forced to pull back. By this time Jaedtke had caught up with the second wave and together they secured control of Rablacken and Landkeim before pushing down into Metgethen from the north. Battlegroup Schröder meanwhile had fought its way through Moditten and on to Metgethen which it entered from the southeast. Battlegroup Malotka, near the northern suburbs of Metgethen, was aided by the arrival of Jaedtke's panzers and together they fought their way through the town. Metgethen was then secured after hard fighting with the defending Soviet infantry.

The Germans then regrouped and resumed their attacks, pushing on towards Seerappen. Advancing along the roadway between the Kobbelbude Forest to the south and high ground to the north, the

German forces came under increasingly heavy Soviet artillery fire. Despite this, the infantry and armour were able to reach Seerappen during the afternoon and after a brief struggle also captured this village. To the south of the village, Bärwalde was also taken. At this point the 5th Panzer Division came under sustained Soviet counter attack using tanks but these were beaten off. Fortunately for the Germans the Soviets did not take advantage of their numerical superiority and instead attacked with small detachments of tanks, around twenty or so at a time.

On the other side of the lines the attack had come as a shock to the Soviets. Almost as soon as the German artillery had started to bombard his position Lyudnikov had reported to Bagramyan that a major attack was underway. The Soviets commanders recognised that the Germans intended to fight their way through from Samland and Königsberg and reconnect the two forces. Bagramyan immediately agreed to provide all available forces to the 39th Army. He ordered Beloborodov to hand over the 54th Rifle Corps to the Lyudnikov and the 3rd Air Army was instructed to assist the ground units, which were to counter attack and halt the German advance. Unfortunately the 54th would not be able to redeploy quickly enough. By the time it had moved south it found the Germans firmly ensconced in a northward facing defensive position.

With their early success the Germans paused to regroup. With Soviet artillery fire continuing to strike his men, Herzog decided to wait until nightfall to undertake his main regrouping, Lasch having forbidden any further advance that day as he was fearful of the Soviets closing the breach behind the 5th Panzer Division. The salient it had driven in the Soviet lines was six miles deep but very narrow. Soviet forces to the north were counter attacking aggressively while those to the south, in the Kobbelbude Forest, continued to resist. In the late evening the Soviets launched yet another counter attack upon Bärwalde but in hard fighting the German infantry held them at bay until armour arrived to repulse the attackers.

To the rear of the attacking units, Lasch began to move the 561st Volksgrenadier Division up to Metgethen. Herzog had wanted to

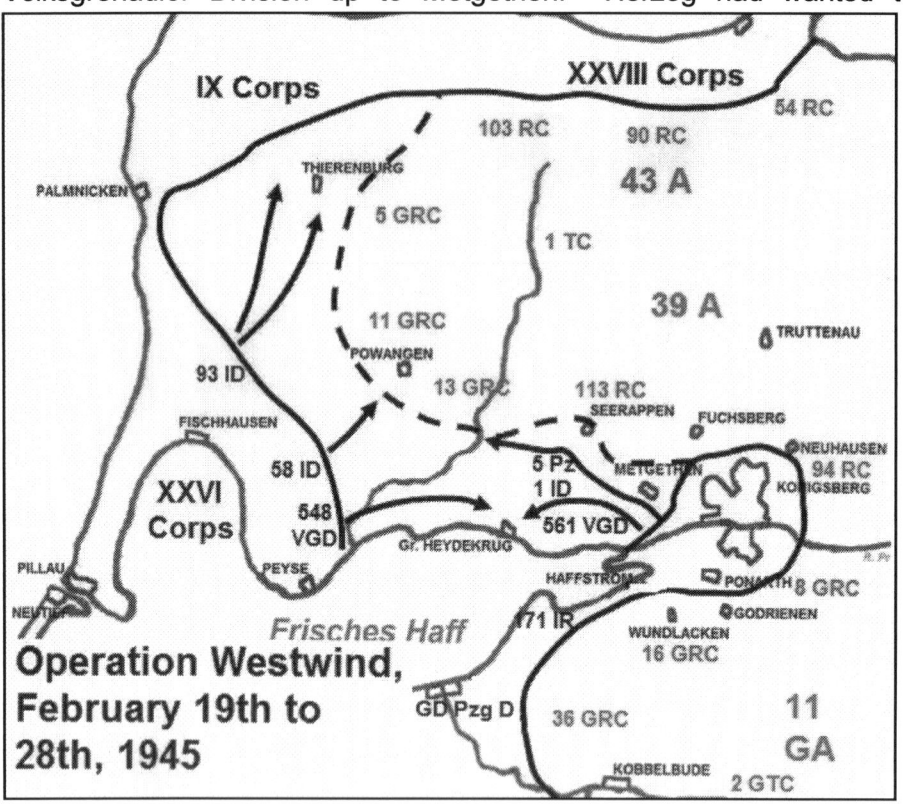

Operation Westwind, February 19th to 28th, 1945

continue his attack so as not to give the Soviets the chance to solidify their defence lines but Lasch was more cautious, being acutely aware that he could ill afford to see his strike force encircled. He intended that the 561st would clear the Soviets out of the Kobbelbude Forest so as to secure the long left flank of the 5th Panzer but fortunately for the Germans, an intercepted Soviet radio transmission revealed that the forces in the forest were about to withdraw. This meant the 561st Volksgrenadier was able to screen the forest and use the bulk of its strength to relieve the panzer troops so that they could concentrate in order to resume the advance to the west. The infantry duly took over the combat line near Metgethen and to the south, enabling the panzer troops to reinforce the battle groups at the tip of the salient in preparation of the next day's attacks. The first day of the attack from Königsberg had been a success for Lasch. Despite meeting considerable Soviet resistance the 1st Infantry Division had punched a hole in the Soviet line and, together with the 5th Panzer Division penetrated deeply into their defences.

While Lasch's forces fought their way to the west, the men of the Samland divisions had begun their attacks. The 548th Volksgrenadier, 58th Infantry and 93rd Infantry Divisions began their attacks at 0530 hours but their frontal assaults, despite the support of the fire of heavy cruiser *Prinz Eugen* lying offshore, resulted in difficult and costly battles with the well entrenched Soviet forces. Heavy fighting saw the Germans achieve a limited advance of just one to two miles. Particularly heavy fighting raged near Gross Blumenau, Kragau and Powangen.

On February 20th the counter attack was resumed. Battlegroup Jaedtke had planned to continue its attack before first light but the Soviets got in first and launched a strong counter attack at Seerappen. The Germans, who had been reinforced during the night by the arrival of those men whose positions had been handed over to the 561st Volksgrenadier Division, were able to hold this attack against their flank and with the bulk of the battle group resumed their own attacks. Hard fighting followed as the Germans encountered stiff resistance from Soviet anti-tank gun positions. Infantry, who were moving up behind the panzers, were able to secure the flanks of the attacking forces and by the afternoon the attack was again making steady progress. The sound of fighting soon began to be heard to the west and at dusk the men of Jaedtke's battle group successfully linked up with the 58th Infantry Division to the north of Gross Heydekrug.

The union of the two forces did not mean an end to the fighting. The Soviets continued their attacks at Seerappen and during the afternoon were able to retake the village. Heavy fighting continued along the new north facing front well into the night, as it did to the south were the now isolated Soviet forces fought hard to escape to the north. The Soviet troops in the Kobbelbude Forest, which stretched along the Haff coast from Metgethen to Gross Heydekrug, had already been ordered to withdraw but they were isolated and had nowhere to go. Men of the 1st Infantry Division, z.b.V. Division Mikosch and the 548th Volksgrenadier Division worked their way through the forest, mopping up the Soviet pockets of resistance as they advanced.

Despite these mopping up battles, the attack had proved an overwhelming success. Lasch's decision to use the 561st Volksgrenadier Division in addition to the whole of the 1st Infantry and 5th Panzer Divisions had been fully justified. By having the men of the 561st following the advance of the panzer troops they had freed up the armour in the face of determined Soviet resistance. It is likely that, had these extra troops not been available, the attack may well have stalled. Credit for the success of the attack rested firmly on the shoulders of Lasch, and he was commended for his brave decision by Gollnick.

Following the success of Operation Westwind the final days of February saw the men of the 5th Panzer Division, together with the 58th and 93rd Infantry Divisions, continued their struggle to widen the corridor from Königsberg. Seerappen was recovered but the German attempts to capture the Galtgarben Height near Thierenburg failed in the face of strengthening Soviet resistance and steady losses. Despite this setback the attack did succeed in freeing the Königsberg to Pillau railway line of Soviet forces so that trains could run through to the port. For the civilians in Königsberg, and indeed for General Lasch, the success of the attack was a great relief. With the road and railway to Pillau open the authorities inside the fortress tried to get as many civilians and wounded out as was possible. Unfortunately, Lasch continued to be hindered by the Party officials who did everything they could to interfere. Gauleiter Koch, who had returned to East Prussia after abandoning the province in fright after his Gross Friedrichsburg estate had fallen to the Soviets in late January, began to exert his malevolent influence once more. He had his Party underlings within the city tear down buildings to build unwanted barricades and even went so far at the lay out an airstrip on the Paradeplatz, despite the fact that there were no planes available to make use of it. Lasch tried his best to mediate between the military and Party authorities but could not prevent the building of the unwanted defences.

Across the battle lines, by February 22nd Marshal Vasilevsky had arrived in East Prussia and got to work reorganising his forces. The Stavka had decided to unite the Soviet forces in East Prussia and so Bagramyan's 1st Baltic Front was wound up. Its elements were grouped into the Samland Operational Group, which was under the command of the 3rd Belorussian Front. Bagramyan, commanding the Samland Group, was also appointed Vasilevsky's deputy in command of the Front. The armies in Samland were placed on the defensive just days later as Vasilevsky decided that he would deal with the Germans in East Prussia step by step. Vasilevsky explained his plan to Bagramyan when the two of them met on the 22nd, saying:

Do not forget the simple truth of the operational art, the enemy cannot be strong everywhere....Our goal, with our slight superiority in numbers is to achieve an overwhelming superiority in those areas where we are going to finish off the enemy. This means we must destroy Army Group North in parts: first we will fall on the main group in the Heilsberg area, then the forces in Samland and finally Königsberg. After thinking for a moment Vasilevsky said 'I believe that after the defeat of the enemy in the Heilsberg area we will focus on Königsberg. Once the fortress has fallen it is be hard for the forces on the Samland Peninsula to resist.' [12]

The Stavka approved Vasilevsky's plans but his request for reinforcements was refused, despite the heavy losses his armies had suffered since the middle of January. Stalin was placing great pressure on the armies on the flanks to complete their work ahead of the Berlin offensive. In response to this pressure Vasilevsky told Bagramyan that the attack on Heiligenbeil must open on time. The renewed attack was scheduled for March 13th, but fighting had been going on without a break since February as the German perimeter was slowly nibbled away. Unfortunately for the Soviets the weather did nothing to help them as rain, sleet and poor visibility kept the air forces grounded.

On March 12th, on the eve of the attack upon the Fourth Army, the Germans also reorganised their forces in East Prussia. Colonel-General Rendulic stepped down as Army Group commander in order to take over control of the German forces in Courland. Command of Army Group North passed over to General Walter Weiss, who had previously commanded the German Second Army. The next day Weiss was faced with a major crisis as the Soviet attacks on the Heiligenbeil Pocket succeeded in severing the narrow link between Königsberg and the Fourth Army. The first attacks by the 11th Guards Army had been repulsed by the *Grossdeutschland* Division, which launched its own counter attack. These in turn were beaten off before the Soviets renewed their assault. The Germans were slowly forced back amid ferocious fighting. On the 15th the southern part of the Heiligenbeil perimeter came under intense pressure as the 5th Guards Tank Army pushed towards Brandenburg. By the 16th the ferocity of the attacks showed clearly that the Soviets meant to finish off the Fourth Army for once and for all. Lasch suggested to Weiss that the remnants of the army attempt a breakout toward Königsberg and Weiss, while in agreement, could only tell Lasch that his suggestion had been denied by Hitler. The Fourth Army fought on, to meet its fate around Heiligenbeil.

After a week of bad weather, with rain and sleet turning the land into a muddy morass, the skies over East Prussia finally cleared on March 18th and the Red Air Force began to pound the Fourth Army relentlessly. German resistance seemed to slacken immediately as the air armies pulverised anything that moved. Under heavy attack the Germans fought back with the desperation of men with no hope.

THE BATTLE OF KÖNIGSBERG

General Grossmann, commanding the VI Corps requested permission to pull his collapsing divisions back but Müller turned him down, the simple fact being there was no longer anywhere to withdraw to. On March 21st Müller requested Hitler's permission to evacuate the remnants of his Army but the Führer predictably refused. By this stage of the battle the fighting had reached Heiligenbeil itself. Two days later Müller ordered the VI Corps to fall back to Balga to concentrate with his few remaining forces. On the 24th, after days of bitter fighting the Soviet forces captured the railway station at Heiligenbeil. The main part of the Fourth Army, now just a ragged band of worn out and exhausted divisions, most with just a few hundred men left, was driven back to the tiny Balga peninsula. Grossmann's VI Corps was separated from the main force and was pushed back upon Leysuhnen. Grossmann then received an order from Müller to fall back to Balga and, despite the urgings of his officers to disregard the order, planned to breakout that night. The attack began at midnight but quickly met with disaster. At Rosenberg the Germans were brought under heavy fire and their force was virtually destroyed. The remnants of the Fourth Army disintegrated on the shores of the Frisches Haff just days later. Only a small force continued to resist on the Balga Peninsula. These survivors of the Fourth Army, few in number and badly demoralised, were subordinated to the command of the *Grossdeutschland* Division on the 28th. On the final day of the campaign, thick fog again grounded the Soviet air armies. This enabled the Germans to evacuate the bulk of their men from the beaches. Covering the retreat was a single infantry division, the 562nd Volksgrenadier. These brave men were unable to get to the evacuation point and fought to the bitter end. Their defeat brought the horrific battle for the Heiligenbeil pocket to an end. The bloody campaign was finally over but at a considerable cost. The Soviets claimed to have inflicted the loss of 93,000 men killed and 47,000 wounded on the Germans, with 605 panzers, 3,600 artillery pieces 1,400 mortars and 130 aircraft destroyed or captured.[13]

As the gunfire to the southwest fell silent, it was clear to the civilians and soldiers in Königsberg that their day of reckoning for the city was not far off. With a great sense of trepidation they awaited the onslaught that would surely follow.

[1] Lasch, *So Fiel Königsberg*, p48

[2] Lasch, *So Fiel Königsberg*, p38

[3] The 13th Guards Rifle and 113th Rifle Corps had been transferred to the 39th Army by Chernyakhovsky to reinforce its drive on Königsberg. The 5th Guards Rifle Corps was operating on the right of the tank corps, the 13th following in its wake and the 113th on its left.

[4] Lasch, *So Fiel Königsberg*, pp50-51

[5] Dieckert & Grossman, *Der Kampf um Ostpreussen*, pp173-174

[6] z.b.V. – zur besonderen Verwendung, meaning for Special Employment, otherwise generally referred to as Special Purpose Division.

[7] Lasch, *So Fiel Königsberg*, pp51-52

[8] Bagramyan, *So We Went to Victory*, pp511-512

[9] Bagramyan, So We Went to Victory, p515

[10] Bagramyan, *So We Went to Victory*, p514

[11] Stalin planned to end his truce with the Japanese and attack their Kwantung Army as soon as the war in Europe had been concluded.

[12] Bagramyan, *So We Went to Victory*, p520

[13] Duffy, *Red Storm on the Reich*, p206

Chapter Six - Fortress Königsberg

On March 16th, while the battle for the Heiligenbeil pocket had still been raging, Marshal Vasilevsky submitted a detailed report to Stalin and the High Command of the plan for the assault on Königsberg. The Stavka had already stipulated that the battle at Heiligenbeil must be concluded by March 22nd, and the attack on Königsberg to be begun no later than the 28th but Vasilevsky was forced to respond that this timetable could not be met. The Heiligenbeil fighting would not be concluded until 25th or even as late as the 28th. The bombardment of Königsberg could therefore not begin until at least the beginning of April. Stalin, in stark contrast to Hitler's behaviour with his generals, accepted Vasilevsky's appreciation of the situation and agreed to the revised timetable. He also offered to send significant reinforcements to try to speed up the destruction of the German forces and promised the assistance of Air Chief Marshal Novikov, the commander of the Soviet Air Force, to coordinate the attacks of the air armies. Golovanov, the commander of the heavy bomber force, was also to make his way to the city to help pound the German defences.

While the Fourth Army was fighting its final bloody battles to the southwest, Otto Lasch despaired of the situation in Königsberg. His efforts in the weeks since being appointed commander of Wehrkreis I and of Fortress Königsberg had been spent tirelessly trying to strengthen the city defences to hold the Soviets back. During March 1945 Army Group command stripped Königsberg bare. The stocks of ammunition which Lasch had worked so tirelessly to organise were shipped off to Müller's embattled Fourth Army in the Heiligenbeil pocket, and many of his artillery pieces and anti-aircraft guns were withdrawn from the city. At the end of March Lasch was so downhearted that he had suggested to Weiss that as the garrison was again in contact with the forces in Samland, responsibility for the defence of the city should fall to the Samland Detachment. He had no clear role anymore he said, and recommended that he be relieved of his command. Weiss sympathized with Lasch's predicament, but explained that his signals to High Command on the subject had gone unanswered. In the absence of any decision, Lasch was to remain on as fortress commander. Weiss himself was soon to leave East Prussia. The destruction of the Fourth Army, and loss of Lasch's carefully hoarded supplies, meant that the necessity for an Army Group command in East Prussia was now redundant. Army Detachment Samland was therefore given responsibility for Königsberg and so Lasch became subordinate to General Müller, who took over command of the Samland forces. Unfortunately the news continued to get worse, as Lasch learned of Müller's intention to withdraw the 5th Panzer and 1st Infantry Divisions permanently from Königsberg. Müller was of the opinion that the Soviets would attack the German forces in Samland before tackling those that remained in Königsberg. Lasch vehemently disagreed but, despite his arguments, Müller pulled the 5th Panzer and 1st Infantry Divisions out, deploying them in the corridor to Seerappen to try to strengthen the line between the city and Samland. This movement stripped Lasch of his main armoured reserve and left him with much weaker infantry. To replace these two relatively powerful units Lasch received in return the 548th Volksgrenadier Division under Major General Sudau.

The original defence plan for Königsberg, which now lay in tatters, had been to hold firm on the Advanced Defence Line which circled the city by following the outlying villages. If this line was breached the Germans would then fall back upon their second defence belt, the Fortress Line, situated on the Ring Chaussee. A third defensive position (the Outskirts Defence Line) followed the outskirts of the city, while the final redoubt, the Inner Defence Line, was anchored along the lines of the heavily fortified city gates and bastions. Should this line be breached the fighting would undoubtedly degenerate into bitter street fighting among the final defensive positions of bunkers, cellars and fortified buildings in the inner city as the garrison fought to the bitter end.

THE BATTLE OF KÖNIGSBERG

The Advanced Defence Line had comprised trench networks with barbed wire obstacles covered by machine gun fire, artillery and minefields. The northern part of this defence line, north of the River Pregel, ran along the line of the settlements Gross Holstein, Tannenwalde, Truttenau, Neuhausen, Lauth and Palmburg while the southern line followed the village line Neuendorf, Ludwigswalde, Gollau, Raulitt, Godrienen, Warthen and Haffstrom. Events had overtaken the Germans in late January and this defensive line was overrun in large parts. In the northeast the Soviets had pressed down and captured Neuhausen and also overrun much of the north western perimeter in their drive to the Haff coast. To the south Ludwigswalde, Gollau, Raulitt and Godrienen had been taken during the 11th Guards Army advance. These losses forced the Germans to use their main defensive line, based on the forts, as their first line of defence.

The Fortress Defence Line circled the city on the Ring Chaussee. The fortresses, which had been built in the second half of the Nineteenth Century, were numbered I through XII, with smaller intermediate Forts numbered Fort Ia, IIa and Va in between the larger structures. Unfortunately, the construction of the Atlantic Wall to defend France against Allied invasion had seen many of the weapons stripped from the forts. They had to be replaced with whatever was available when the crisis threatened East Prussia in the winter of 1944. The garrisons in the forts were also of doubtful quality, being made up in many instances by the so-called 'stomach and ear' battalions. These were men who were suffering from various ailments and were not considered fit for front line duties.

Let us now take a more detailed look at the fortresses which surrounded the city. Fort I was located east of the city, between the villages of Lauth and Palmburg, and guarded Reichsstrasse 1 as it made its way into Königsberg. It was known by the name '*Stein*' after Heinrich vom Stein, the Prussian statesman had laid the foundations for the modern state of Prussia. At the time of the Soviet offensive in April 1945 the fortress was commanded by Reserve Major Heisel. Intermediate Fort Ia '*Groeben*' was to the north of Fort I, situated east of

Devau. It had been named after Karl von der Groeben, a Prussian general who had fought in the wars against Napoleon before holding corps and army commands for the remainder of his career. Fort II *'Bronsart'* was south of the village of Mandeln and the Bäckerburg Mount and covered the approaches to the city along Reichsstrasse 126, which ran northeast out of the city. It had been named in honour of General Paul Bronsart von Schellendorff who had served as War Minister from 1883 to 1889. Intermediate Fort IIa *'Barnekow'* lay on the eastern approaches to Quednau. It had been named for General Albert von Barnekow, who had served in the Franco-Prussian War of 1870-71 and afterwards had commanded the I Corps in East Prussia from 1873 until his retirement in 1883. Fort III *'Friedrich Wilhelm I'*, originally named Fort Quednau, was renamed in honour of the King of that name. A number of the other forts were also named after former monarchs of Prussia. Fort III was situated to the north of Quednau, on a high point east of Reichsstrasse 128 which led out of Königsberg. Its garrison was commanded by Reserve Major Dziobaka. Fort IV *'Gneisenau'* was north of Beydritten and was named for August von Gneisenau, the famous Prussian general of the Napoleonic Wars. Fort V *'Friedrich Wilhelm III'* lay to the north west of the city, on the western edge of the village of Charlottenburg. Intermediate Fort Va *'Lehndorf'* covered the northern approaches to Juditten while Fort VI *'Konigin Luise'* was west of Juditten. Fort VII *'Herzog von Holstein'*[1] protected the entrance to the River Pregel at the very western edge of the northern defensive belt.

Fort VIII *'Friedrich Wilhelm IV'* was the outermost fort on the southern defensive belt, lying somewhat inland from the coast near the village of Kalgen in order to protect the south western approaches to the city along Reichsstrasse 1. Fort IX *'Dohna'* was west of Altenberg and Fort X *'Kanitz'* was to the east. Fort IX had been named for Karl Friedrich Emil zu Dohna-Schlobitten, another Prussian general who rose to the rank of Field Marshal in 1854 when he retired. Fort X had been named in honour of August Wilhelm Graf von Kanitz, Prussian Lieutenant-General and Minister of War in 1848. Together these forts covered the southern approaches to the city. Fort IX *'Dohna'* would take no part in

The Konigsberg Fortifications

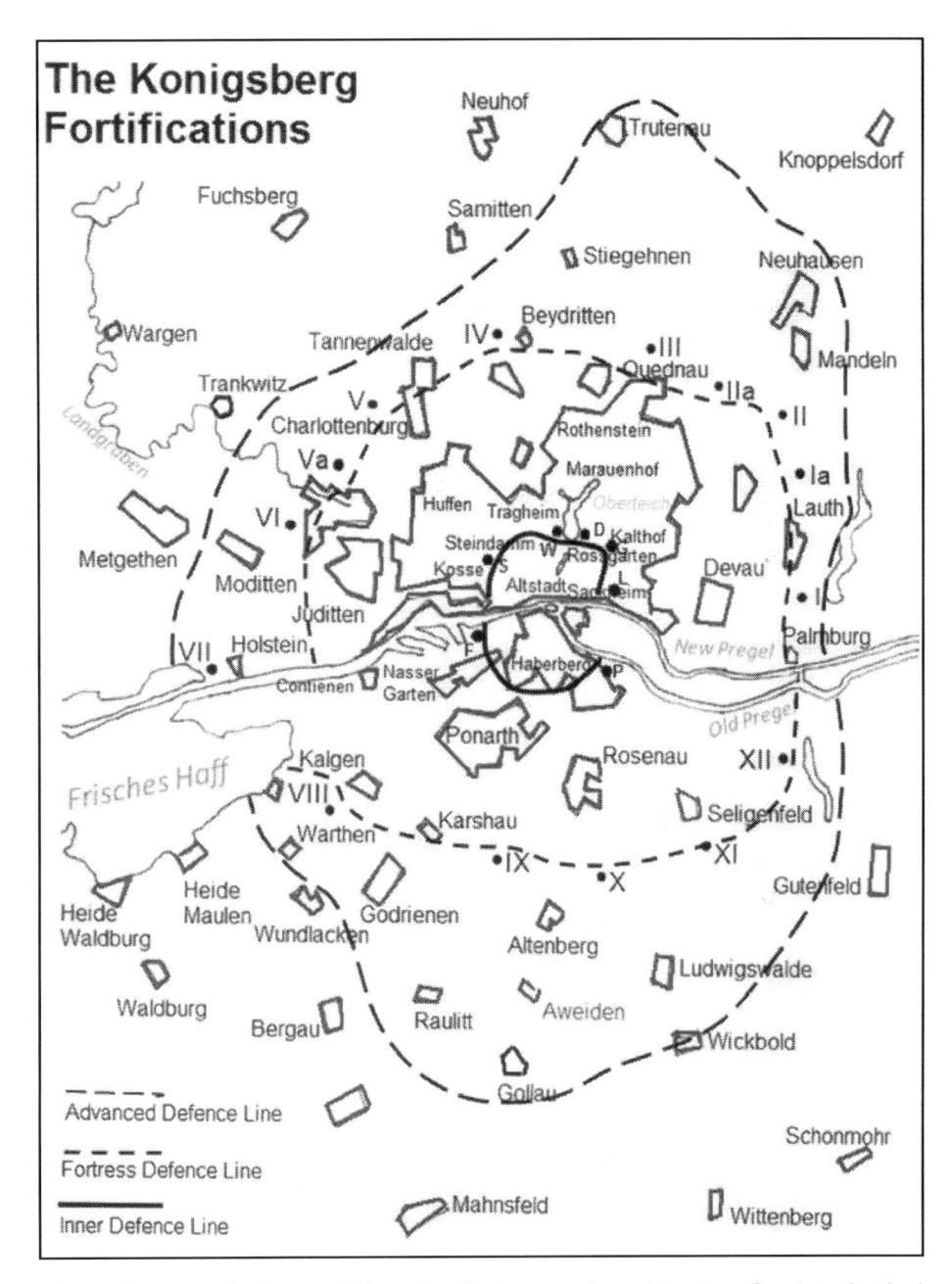

Advanced Defence Line
Fortress Defence Line
Inner Defence Line

the subsequent siege of the city, being captured by the Soviets in their early advance on the city on 28th January 1945. Fort XI *'Dönhoff'* was near Seligenfeld and had been named after August Heinrich Hermann von Dönhoff, a leading Prussian diplomat. He had been appointed Prussian Foreign Minister in 1848. Fort XII *'Eulenburg'*, near Neuendorf, together with Fort XI covered the south eastern approaches. Fort XII completed the ring of defences which circled the city. It had been named for Botho Graf von Eulenburg, former Interior Minister and Prime Minister of Prussia. The areas between each of the forts were augmented by the construction of a series of formidable anti-tank ditches, barbed wire obstacles, concrete bunkers and minefields.

The Outskirts defence system comprised a trench line with bunkers, machine gun and artillery positions, minefields and mutually supporting fire points surrounding the city. It was an intermediate position and not as strongly fortified as either the Fortress line or Inner Defence Line but was meant to serve the purpose of slowing down the Soviet advance and bleeding their units before the attack could reach the city proper.

The final defence line, the Inner Defence Line, circled the perimeter of 'old Königsberg'. When built in the Nineteenth Century this defence network was sub-divided into smaller defensive sections centred on a number of fortified bastions. Working our way around the northern sector in a counter clockwise direction from the east, there was the Lithuanian Bastion, which protected the eastern approaches to Sackheim on the north bank of the Pregel. To the north was the Copper Pond Bastion and defensive walls leading to the Grolman and Oberteich Bastions, which protected the Rossgarten district of the city. Also located close to the Grolman Bastion was the main barracks, the Kronprinz (Crown Prince) Barracks. The Grolman Bastion was a considerable defensive position, its structure being added to in the second round of defensive works building in the 1870's. The Oberteich (the Upper Pond) sector comprised the Dohna Tower and Wrangel Tower at the base of the Oberteich and covered the northern approaches to the city centre. To the west, covering the north western approaches to Tragheim, were the Tragheim and Krauseneck Bastions,

Figure 27 - The Wrangel Tower

with defensive redoubts in between, before heading on to the Observatory Bastion (later called the Sternwarte Bastion) close to the Königsberg Observatory. The Observatory/Sternwarte Bastion was somewhat demolished in the early 1900's, its outer defensive walls being pulled down. Behind these defences was the Trommelplatz Barracks. The final defence sector in this northern section of the perimeter stretched from the Sternwarte Bastion to the Pregel and included the Butterberg and Laak Bastions. South of the river was the Friedrichsburg Tor Fortress and the Old Garden and Brandenburg Bastions while in the Haberberg suburb was the Haberberg Bastion, three ravelins (the Haberberg, Friedland and Cavalier positions) and the Pregel Bastion.

Figure 29 - The Königstor

Every major route into the city was protected by a formidable defensive gate, there being ten in total. The Königstor (King's Gate) stood south of the Grolman Bastion, on the eastern side of the city. The foundation stone for this gate had been laid in the presence of King Friedrich Wilhelm IV in 1843 and on its completion in 1850 its was adorned on its front face with statues of King Ottokar III of Bohemia, King Friedrich I of Prussia and Duke Albrecht. The Sackheimer Tor was to the south of the Königstor on the main route out of the Sackheim district. The Rossgarter Tor was close by the Dohna Tower, close to the eastern shores of the Oberteich. The Ausfalltor and Eisenbahn Tor (Railway Gate) were across the city to the west, protecting the routes out of the city into Samland. They were situated a little to the east and south of the Sternwarte Bastion respectively. In the south of the city, on the outskirts of Haberberg, were the Friedländer Tor and Brandenburger Tor, which stood east and west respectively of the three ravelins.

Figure 30 - The Sackheimer Tor

The most formidable gate of all, protecting the southern bank of the Pregel into the city from the west, was the Friedrichsburg Tor Fortress. This massive structure had been an imposing fortress in its heyday but in the early Twentieth Century much of its outer defence works, walls and gates were pulled down, leaving only the massive inner towers intact. Despite this, the fortress still represented a major obstacle to an attack into the city along the line of the river.

THE BATTLE OF KÖNIGSBERG

Figure 28 - The Friedrichsburg Tor Fortress

Figure 31 - The Friedlander Tor

These bastions proved to be some of the last points of German resistance when the end of the siege came. The growth of the city in the late nineteen and early twentieth centuries had led to many of the fortified gates being partly dismantled, and the bastions and earth banks were allowed to deteriorate. It was only with the imminent threat to the city in 1945 that the Germans belatedly re-armed these forts and bastions in preparation to fend off the Soviet assault.

At the end of March 1945 the German forces arrayed around the city were shattered remnants compare to those that had marched out to invade Poland in 1939. To fend off the formidable Soviet armies Lasch had at his disposal four burnt out infantry divisions, the remnants of a number of other units plus Volkssturm and Police troops.

To the northwest of the city was Major General Erich Sudau's 548th Volksgrenadier Division. Its left flank rested north of Metgethen, against the right flank of the 561st Volksgrenadier Division. The central part of the 548th was situated before Fort Va *Lehndorf* and its right before Fort V *Friedrich Wilhelm III* and the settlement of Charlottenburg. By the time the division had been forced back to Königsberg after its battles at Tilsit and in Samland, it had been reduced to just two regiments, the 1094th and 1095th Grenadier Regiments commanded by Lieutenant-Colonel Hans-Heinrich Wendlandt and Lieutenant-Colonel von Bernhardi respectively.

The 561st Volksgrenadier Division took a relatively minor part in the battle outside the city. It was not part of Lasch fortress command but did become involved in trying to rebuild the shattered Samland front after the city was isolated by the attacks of the 39th and 43rd Armies. The division had been commanded by Colonel Felix Becker since March 1945 after its former commander, Walter Gorn, had been appointed the commander of an infantry division on the Western Front. The division was deployed to cover Metgethen and Seerappen. Held in reserve in Samland near Seerappen, and no longer available to Lasch, was Colonel Herzog's 5th Panzer Division. This unit, which had fought so long and hard to secure the southern approaches to the city in January and February, and had been so instrumental in the success of Operation Westwind, was to be used to counter any Soviet effort to sever the city from the peninsula.

Situated to the right of Sudau's 548th Volksgrenadier Division were the remnants of Lieutenant-Colonel Gross' 75th Security Regiment, formerly attached to the 61st Infantry Division. It secured the junction between the right wing of the 548th Volksgrenadier Division and the left wing of the 367th Infantry Division around the village of Beydritten and Fort IV *Gneisenau*. Lieutenant-General Hermann Hähnle's 367th Infantry Division held the perimeter from the north eastern face before Fort IV *Gneisenau* to the east of Reichsstrasse 126, its right wing being secured south of Neuhausen, near Fort II *Bronsart*. By the time it reached the city in late January 1945 the division, like the 548th to the north, was considerably reduced in strength. In April it comprised the 974th Grenadier Regiment under Colonel Hesselbacher and 976th Grenadier Regiment under Colonel Werner, plus support units. Its 975th Grenadier Regiment had been destroyed at Heiligenbeil after having fought long and hard battles in the Haff corridor.

The remnants of the 61st Infantry Division held the eastern face of the pocket from Fort II *Bronsart* in the north, to banks of the New Pregel in the south. In March 1945 the division had been smashed in the fighting at Heiligenbeil. Largely destroyed, the remnants had fled into Königsberg. During the battle for the city the division had the strength of a large battle group, its three original grenadier regiments having been largely destroyed. By April it largely comprised the remnants of Major Thorwald Lewinski's 192nd Grenadier Regiment, supplemented by detachments of Volkssturm and Hitler Youth. From 11th December 1944 the division had been commanded by Lieutenant-General Rudolf Sperl. He had previously commanded the 15th Panzergrenadier Division in Italy from November 1943 to September 1944 and had been involved in the bitter fighting around Monte Lungo and Monte Cassino.

THE BATTLE OF KÖNIGSBERG

South of the River Pregel were the men of the badly depleted 69th Infantry Division. They were deployed on an arc from Neuendorf in the east to Prappeln in the west. Following the disastrous battles of January 1945 the remnants of the division were forced into Königsberg. After the death of Lieutenant-General Rein in January, it had been commanded by Colonel Grimme. He relinquished command to Colonel Kaspar Volker, who was appointed divisional commander on 9th February 1945. Volker was promoted to Major-General on 1st April 1945.

Securing the right wing of the 69th Infantry Division were the remnants of another infantry division. The survivors of Lieutenant-Colonel Rieger's 171st Grenadier Regiment of the 56th Infantry Division, who had escaped from Heiligenbeil, were subordinated to the 69th Infantry Division. In the January offensive the division suffered heavy losses and was virtually wiped out at Heiligenbeil in March. The surviving headquarters personnel made their way west to Pomerania while the remnants of 171st Grenadier Regiment escaped to the dubious refuge of Königsberg.

Situated on the southern sector of the defensive perimeter near Ponarth was Battlegroup Schuberth. This formation, comprised in the main of Police troops and regional SS units, had also suffered badly in the Heiligenbeil pocket, fighting there as part of Battlegroup Hannibal. Shortly before the German forces in the pocket were destroyed, its remnants escaped to Königsberg. The resultant battle group came under the command of Major-General of Police Fritz Schuberth. It comprised the remnants of Police Regiment 31 under Major Voigt; Police Regiment Schulz commanded by Major Schulz and a mixed force of SS remnants in SS Regiment '*Böhme*' commanded by SS Oberführer Horst Böhme. Böhme had previously served as commander of the SD[2] in East Prussia.

The Army, SS and Police units in the city constituted anywhere from 25-35,000 soldiers[3]. To provide armoured support there was a small force of around fifty assault guns. Unlike many of the units in the East, there was enough fuel for the armoured vehicles in the city, the port facilities holding a sufficient supply to keep the Germans mobile. Fortress Pak Regiment 1, armed with towed anti-tank weapons, provided support to the infantry against tank attacks and was deployed around the city perimeter, with particular emphasis on the coast road to the southwest. The German artillery was seriously short of ammunition, having reserves sufficient to last for only a single day of intense combat. Lasch's forces also lacked aerial support, the Luftwaffe units in Samland could field barely 100 planes and they were more often than not grounded by a lack of aviation fuel.

The German forces in the city were further impeded by the presence of 120,000 or so civilians and foreign labourers who remained. Everyone in the city, soldiers and civilians alike, knew that with the collapse of the German forces in Heiligenbeil, the Soviet juggernaut would turn against them soon.

There were eight Volkssturm battalions within Königsberg, which were split up between the various defence sectors as directed by Lasch. Being Volkssturm they were under the authority of the Party until they actually entered combat. Because of this, Lasch's orders were frequently interfered with by those Party representatives who resented any form of Army control. The Volkssturm forces to the north of the city were commanded by S.A. Standartenfuhrer Lange and those to the south by Reserve Captain Wachholtz. Total Volkssturm numbers were in the region of 5 - 10,000 men and boys. These troops had helped the regular forces in the fighting around the city since January 1945, indeed one Volkssturm member, Battalion Leader Ernst Tizbury, had been awarded the Knights Cross at the end of February in recognition of his action in destroying five Soviet tanks during an intense period of fighting on February 10th. As we have already learned, Kreisleiter Wagner had also been awarded the Iron Cross for his actions near Neuhausen in January. During the final battle for the city the men and boys of the Volkssturm fought valiantly, and gave their lives, alongside their regular army comrades.

THE BATTLE OF KÖNIGSBERG

* * *

Having cleared the Heiligenbeil pocket the Soviets immediately began to redeploy their forces to destroy the Germans in Fortress Königsberg. Such was the German shortage of ammunition and lack of aerial support that the Soviets were able to redeploy without interference by enemy artillery. In order to carry out the new operation Vasilevsky suggested the redeployment of the 43rd Army from its positions in Samland to the northern face of the Königsberg perimeter, while the 50th Army was brought across from Brandenburg to take up positions to the north and east. The removal of the 43rd Army from Samland was made possible by the arrival of 2nd Guards Army and 5th Army. The 39th Army now held a considerably shorter line between Königsberg and Samland.

The Soviet armies were superior in all numerical aspects to their opponents, having more men, artillery, tanks and aircraft and lavish quantities of supplies. Nevertheless, the siege was expected to be one of the largest and most difficult urban assaults undertaken so far by Soviet forces. Aerial reconnaissance had shown how effective the preparations made by the Germans in the last few weeks had been; with powerful forts, innumerable pillboxes and foxholes and well-constructed fortified buildings presenting an enormous challenge. To support the ground assault Marshal Vasilevsky had secured from the Stavka all Soviet aircraft operating in East Prussia together with a considerable force of heavy artillery released from Leningrad.

The assault on the city was planned by General Bagramyan. As early as February 1945 he and his army commanders had realised that a full scale assault on the German lines would lead to excessive casualties. It was therefore decided that the main thrust should strike the Germans to the west of the city, with attacks from the north and south severing the connection between the city and Samland before the garrison was destroyed by a drive into the city centre. Training for the task at hand began in early March. To help the attacking forces a 1:3,000 scale model of the city was built, detailing the external and internal fortifications and the forts in particular. Army and corps commanders were encouraged to familiarise themselves with their assault sectors and work out the best way to disable the German defences. Bagramyan's plan was approved by Vasilevsky and the Stavka on March 17th and in the days following preparations moved into high gear. The 11th Guards Army was to form the southern arm of the Soviet pincer while the 43rd Army attacked from the north. The two forces were to meet up west of Königsberg before turning inward to crush the Germans in the city centre. Meanwhile, the bulk of the 50th Army (two of its three corps) would attack alongside the 43rd but would aim to break into the rear of the German forces to the east of the city, rather than push directly into the urban area. Vasilevsky issued strict orders to the attacking forces that they were not to get held up attacking the German forts, they were to be screened so that the attacking forces could push on to keep the German defenders off balance.

Before the main land assault began the Soviet artillery and air forces would soften up the German defences, targeting their front lines, artillery emplacements and communications network during four days of intense bombardment. The purpose of much of this fire was to remove the earth banks the Germans had built up on their defensive works. Not until three hours before the main assault was the heaviest fire to begin. This final barrage was to destroy all remaining buildings and defence positions in the attack sectors, and then cover the attacks of the infantry and tank forces against the first line of defence.

The Soviet assault force consisted of 137,000 men supported by 5,000 artillery pieces and mortars, 538 tanks and self propelled guns and 2,444 aircraft (including 1,124 bombers, 470 ground attack and 830 fighters).[4] The Baltic Fleet also contributed naval air forces. Half of the artillery that was available consisted of heavy pieces of 203mm to 305mm calibre. There were also 300 Katyusha rocket launchers, the dreaded Stalin Organs which the Germans feared so much. Some of the Soviet tanks included the Lend-Lease US Sherman, which were inferior to the Soviet built T-34's and IS-II Stalin tanks. The T-34/85 formed the greater part of the tank forces, together with contingents of the heavy Stalin tanks.

The Soviet infantry and armoured units had practiced for the urban warfare to be expected in the city and each division had its regiments establish assault groups. These assault groups comprised:

A rifle battalion, a company of engineers, a section of 76mm guns, one flamethrower section, a battery of 120mm mortars, a tank company and SP guns; battalions and companies formed similar assault groups supported by two anti-tank guns, two guns and two or three tanks. Every rifleman in the assault groups was equipped with six grenades and rigged out with all the equipment that arduous experience of street fighting dictated.[5]

Facing the German forces in the southern part of the Samland corridor was Colonel-General Lyudnikov's 39th Army with its 94th, 5th Guards and 113th Rifle Corps. Lyudnikov had been caught napping by the Germans in February when Lasch and Gollnick had launched Operation Westwind. He was to pay them back by cutting Army Detachment Samland off from Königsberg once again. This would be achieved by a thrust across the railway line that ran west from Königsberg to Pillau between Seerappen and Metgethen. Lyudnikov's army would play a largely supporting role in the battle for the city. His primary purpose was to tie down the German reserves to prevent a counter attack to aid the city defenders. Its previous position on the northern approaches to Königsberg had been taken over by the 43rd Army, while those to the east were now held by the 50th Army.

The northern strike force of the Soviet pincer was formed from Beloborodov's 43rd Army. Before the assault began the army comprised the three rifle corps. The 90th Rifle Corps was deployed on the right wing before Trankwitz, with the 26th, 70th and 319th Rifle Divisions. Lopatin's 13th Guards Rifle Corps secured the centre of the army with its 33rd and 87th Guards Rifle Divisions in the first echelon and 24th Guards Rifle Division in the second. Their task would be to storm and capture Fort Va. The 54th Rifle Corps, situated west of Tannenwalde, had the 263rd and 235th Rifle Divisions. They were to take Fort V and the southern part of the village of Charlottenburg in order to secure the left wing of the army.

The 50th Army faced the northern and eastern face of the German perimeter but was deployed with the bulk of its strength amassed on its right wing. The army deployed Lieutenant-General Zakharov's 81st Rifle Corps around Tannenwalde with its 363rd and 307th Rifle Divisions in its first echelon and 2nd Rifle Division in the second echelon. Lieutenant-General Ivanov's 124th Rifle Corps was south of the village of Sudau with the 208th and 216th Rifle Divisions in the first echelon and 51st Rifle Division in the second. These two corps' were to operate on the left wing of the 43rd Army and were tasked with the capture of Fort IV during the initial stages of the offensive, before moving into the rear of the German forces that were deployed on the eastern face of the perimeter. The 69th Rifle Corps, commanded by Lieutenant-General Multan, comprised four rifle divisions and held an extremely long front, stretching right around from the north and along the whole eastern face of the perimeter. It included the 153rd Rifle Division deployed on the northern face of the pocket on a relatively narrow front next to the 216th Rifle Division. The 110th Rifle Division held the north eastern face of the perimeter around Neuhausen and the 324th Rifle Division was deployed on the eastern face of the perimeter from the Bäckerberg in the north to the New Pregel in the south. The fourth division of the corps was positioned to cover the line from the southern bank of the New Pregel to Seligenfeld, where its left flank linked in with the right wing of the 11th Guards Army. The 69th Rifle Corps would have a limited role in the battle to come, acting as a holding force and mainly coming into play during the closing stages of the battle. Lieutenant-General Fedor Petrovich Ozerov had

THE BATTLE OF KÖNIGSBERG

commanded the 50th Army since General Boldin, the previous commander, had been dismissed by Rokossovksy in January 1945 for mishandling his army during the breakout from the Narew. Ozerov had previously served as commander of 5th Rifle Division in 1941 before being appointed Chief of Staff of 34th Army. During 1942-43 he commanded the 27th Army and in 1943 and 1944 was Chief of Staff of the Volkhov Front and 18th Army before being appointed commander of 50th.

The 11th Guards Army was south of the city. Galitsky and Bagramyan were old colleagues and worked well together. Galitsky was a man of few words but, as had been demonstrated from the battles of October 1944 onwards, was a reliable and competent commander. In April 1945 his veteran Guards Army comprised the three rifle corps which had served him well throughout the East Prussian battles. The 36th Guards Rifle Corps was deployed against the Frisches Haff between Heide-Maulen and the railway line which ran into the south western suburbs of the city. It included the 16th, 84th and 18th Guards Rifle Divisions. The 16th and 84th were in the first echelon of the attack and the 18th was held in the second. The 16th Guards Rifle Corps was in the centre of the 11th Guards Army between Godrienen and Altenberg. It comprised the 31st and 1st Guards Rifle Divisions in its first echelon. The 16th had already breached the fortress belt in fighting south of the city during January and occupied Fort IX in the centre of its area of attack. The 8th Guards Rifle Corps was on the right flank of the army, from Altenberg to Fort XI, with its 26th and 83rd Guards Rifle Divisions. The 5th Guards Rifle Division was held back in the second echelon until the initial breakthrough had been achieved. In army reserve there was also the 11th Guards Rifle Division, ready to be committed as the battle developed.

Air support for the offensive was provided by the 1st, 3rd and 15th Air Armies while another two air corps were released from the 18th Air Army (the heavy bomber force), and aircraft of the Baltic Fleet. The 1st Air Army was to launch its attacks from the east, the 15th Air Army from the north, Baltic Fleet air forces from the west and 3rd Air Army from the south. Air Marshal Alexander Novikov, the commander of the Soviet Air Force, co-ordinated the operations of these forces. His operations plan involved the use of low level attacks by the heavy bomber forces in order to drop a high tonnage of munitions on the Germans with a great degree of accuracy. As Marshal Novikov wrote:

The plan provided for carrying out preliminary air preparation for two days before the city was to be stormed. The objective was to destroy the forts and key strongpoint's in the zones of the advance of the 43rd and 11th Guards Armies, to mount massive raids on the enemy air force on the ground and destroy their runways. Strikes by attack-plane formations were to complete the destruction of the enemy air force.[6]

The size of the opposing forces involved in the forthcoming battle has been both under- and over-declared by each side. German sources generally place the number of attacking Soviet troops at 250,000 and their own at just 35,000, making the Soviet victory appear totally inevitable. The Soviets in their place gave their own strength at 137,000 troops and that of the Germans at 130,000, thereby giving the impression that the attacking forces had to overcome not only a force equal to their own, but one ensconced in formidable fortified defences. It was usual Soviet practice to multiply the number of enemy divisions opposite them by their full strength complement, a strength the Germans clearly did not possess. By over-estimating the German strength the rapidity of the Soviet victory in the final battle seems all the more spectacular. Similarly the Germans writing after the war overestimated Soviet numbers so as to give the impression that they were fighting against insurmountable odds and had no hope of success.

The truth, as is usual in such cases, probably lies somewhere in between. It is most likely that the German strength of 40-45,000 men and the Soviet strength of 137,000 is the most plausible. The German divisions inside the city had suffered heavy losses but during the lull between February and April they had been able to take in a small number of replacements. An approximate strength of around 5-6,000 men per division, plus the additional battle groups attached to the garrison, extrapolates an approximate strength of between 30-35,000 regular troops. The Volkssturm contingent would have numbered between 5- and 10,000. Assuming each Volkssturm battalion was at full strength, given the high number of civilians still inside the city, a battalion of 600 men was entirely likely, although Volkssturm battalions of 1,000 men were not unknown. Extrapolating these figures a force of 5-8,000 Volkssturm is certainly credible. Lasch comments in his work, *So Fiel Königsberg*, that as many as 8,000 Volkssturm were present at the start of the offensive, alongside 30-35,000 military personnel.[7] He does quantify his comments though by saying that all records of personnel strength were lost during the final battle and the above figures are an estimate only.

For the Soviet forces, the losses they had incurred in the opening months of 1945 had taken a heavy toll. With the lion's share of reserves being sent to the Berlin sector, the formations in East Prussia were to some degree left to their own devices. Vasilevsky's requests for reinforcement from the High Command were denied a number of times and it was only after the difficult battle for control of the Heiligenbeil pocket that Stalin agreed to send up a sizeable contingent of replacements.

* * *

Easter Sunday, April 1st 1945, was a beautiful spring day in Königsberg, in contrast to the rain and sleet which had fallen over the previous two weeks. Soviet aircraft were active in the skies over the city, keeping the defenders and civilian's heads down but otherwise there was little activity around the battle lines that circled the city.

Easter Monday was a different story, as it dawned wet and miserable, much to Vasilevsky's chagrin. The saturation of the ground meant the opening of the preparatory artillery barrage had to be delayed, and the air armies remained firmly on the ground. Inside the city General Müller arrived for a meeting with Lasch and the senior commanders and Party members. Lasch gave Müller an outline of the general situation, the state of the defences and perilous ammunition situation. His accurate appreciation of the situation did nothing to inspire confidence in Müller, who went on to outline his own plans. To an incredulous Lasch he explained how he envisaged driving the Russians from East Prussia. As Lasch later recalled:

> ... [Müller] summoned an assemblage of divisional and unit commanders and Party leaders. In the cellar of the University he delivered an enthusiastic speech which was brimming with optimism and confidence in final victory. He would bring the survivors of the 4th Army into Königsberg. From here there would be a new large scale attack which would sweep the Russians out of East Prussia[8].

Lasch, ever the realist, questioned where the forces needed, around four or five divisions, would come from. Müller had to admit he did not know but merely assured his audience that he felt everything would turn out well. Müller then met with Lasch privately and told him he was arranging to have him relieved as commander of Fortress Königsberg:

> [Müller] told me I would be replaced shortly. He had the impression that I no longer had sufficient confidence in the defensive capability of the fortress, and that only a fresh unbiased commander would suffice. When I asked when I could expect to be replaced, he told me there were still some problems to overcome as the previous commander had given such a good

review of my performance that nothing could be done immediately. However, he told me he had a long reach and would apply directly to the Führer to bring about my replacement. [9]

While Lasch dealt with Müller, Vasilevsky was having his own troubles. With the opening of the Berlin offensive just days away, Stalin was putting increasing pressure on him to mop up the Germans in East Prussia for once and for all, and excuses that the weather was no good simply did not wash.

On Wednesday April 4th a light drizzle continued to fall across a landscape blanketed with a veil of mist. The bad weather kept the air force on the ground for much of the day so Vasilevsky had to use just his heavy artillery against the German outer fortresses and defensive positions. This was the beginning of the barrage which would last until the fall of the city. Unfortunately the bad weather, which had seemed to plague Soviet operations in this region from October 1944 onwards, impaired the effectiveness of the bombardment, whose purpose was to blow away the protective banks of earth around the forts. Soviet raiding parties also began to probe the German defences. In the north the 43rd Army launched strong attacks upon the 548th Volksgrenadier Division around Charlottenburg while on the southern sector the 69th Infantry Division lost control of a number of bunkers on its forward positions close to Godrienen as the 11th Guards Army conducted its own attacks. As was usual in such circumstances, the Germans launched counter attacks but were unable to fully recover the lost positions, the intensity of the Soviet counter fire proving too much. While the fighting raged, Soviet loud speakers began to loudly blare out around the city. The Soviets informed the Germans that the attack would begin soon, unnerving the defenders, and urging them to surrender.

Through interrogation of prisoners Lasch was able to ascertain that the Soviets would indeed launch their attack on either April 6th or 7th. Unlike the situation in January, when Raus and Hossbach were able to evacuate their forward positions to avoid the severest Soviet artillery fire, Lasch did not have that luxury. Having been forced back to their fortress defence line, the Germans could ill afford to lose any more territory, and were stuck in their trenches and bunkers, having to wait out the Soviet bombardment and hope enough of them survived to fight off the infantry and tanks that would inevitably follow. The continual Soviet artillery fire knocked out the electricity supply, making an already terrible situation all but unbearable. Following Müller's visit, Koch also visited the city, his last visit before its capture. His visit was fleeting, the Gauleiter doing nothing to help the civilians, or to bolster the morale of the Volkssturm who were braving the Soviet bombardment and manning their defences.

The probing attacks and artillery fire continued throughout the 5th. Worryingly for Vasilevsky the weather did not improve this day either but after nightfall the rain finally stopped falling. In spite of the rain, the ground preparation continued with more strong reconnaissance attacks by the 43rd Army and the 11th Guards Army. Being short of artillery ammunition the Germans were unable to do any major counter-battery work. Lasch was conserving his artillery until the Soviet offensive had actually begun, and planned to launch his counter battery against specific targets at that point.

As night fell on the 5th Vasilevsky and Lasch both waited nervously for the new dawn. For Vasilevsky the weather was the key to his decision. More rain and cloud cover would keep his planes on the ground and he would have to decide whether to attack without their support. Only the dawn would tell what fate held for the beleaguered city.

[1] Herzog von Holstein translates as Duke of Holstein.

[2] SD: Sicherheitsdienst, the security service which acted as a sister organisation to the Gestapo.

[3] The destruction of records at the end of the siege has meant it is impossible to establish a true figure for German strengths.

[4] *Battles Hitler Lost*, New York 1986, 12. The Storming of Königsberg, p173

[5] Bagramyan, *So We Went to Victory*, p 530

[6] *Battles Hitler Lost*, New York 1986, 12. The Storming of Königsberg, p174.

[7] Lasch, *So Fiel Königsberg*, p116

[8] Lasch, *So Fiel Königsberg*, p84

[9] Lasch, *So Fiel Königsberg pp84-85*

Chapter Seven - The Final Battle: The First Day

As dawn broke on April 6th Vasilevsky had a difficult decision to make. His artillery had bombarded the German defences for two days but, crucially, the air force had not been able to provide any real support. As daylight approached, the weather cleared a little, although the overcast sky did not bode well for the morning. With Stalin's words fresh in his mind, Vasilevsky gambled and gave the order to begin the attack.

As Marshal Vasilevsky made his difficult decision, a military hospital train pulled out of Königsberg's Pillau station and built up speed as it headed west for the port of Pillau. Loaded with hundreds of wounded soldiers and refuges, no one aboard knew it, but they would be the last to leave the city before the Soviet assault began.

After the artillery fire of the last few days, which had rolled around the perimeter striking strong points, fortresses and trench positions, the barrage which began at 0800 hours in the 11th Guards Army sector was truly terrifying. An hour later the artillery of the 43rd Army also began to pound the Germans northeast of the city. The Soviet fire literally smashed the German lines to pieces, obliterating trenches and killing or dazing the defenders. Marshal Novikov, who was with Bagramyan at Beloborodov's forward observation post near Fuchsberg, relates:

The pounding of the enemy defences lasted for more than two hours. The ground literally shuddered from the salvoes of super powerful guns. Rockets screeched as they left their fiery trails. "The God of War" as we called artillery, performed its part with precision, skill and a good display of strength...Vasilevsky found a moment to put down his binoculars and say, "That's quite a concert!"[1]

THE BATTLE OF KÖNIGSBERG

In the main attack sectors the Soviets had amassed thousands of artillery pieces, concentrating upwards of 250 guns to each kilometre of front. The results were stunning. As one unfortunate German soldier who suffered under this deluge of fire recorded:

> 'The German positions were smashed, the trenches ploughed up, embrasures levelled with the ground, companies buried, the signals system torn apart, and ammunition stores destroyed. Smoke clouds hung over the ruined house of the city. In the streets were ruined walls, battered motor cars, the dead horses and corpses of the fallen. '[2]

After two hours of ferocious artillery fire all fell silent. The sudden silence was soon broken by the roar of hundreds of engines as tanks and infantry rushed forwards to attack the German lines. This was the moment that Lasch unleashed his carefully plotted counter battery. Shells struck Soviet command posts and lines of communications, inflicting considerable damage. Beloborodov's command post, in a grand house on the hill near Fuchsberg, was one of the locations targeted by the German fire that sent the Soviet commanders diving for cover. As Air Marshall Novikov recalled:

> The command post was fired at suddenly by at least a battalion of enemy artillery...The shells exploded next to the house. The windowpane in the room where Bagramyan and Beloborodov were was shattered by the blast wave. Beloborodov was hurled into a corner, and Bagramyan's face was cut with glass splinters.
>
> This was clearly no accident. After Königsberg had been taken, one of the Nazi generals taken prisoner admitted during interrogation they had some time previously noticed the big house on the hill and watched it in expectation of a suitable opportunity to shell it.[3]

THE BATTLE OF KÖNIGSBERG

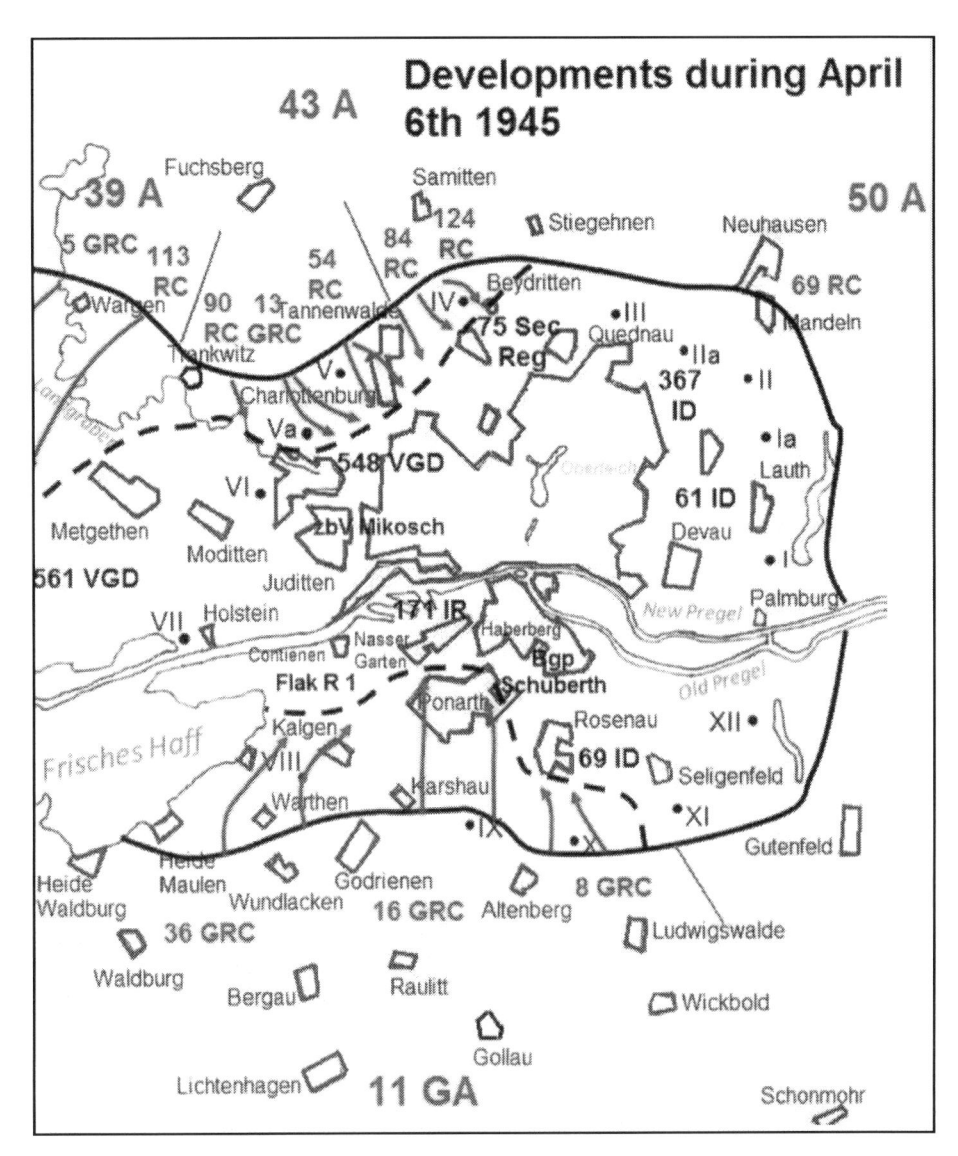

Developments during April 6th 1945

The main attack from the north began at 1000 hours as Beloborodov's 43rd Army smashed into Sudau's 548th Volksgrenadier Division. The 90th Rifle Corps pushed due south toward Fort VI, pummelling the left wing of the 548th. In hard fighting the 26th and 70th Rifle Divisions were able to make steady progress but German resistance was dogged, with repeated counter attacks having to be fended off as the Germans tried to restore their original positions. The Soviet forces were held off some way short of Fort VI and the railway line to Pillau.

In the centre of the 43rd Army, the 33rd Guards Rifle Division of Lopatin's 13th Guards Rifle Corps was embroiled in heavy fighting before Fort Va as it penetrated the German forward positions and pushed on toward the Landgraben Canal and Juditten. Soviet artillery pounded the fort remorselessly, over 500 heavy calibre shells striking it. The 83rd Guards Rifle Division reached Fort Va at noon but moved around it, following strict orders to circumvent the fort and leave its capture to the second echelon. The defenders of the fort nevertheless put up a ferocious defence and refused to crumble under the intense Soviet artillery fire. Bitter resistance right along the line meant that Soviet progress was very slow. However, by the end of the day the men of the 33rd Guards Rifle Division had managed to cross the Landgraben and penetrate almost to the outskirts of Juditten. To the left of the 33rd, the 87th Guards Rifle Division had also pushed on. It was able to advance deep into the centre of the 548th Volksgrenadier Division but fell short of reaching the outskirts of the Huffen district. The left flank formation of the 43rd Army, the 54th Rifle Corps, was also able to make steady progress as it developed its attacks around Fort V and pushed back the right wing of Sudau's 548th. The 263rd Rifle Division launched a successful attack on Fort V, quickly surrounding it, and then moved on to overrun the southern parts of Charlottenburg. The 235th Rifle Division, fighting alongside the 263rd, gained control of the northern part of Charlottenburg and advanced along the railway line heading into Königsberg. The Germans fought back with a fierce tenacity despite the overwhelming fire that the Soviet forces brought down on their heads. As soon as one position was lost the Germans immediately launched counter attacks in order to recover it. Unfortunately for them the Soviet numbers were so overwhelming that little could be achieved, and the counter attacks merely sapped at their strength.

Beloborodov had cause to be pleased with the progress of his divisions during this first day of the offensive. The German defences had been pushed back all along his front although they had not been pierced. Strong resistance by Sudau's 548th Volksgrenadier Division had held back the attacking troops at the edge of the urban area, but the two formidable fortresses in the path of the 43rd Army had been encircled, allowing the army to successfully develop its attacks.

The men of the German 75th Security Regiment, holding the line between Tannenwalde and Sudau, found themselves under fierce attack from Ozerov's 50th Army. The Soviet 81st Rifle Corps hit the German positions east of the railway line heading into Königsberg. The 343rd and 307th Rifle Divisions advanced toward the Oberteich and Marauenhof suburb. This first day of fighting saw the Soviet troops smash the 75th Security Regiment. The Germans suffering crippling casualties as the 81st secured control of much of Charlottenburg. To their left, the 124th Rifle Corps struck out from Sudau towards Fort IV, its 216th and 208th Rifle Divisions isolating the German garrison after a bloody battle on the approaches. A fierce battle here kept the 216th from pushing forward to Beydritten. The remainder of Ozerov's army, the 69th Rifle Corps, remained largely static throughout the day, occupying the 367th and 61st Infantry Divisions on the eastern face of the pocket with harassing fire and nuisance attacks. The 153rd Rifle Division, deployed alongside the 216th, managed a limited advance to protect the flank of their neighbouring division. Among the places captured by Ozerov's troops was the city transmitter station.

In Samland Lyudnikov's 39th Army launched a fierce attack against the corridor that connected the Königsberg defenders with the Samland Detachment. The 94th, 5th Guards and 113th Rifle Corps each attacked, striking Becker's 561st Volksgrenadier and Thadden's 1st Infantry Divisions hard. All three formations were able to make significant gains into the German positions. The 5th Guards Rifle Corps pushed close to the outskirts of Seerappen but it was the 113th Rifle Corps which penetrated the deepest, throwing forces across the railway line to Pillau and partially severing communications between the city and Samland.

The bitter fighting across the northern face of the perimeter had been shrouded by poor weather for much of the morning. As the weather cleared after midday Novikov was able to put his aircraft aloft during the late afternoon, but not in the large numbers he had originally planned. The focus of their attacks were against the north western suburbs and the railways yards, harrying the Germans as they tried to mount counter attacks against the advancing Soviet armies. Of the 4,000 sorties that Novikov had planned to mount, fewer then 1,000 were flown. Nevertheless, the Soviets had uncontested control of the air when they were aloft, the Luftwaffe remaining firmly on the ground during this first crucial day of the battle.

While Lyudnikov, Beloborodov and Ozerov pounded the Germans north of the city, Galitsky unleashed his army against the defenders south of the River Pregel. The bombardment by the 11th Guards Army had been as successful as that to the north, smashing up the German trenches, knocking out their lines of communications and inflicting heavy casualties on the front line troops. After pulverising the 69th Infantry Division, the remnants of 56th Infantry Division and Battlegroup Schuberth under a hail of fire, Galitsky launched his massed infantry and armour into the attack. From the Haff shore to Seligenfeld, the 11th Guards Army clawed its way through the first German defence line.

One German gun commander, named Dröger, with Fortress Pak Regiment 1, recalled the intensity of the attack by the 36th Guards Rifle Corps on the left wing of the 11th Guards Army:

> After furious drumfire there was a massed infantry attack at 1200 hours, supported by tanks. The anti-tank platoon near Prappeln was caught by surprise and one of our guns took a direct hit. About 200 metres left of Kalgen the Russians broke through to Ponarth. The anti tank obstacles from Kalgen to the Haff brought the attack to a halt....As the attack continued in a series of waves a few Russians succeeded in getting close to the guns;

despite this we were able to extract ourselves from the dangerous situation with a few hand grenades....As we had used up our ammunition and our left wing was open, we had to pull back that evening after rendering our guns unusable. [4]

Amid such desperate scenes Guriev's 16th Guards Rifle Division quickly overran Warthen and moved to outflank the Germans in Kalgen. The 84th Guards Rifle Divisions pushed towards Kalgen, throwing units around Fort VIII as it advanced. The German defenders in the outer works put up a stiff fight, defending their positions to the last man against wave after wave of Soviet attacks. The outer defences of Fort VIII were quickly overcome but the defenders inside the fort itself obstinately refused to surrender. Determined German resistance forced the commitment of the 18th Guards Rifle Division to the attack on the right wing, bypassing the defenders of the fort in order to close up to Prappeln. They were met by fierce counter attacks between Prappeln and Kalgen and only with difficulty were the Germans held off. The Soviet penetration near Prappeln prompted Lasch to throw reinforcements into the battle in this sector in an effort to restore the crumbling line. Police Regiment 31 and SS Regiment *Böhme* of Battlegroup Schuberth entered the fighting and were able to blunt the Soviet thrust, although at a heavy price. An officer with Battlegroup Schuberth described the desperate struggle against the Soviet attack:

'On the morning of 6th April 1945 the enemy began his assault. After prolonged artillery bombardment, supported by the fire of tanks and air support the Russians began their attacks from the southwest and south between Kalgen and Klein Karschau and penetrated as far as the defensive position just south of Ponarth. Here his attack was halted by two battalions of the Battlegroups' Police Regiment 31 and SS Regiment Böhme together with elements of the 69th Infantry Division.

By the evening of the 6th April, the enemy had also managed to break through the south eastern positions of the 69th Infantry Division at Seligenfeld and Adlig-Neuendorf.

Our positions, command posts and major transportation routes were almost continuously under heavy enemy artillery bombardment. Our artillery was inferior to the enemy and could not respond effectively. We had to economize with our ammunition because the there were no further supplies....[5]

In the centre of the 11th Guards Army front, the 16th Guards Rifle Corps developed its attack towards Ponarth, smashing the 56th Infantry Division. The 31st Guards Rifle Division was able to push rapidly forwards and outflanked the defenders of Prappeln from the east before pushing on to enter the Outskirts Defence Line at noon. This line was also breached and by dusk Soviet troops had fought their way into the suburbs of Ponarth. Next to the 31st, the 1st Guards Rifle Division pushed forward from its positions around Fort IX, aiming for Ponarth as well. It was also able to reach the Outskirts Defence Line and, after fighting off a strong German counter attack, was also able to overrun the southern parts of Ponarth. The Soviet troops continued their attacks through the night and secured control of Ponarth, beating off yet more German counter attacks.

On the right wing of the army the 8th Guards Rifle Corps made a deep penetration with its 26th Guards Rifle Division, penetrating the Outskirts Defence Line to close up to Rosenau. The success of the attack prompted Galitsky to send the 5th Guards Rifle Division into action in this sector, reinforcing the attack as the Germans mounted repeated counter attacks to slow the Soviet progress. A counter attack from Aweiden into the flank of the 26th Guards Rifle Division was beaten off and then driven back by the advance of the 83rd Guards Rifle Division. This division, having isolated the defenders of Fort X, moved on to take Aweiden. Its progress was then held up on the Outskirts Defence Line as the 69th Infantry Division put in yet another counter attack.

The defenders of Fort VIII and X, now isolated behind the Soviet front line, continued to hold out against repeated attacks and intense artillery bombardment. The moats and thick walls of the fortresses proved difficult obstacles for the Soviet troops to overcome. Nevertheless, Galitsky's opening attacks had been extremely successful, and he pressed his men on to attack throughout the night. The Germans, having been pushed back from their Forward and Outskirts defence lines, abandoned the defences around Forts XI and XII during the night, although the garrisons of the forts remained. The men of the 69th Infantry Division also pulled back to Seligenfeld and Schönfliess to await the new dawn and further Soviet attacks.

The first day of fighting had proven extremely trying for the Germans. Lasch was fully aware of just how threatening the situation had become. Gross' 75th Security Regiment was a spent force, having suffered crippling casualties under the attacks of the 50th Army. During the night Lasch had to extend the left wing of the 367th Infantry Division to maintain the junction with the 548th Volksgrenadier Division. South of the Pregel, the situation was most worrying. Galitsky's men had made a deep penetration into their lines and inflicted crippling losses on the 56th and 69th Infantry Divisions.

As the crisis at Königsberg developed, Lasch sent an urgent message to Müller requesting that the 5th Panzer Division be released from Samland to repel the Soviet forces south of the city. If the armour could be brought into the city the breach punched in the German line could be nipped shut before a disaster overtook the defenders. Unfortunately for Lasch and his men, the panzers were not released and Lasch was left to fight on without any additional support.

THE BATTLE OF KÖNIGSBERG

---

[1] *Battles Hitler Lost*, 12. The Storming of Königsberg, p177

[2] Dieckert and Grossman, *Der Kampf um Ostpreussen*, 1960, p197

[3] Novikov, in *Battles Hitler Lost*, 12. The Storming of Königsberg, p178

[4] Lasch, *So Fiel Königsberg*, p88

[5] Lasch, *So Fiel Königsberg*, p89

Chapter Eight - The Second Day of the Assault

Under clear skies April 7th began with yet another colossal Soviet artillery barrage against the German defences. The heavy guns continued to bombard the outer forts while the mass of the remaining artillery pounded the German positions throughout the city. Above the battlefield the clear skies brought up massive waves of Soviet fighter-bombers. They struck targets in the city and the surrounding defences from dawn onwards. Towards noon Novikov decided it was time to bring up the heavy bombers of the 18th Air Army and so he ordered Golovanov to launch his planes against the city. Golovanov protested that the use of these slow aircraft in daylight would leave them easy prey for the German fighters but Novikov dismissed his concerns, stating:

> 'Don't worry yourself on that score. I will give your bombers an escort of 125 fighters so not a single "Messer" will touch you. In addition, 200-300 shturmoviks with heavy fighter escort will cover the city constantly and in co-operation with our artillery will make sure that the German anti-aircraft guns won't utter a peep...'[1]

Golovanov nevertheless still tried to argue but Novikov ordered him to get it done. Twenty minutes before the bombers arrived over the city more than a hundred fighters of the 11th Fighter Corps swept the German airfields and air defences. Then the low rumble of 516 heavy bombers, flying in three waves, grew louder over the city. The Soviet planes dropped 550 tons of bombs on the Germans, destroying entire streets, levelled fortifications and reduced weapons and vehicles to scrap, creating a confused landscape of rubble and debris.[2] Hardly had the dust of this terrible pounding settled than the next wave of aircraft

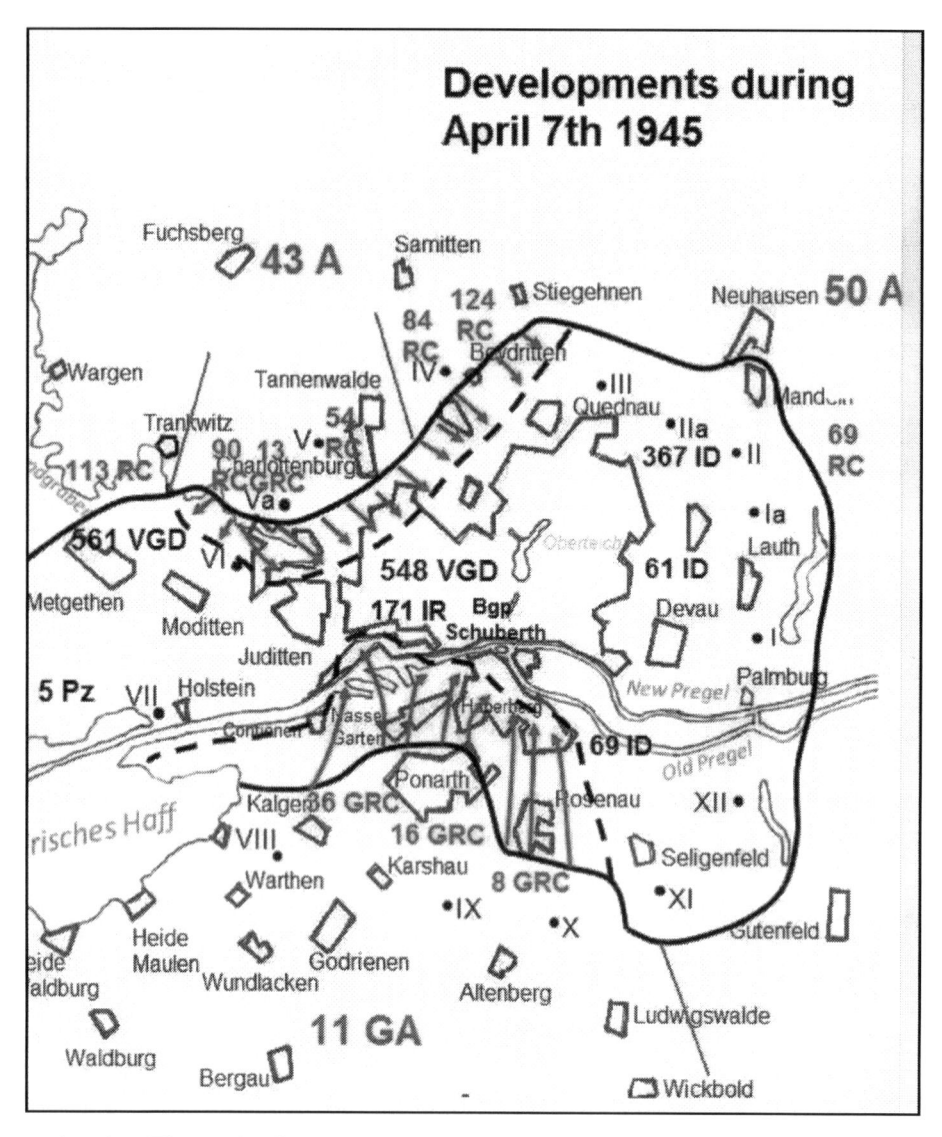

arrived. The 5th Guards Bomber Corps, together with Baltic Fleet aircraft also struck the city and its naval base. The Germans had tried to put up their aircraft to fend off the hordes of Soviets machines but were simply overwhelmed. Soviet airmen claimed twenty-two enemy planes shot down and thirty-six more destroyed on the ground for the loss of twenty-five of their own. Over the course of the day the Soviets had flew a staggering 4,700 sorties, and had more planned for the next day.

While fire rained down from the skies, on land the Soviet armies continued their bitter attacks. To prevent the Germans from bringing reserves across from Samland Lyudnikov's 39th Army launched a series of attacks aimed at pinning down Herzog's 5th Panzer, Schittnig's 1st Infantry and Becker's 561st Volksgrenadier Divisions. The left wing of the 561st was very heavily attacked, while the 5th Panzer, which had been trying to deploy east of Juditten in order to move up to Königsberg, was pinned down by continuous Soviet air attacks which lasted from sunrise to sunset. The 1st Infantry Division also came under sustained attack, preventing any of the Samland forces from helping relieve the pressure on the defenders of Königsberg.

After their successes during April 6th the divisions of Beloborodov's 43rd Army renewed their attacks across the Landgraben, but faced more German counter attacks. Progress was slow as Sudau's 548th Volksgrenadier Division fought back with a fierce determination. The German troops were well aware that they had nothing to lose, if their front collapsed, they would be destroyed. The 90th Rifle Corps made only limited progress toward Fort VI and the railway line east of Metgethen. The neighbouring 13th Guards Rifle Corps turned its attack from a southerly to south-easterly direction, introducing the 24th Guards Rifle Division to the battle on its right wing. Together with the 33rd and 87th Guards Rifle Divisions, the 24th moved towards the Outskirts Defence Line but ferocious German resistance held the 33rd and 24th Divisions short of their objective. On the left wing the 54th Rifle Corps renewed its attack and did manage to break through the Outskirts defences and pushed down towards the Ratshof and Huffen suburbs. Progress here was also painfully slow. The Germans again launched repeated counter attacks against any new Soviet breaches in their line but the continual battles were taking a terrible toll, the 548th literally bleeding to death on the battlefield. As Soviet troops entered the urban area of Ratshof the fighting degenerated into bloody close quarter fire fights.

Behind the front line the Soviet heavy guns had continued to pound the German forts that had been isolated during the previous days fighting. Forts V and Va were hit by hundreds more heavy calibre shells but their beleaguered defenders refused to give up. Fort Va finally fell to the 83rd Rifle Division during the early hours of the morning after a night time assault forced the garrison to surrender. Fort V continued to resist the attacks of the 263rd Rifle Division until the evening, when its battered defenders were also compelled to surrender.

To the east Ozerov's 50th Army was meeting increasingly strong German resistance but made gains, although they were slow and costly. The 81st Rifle Corps developed its attacks southeast of Charlottenburg, where its 343rd Rifle Division was able to break through the Outskirts Defence Line. The 343rd then supported the attack of the 54th Rifle Corps' 235th Rifle Division to its right. Meanwhile, the 307th Rifle Division found itself held up before the German defence line as were the divisions of the 124th Rifle Corps, which secured control of Beydritten after a bloody struggle. Fort IV was attacked by the 216th Rifle Division and fell at 0800 hours. The German 367th Infantry Division, which had extended its left wing to cover the sector held by the shattered 75th Security Regiment, now also came under heavy attacks on the northern and eastern faces of the perimeter. The 153rd Rifle Division of the 69th Rifle Corps developed its attack towards Rothenstein, threatening to break into the rear of the German defences at Quednau while to the east the 324th Rifle Division began a slow advance toward Mandeln and Fort II.

The 548th Volksgrenadier and 367th Infantry Divisions had slowed the rate of the Soviet advance appreciably throughout this second day of intense combat. However, the German troops were close to the end of their strength and collapse was clearly not far off. Ammunition supplies were running dangerously low and fatigue was taking its toll on the defenders. Lasch could take some comfort from the fact that the Soviets had been prevented from achieving a break through north of the city but, more worryingly, a dangerous crisis was developing to the south, where Galitsky continued his assault.

THE BATTLE OF KÖNIGSBERG

The 36th Guards Rifle Corps of Galitsky's 11th Guards had continued its attacks between Kalgen and Ponarth through the night of the 6-7th and followed them up with a relentless series of blows against the German defenders all through the 7th. By dusk they had reached the south bank of the Pregel after smashing the German defenders to pieces. The 16th Guards Rifle Division was involved in heavy fighting for control of Contienen on the southern bank of the Pregel while the 84th and 18th Guards Rifle Divisions were involved in a hard fought action to gain control of Nasser Garten. This penetration took Soviet troops into the rear of those Germans who were trying to hold back the 16th Guards Rifle Corps. This unit was launching its own attacks and broke through the German lines near Shönbusch and Ponarth to push into the southern suburbs of the city. Bitter fighting erupted around the Main Railway Station. The Soviet attacks in these sectors succeeded through sheer weight of numbers, the 11th Guards Rifle Division adding its weight to the attack.

The German defensive positions had simply been swamped under the onrush of Soviet assaults. Elements of the 69th Infantry Division, Fortress Pak Regiment 1 and the remnants of the 56th Infantry Division were pounded by overwhelming fire and massed infantry and armour assaults. German losses in these defensive battles were extremely high. Fortress Pak Regiment 1 was again in action, this time near the Main Railway Station. Gunner Dröger, involved in this action, again recalled the fighting:

> ...by early 7 April [we] were in Schönbusch. As the enemy was pushing into Schönbusch from Ponarth we could only retreat to Nasser Garten. The meadows on either side were flooded and under Russian fire. Sheltering behind the road embankment and some of the time in the water itself, we fortunately got through... Some units were in position in Nasser Garten, including two anti tank guns.
>
> The rest of the company went into position by the truck garages of the Linger Barracks. Several Russian 120mm guns took up

position on the Schönbusch road, but these were struck again and again by well-aimed shots from our anti-tank guns. The infantry gathering on either side of the road were also shot up.[3]

The Germans continued to come under intense attack from ground and air forces, forcing them to give ground:

Aircraft attacked us until dusk. As the road back to the main railway station was already in enemy hands we had to pull back to the Shichau works. From there we went further along the Pregel. At dusk – in constant contact with the Russians – we crossed the railway bridge, which was blown up shortly after our crossing.[4]

The men of Battlegroup Schuberth, who had been committed to the fighting the previous day, were also involved in bloody fighting at Ponarth and the Nasser Garten. Initially holding up the Soviet advance with a fierce counter attack, the Germans were struck in the flank by a renewed enemy assault and suffered crippling losses, the bulk of Battlegroup Schuberth were killed or captured in this fighting, leaving the remnants to struggle to break free and pull back across the Pregel, from where they took up the battle inside the city itself. An officer with the battle group described their struggle:

In the early morning hours of 7 April, the enemy continued his attacks at all costs. The defensive positions to the southwest, south and southeast of Ponarth and Rosenau were only able to hold off the superior strength of the enemy temporarily. In the evening the enemy was just outside the inner city position. He had initially managed to break through with a tank group to the south of Ponarth and pushed forward into the area of Nasser

Garten. From here he cleared Ponarth of German troops by means of a flank attack. Of the two battalions of Battle Group Schuberth deployed there hardly a man came out alive. Most of the soldiers were killed, only a few were taken prisoner. The enemy attacks from the south-east also met with success in the course of the day, as they penetrated almost to the Friedländer Tor. The centre of the positions in the south had to be reinforced by the men of the 69th Infantry Division.[5]

The 8th Guards Rifle Corps was able to push forward and reached the Pregel after forcing its way through Rosenau. Despite fierce resistance by the 69th Infantry Division the Soviet advance could not be stopped. With mounting numbers of dead and wounded flooding their positions the Germans were compelled to abandon any hope of holding on to the southern bank of the Pregel. Pockets of desperate defenders continued to resist, the men in the Friedländer Tor putting up a stubborn fight even though they were surrounded by enemy forces.

Behind the advancing front line the Soviets continued their struggle to overcome the isolated fortresses. Fort VIII, which had been encircled early the previous day, came under repeated attack by the 84th Guards Rifle Division of the 36th Guards Rifle Corps. Under the cover of a smokescreen Soviet troops were able to get in close to the fortress walls and then made use of their flamethrowers. Their fire enabled other infantry, supported by tanks, to break into the rear entrance of the fortress. Bitter fighting spread inside the confined spaces of the fortress interior but eventually the Germans were overcome and the survivors surrendered at 1100 hours. Fort X, also bypassed during the previous days fighting was captured by the men of the 83rd Guards Rifle Division during the afternoon, as were Fort XI and XII.

Galitsky had made excellent progress, having shattered the German forces south of the river. By dusk his front line ran along the coast, on to the Main Railway Station and from there into Haberberg, Friedländerstrasse and Alte Wiesenschantze. After confused and bitter fighting in its marshalling yards and buildings the Railway Station was secured by Soviet forces after dusk. The fighting continued on through the night. Large parts of Haberberg were overrun during the hours of darkness as the 36th and 16th Guards Rifle Corps prepared to launch their attacks across the Pregel the following day.

Lasch knew he was fighting a losing battle. The loss of the southern sector brought Soviet forces to the fringes of the Inner Defence Line. He expected them to attempt a crossing of the Pregel during the night or the following morning to break into the rear of those forces still fighting to the north. To prevent just such an attempt Lasch brought a number of battalions of the 61st Infantry Division from the eastern face of the pocket, where everything remained disquietingly peaceful, to the west. The troops tried to move under cover of darkness but due to continuous enemy artillery fire, which had left the streets full of rubble following continual artillery fire and air raids, they were unable to deploy in time to have any impact on the next days fighting. Lasch also ordered the fortresses in the west to be abandoned. The garrisons of Fort Ia, II and IIa were to pull back and reinforce those already fighting close to the city centre.

Lasch again signalled Müller, advising him of the deterioration of the situation. He urgently requested a decision on his request to evacuate the entire garrison, together with the thousands of civilians who remained in the burning city. He aimed to launch a breakout towards Samland, where the 5th Panzer Division would also counter attack. Müller denied the request in the strongest terms relayed the same old order; Königsberg must be held to the last man.

THE BATTLE OF KÖNIGSBERG

[1] Bagramyan, *So We Went to Victory*, p560

[2] Novikov in *Battles Hitler Lost*, 12. The Storming of Königsberg, p179

[3] Lasch, *So Fiel Königsberg*, p88

[4] Lasch, *So Fiel Königsberg*, pp88-89

[5] Lasch, *So Fiel Königsberg*, p90

Chapter Nine - Encirclement Complete

Two days of ferocious fighting had seen the German defences north and south of Königsberg torn apart. The formidable German defences had been breached and the Soviet armies had thrown the enemy back from one position to the next. To make matters worse, clear weather on April 8th again saw the Soviet air forces over the city in strength. Novikov put up over 6,000 sorties through the course of the day. With so many aircraft in the air, the Germans were harried from one end of Samland to the other. Heavy bombers attacked the installations at Pillau and Fischhausen while ground attack planes concentrated on Königsberg and the German forces west of the city.

The third day of the offensive began with another massive artillery barrage that smothered the German positions under a rain of explosives. In the 50th Army sector the 81st and 124th Rifle Corps continued their advance into the northern suburbs. Elements of the 81st fought their way close to the northern shores of the Oberteich while the 124th entered the urban area at Marauenhof and Rothenstein. Quednau and Fort III were in danger of encirclement as Soviet forces pushed into the rear of the German defenders. On the left wing of the 43rd Army, operating alongside the 50th Army, the 54th Rifle Corps introduced its second echelon 126th Rifle Division into the centre of its assault. Forward elements of this division were soon up against the Outskirts Defence Line while the 263rd Division to the right and 235th Division to the left also closed up to the German defences. Elements of the latter closed up to the western fringes of the Oberteich and the Wrangel Bastion at the lake's southern tip. Meanwhile, the 263rd was fighting its way into the North Railway Station and towards the Sternwarte Bastion. The remnants of Fortress Pak Regiment 1, which had been fighting on the south bank of the Pregel at the start of the offensive, had now fallen back to the northern bank. This did not help them as they continued to come under intense attack. During the afternoon it was involved in bitter fighting around the Walter Simon Platz. To the rear the battle for the forts continued, although a great many had now fallen to the Soviet forces. After a bitter struggle, which had lasted all through the night, the defenders of Fort VI gave up their struggle and surrendered at 0300 hours.

Figure 33 - Soviet troops fighting inside the city

The right wing and central elements of the 43rd Army continued their drive south in an effort to link up with the 11th Guards Army. Their objective was to make contact with the guardsmen close to the bridgehead that had been established at Kosse. As the 90th Rifle Corps attacked it swung its divisions to the west to form a protective barrier against the German forces in Samland. In an effort to halt the attacks of the 90th Rifle Corps the Germans were compelled to swing elements of the 561st Volksgrenadier Division back upon Holstein and Moditten to establish a new front facing east. Meanwhile the 5th Panzer Division continued its fruitless efforts to launch a counter attack towards the city. The 13th Guards Rifle Corps attacks were now being launched in conjunction with the northward thrust of the 11th Guards Army. Galitsky's men had crossed the Pregel during the night, elements of the

36th Guards Rifle Corps using small boats to reach the northern bank. Despite heavy enemy fire, by dawn the brave men of the crossing party had established a bridgehead on the northern bank at Kosse. They were amply supported by the air force, as Novikov recorded:

> Our attack planes were a great help to the ground troops. The first to reach the River Pregel was the 16th Guards Rifle Division commanded by General Pronin; but because of strong enemy fire, the division's troops could not make a forced crossing from march column. Then the air force representative in the division called in attack planes. Three six-plane groups first put an end to the enemy artillery, then held down the Nazi infantry by bomb-and-gun fire. Covered by attack planes the Soviet infantry crossed the river quickly.[1]

Dawn brought a renewed Soviet artillery bombardment of overwhelming power. The exhausted and shattered German troops could only take cover in the ruins of their positions as thousands of shells smashed up their hastily erected defensive lines. Following this terrible pounding the 36th Guards Rifle Corps pushed its 1st Guards Rifle Division north where they were able to link up with the men of the 87th Guards Rifle Division, part of the 13th Guards Rifle Corps. The two spearheads met between Juditten and Ratshof, completing the encirclement of Lasch's divisions. The tenuous link was quickly strengthened as the remaining divisions of the two Guards corps linked up, conquering a wide swathe of territory.

Developments during April 8th 1945

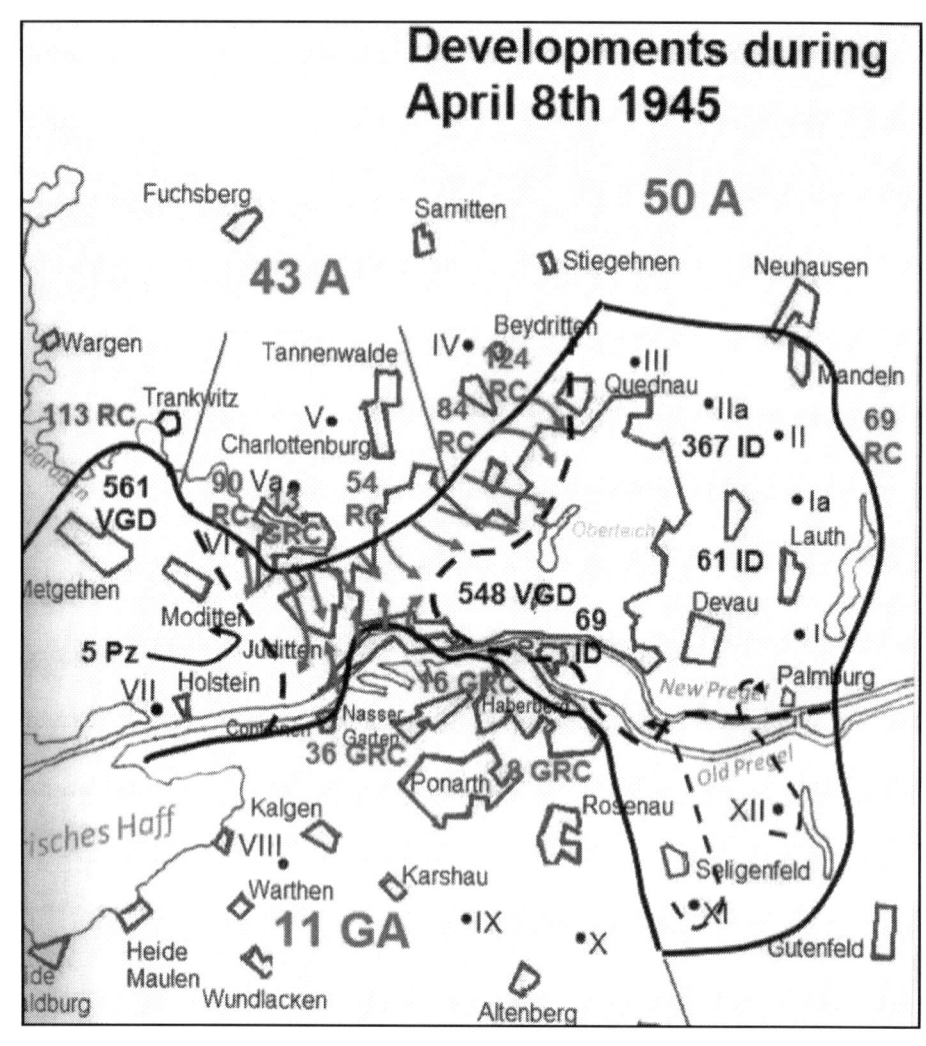

The success of the 13th and 36th Guards Rifle Corps seriously undermined the remaining German defences south of the Pregel. Lasch knew that his remaining forces south of the river would be destroyed unless they were pulled back and therefore, late in the afternoon, he ordered that they be pulled back into the city centre in order to strengthen the forces now fighting on the northern bank of the Pregel. As the German soldiers tried to pull back the Soviets continued their fierce attacks. Battlegroup Schuberth was struck by heavy artillery fire before the attack resumed:

> [The enemy's] *intention was clear, to break through to the southern shore of Pregel to our west and then advance into the rear of the troops the holding the centre position of the southern defences. If this was successful, the enemy would cut off the German forces in the southern part of the city from those in the northern part of the town. To counter this threat the Battle Group extended its flanks. Nevertheless the enemy was able to attack the flanks. Around 16:00 he was attacking from the direction of freight station... A thrust from the direction of the Schönfliesser Avenue overcame the Friedlander Gate and penetrated to the Cattle Market. Up to that point, the enemy in the other sections of the southern position had held down our troops with heavy artillery fire and bombing. His repeated attacks were repulsed. At 16:30 the enemy pushed east from the freight station and Cattle Market into the rear of our forces, only then did the southern front begin to crumble. One strongpoint after another was lost. The situation was clear, and so the commander of the fortress ordered the withdrawal of the battle group into the city centre to the north.*[2]

The men of the 16th and 8th Guards Rifle Corps quickly closed up to the Pregel, overrunning Haberberg and the area between the New and Old Pregel. The bitter struggles around the Main Railway Station and the Friedländer Tor gradually died down as the Germans were overcome. The isolated defenders of the Pregel Bastion, comprising the survivors of a Police Battalion, refused to give up their struggle despite being surrounded. However, after hours of bombardment and repeated attacks the commander of the Bastion, Major Vollmer, gave in to the inevitable and reluctantly agreed to surrender to the Soviet troops, Some of the younger officers wished to continue the struggle but

Vollmer won the day and resistance came to an end. The men holding the Friedländer Tor also gave up their struggle but rather than surrender they managed to break out to carry on the fight in the city centre.

The southern face of the German perimeter was being held by a collection of ragged groups. The badly depleted remnants of Battlegroup Schuberth held the central part of the line, around the castle and western Sackheim suburbs while the 69th Infantry Division held the rest of Sackheim up to the Lithuanian Bastion. The z.b.V. Division Mikosch was to the west, in the Laak area. Vasilevsky could see that it was only at matter of time before the German defences collapsed entirely and during the afternoon he gave the defenders the chance to surrender. Lasch knew he would have to surrender the city eventually but did not give up the hope of being able to breakout. While such a hope, existed the Germans would continue their resistance and the chance to surrender was turned down.

The arrival of Soviet troops deep inside the city gave the Party officials a dreadful shock. They finally began to realise that all was lost, their Führer's demand that they hold to the bitter end might actually mean a bitter end for them. A deputation of officials took this moment of crisis to descend on Lasch and demand that the military, who they had tried for so long to hinder and undermine, now organise a breakout attempt so that they and the civil populace could escape to the Samland peninsula. Deputy Gauleiter Ferdinand Grossherr called Koch from Lasch's headquarters to request immediate assistance but Koch, who was in the safety of his Neutief bunker, refused his request to breakout. Instead he referred the matter to General Müller. Lasch for his part proposed to General Müller that he launch a major counter attack westward in an effort to take as much of the garrison and as many civilians as possible into Samland. Müller merely reiterated that the city must be held at all costs, condemning Lasch and his men to certain defeat inside the city. However, Müller did allow Lasch to attempt a breakout with a small force so that the civilians and Party members could escape.

A frustrated Lasch called Müller again that evening and explained that a limited attack would be doomed to failure. He urged instead a major breakout attempt. The obstinate Müller again denied Lasch the opportunity to break out with the majority of his men, repeating his orders that only a small strike force should attack to the west to link up with the 561st Volksgrenadier and 5th Panzer Divisions and allow the civilians to be funnelled through. Lasch knew that an attempt with only limited forces would fail, but it must nevertheless be attempted and so during the night he tried to gather his forces.

THE BATTLE OF KÖNIGSBERG

---

[1] Novikov, *Battles Hitler Lost*, 12. The Storming of Königsberg, pp180-81

[2] Lasch, *So Fiel Königsberg*, pp90-91

Chapter Ten - The Bitter End

After three days of relentless struggle the Germans struggled during the early hours of April 9th to assemble their forces for a breakout attempt. The breakthrough force would comprise elements of Sudau's 548th Volksgrenadier Division, Sperl's 61st Infantry Division and Hähnle's 367th Infantry Division. It was supposed to begin the attack at 2300 hours on the 8th but considerable problems in redeploying prevented this. Around midnight some elements of the 548th Volksgrenadier Division were ready to begin their attack from the Northern Railway Station but the 61st Infantry Division had still not reached its staging area at the Sternwarte Bastion, and could only begin its attack at 0200 hours. Before the 61st Infantry Division could even begin its attack its commander, Sperl was seriously wounded by Soviet artillery fire. To make matters worse none of the artillery of the 367th Infantry Division was able to make it through the rubble of the city centre.

While the soldiers were making their preparations, at 0030 hours the Party authorities in Königsberg announced to the inhabitants that the city was about to fall, and ordered them to assemble on the Pillau road. From here they would march west towards Samland. Neither Lasch nor any of the divisional commanders had been informed of this decision, or the announcement, and the breakthrough units were unexpectedly flooded with thousands of refugees while they were trying to concentrate for their attack.

The 548th Volksgrenadier Divisions should have attacked at midnight from the North Railway Station and Post Office areas, but their deployment had also been difficult and meant the attack began later than planned. Sudau had launched his attack despite the lack of support from the other units and the area being swamped with frightened civilians. With vehicles mounting quadruple machine guns and armoured cars in the lead, Sudau and his men led a vast column of civilians forward. At 0200 hours, with the roads crowded with thousands of terrified civilians, all desperate to escape the approaching Russian forces, the attackers moved off. Unfortunately such a mass of people quickly attracted the attention of the Soviet troops, who poured artillery and machine gun fire onto the helpless mass. The result was a massacre, as described by one of those present:

'The enemy opened up with infantry weapons of all kinds, mortars, artillery and Katyusha's against this ill-led and confused mob of soldiers, Party officials and civilians. The result was a frightful bloodbath...Heartbreaking scenes were played out among the civilians. Many of them tried to drag their badly wounded relatives back into the city, and were themselves struck down.' [1]

It was during this fighting that Major General Sudau was killed. He had been at the head of the column in an armoured car. His death seemed to herald the collapse of the German attack as both soldiers and the surviving refugees fled for their lives back toward Königsberg.

To the south the 192nd Infantry Regiment of the 61st Infantry Division, under the command of Major von Lewinski took up positions in an orphanage next to the Sackheim Tower before moving west across the city to its attack sector. They tried to work their way through but, despite the use of guides, quickly became lost in the rubble strewn and cratered landscape. By 0035 hours Lewinski and his command staff had reached the Botanical Gardens, close to the Sternwarte Bastion from where he was to begin the attack. Lewinski was joined by Captain Berthold and the remnants of the 171st Infantry Regiment. This regiment had been reduced to just 150 men after its hard battles south of the Pregel. Lewinski described the difficult situation before the attack began:

...The detonations of bombs, mortars and heavy rockets crashed again and again, tumbling the remaining building frontages into the streets and leaving huge craters. Rear-area units, trucks, artillery and assault guns came into this hell from north and south, until they were so tightly wedged together that they could neither move back nor forward. The regiment had to work its way through this inferno, constantly seeking routes, constantly turning back from anti-tank barriers and gigantic craters. Our artillery and support column was in a short time completely stuck, wedged in between trucks of all kinds, its route blocked by new craters and rubble.[2]

The 192nd and 171st Infantry Regiments began their attack in the early hours of the morning, even though not all of their men have managed to reach the start line. The artillery of the 367th Infantry Division, which was supposed to assist in the attack, was still stuck in the city centre, only 30 men having arrived to try to join the break through with Lewinski. Lewinski described the beginning of the attack:

At about 0200 hours we set off with the reinforced 1st Battalion on the right and 171st Infantry Regiment on the left. There was a deep railway cutting in front of our trench, the line from the main railway station to the northern station, and we had to cross it. The first Russian lines were swiftly overrun and we pushed on into the cemeteries that lay behind. Here we encountered the first difficulties. There was flank fire from all sides, with salvoes of Stalin Organs landing on the cemeteries. It was almost impossible to keep a sense of direction in the overgrown landscape with its barbed wire entanglements and only a few paths...The regimental staff was right behind the battalion with an assault company. We encountered only isolated resistance, which we overcame with our assault rifles. Half right from the regimental staff, the 1st Battalion was held up in a heavy fire fight. Apparently it was too far to the right and had ventured into housing along the old Pillau road...We halted after we had crossed the high wall around the cemetery on our left.[3]

The attack quickly broke up and men scattered in all directions, some fleeing back into the city while others tried to make their way west through the enemy lines in small groups. The 192nd and 171st Infantry Regiments lost contact with one another. Under heavy fire Lewinski pulled his regiment back:

We crossed the railway line where we came under heavy fire from both sides and had to pull back; even though we originally wanted to press on from there....we pushed into a completely devastated factory area, where the enemy's tanks were meant to be forming up, without meeting any opposition.

Suddenly and unexpectedly we found ourselves on the Holsteiner Damm and the shore of the Pregel. It was already growing light but we had no choice, on we went along the Holsteiner Damm, heading west. We were now a group of around 40 or 50 men. We had already lost a lot of men in the cemetery. We managed to pass several houses occupied by the Russians without being noticed, until our vanguard came under fire near the grain silo. In a few moments all hell broke loose. We came under fire from every window and even from the opposite bank. Shot at from all sides, we managed to reach the end of the row of silos. [4]

The depleted group managed to move on and took refuge between Moditten and Gross Holstein. As it was growing light they decided to take cover for the day and try to move again at night.

THE BATTLE OF KÖNIGSBERG

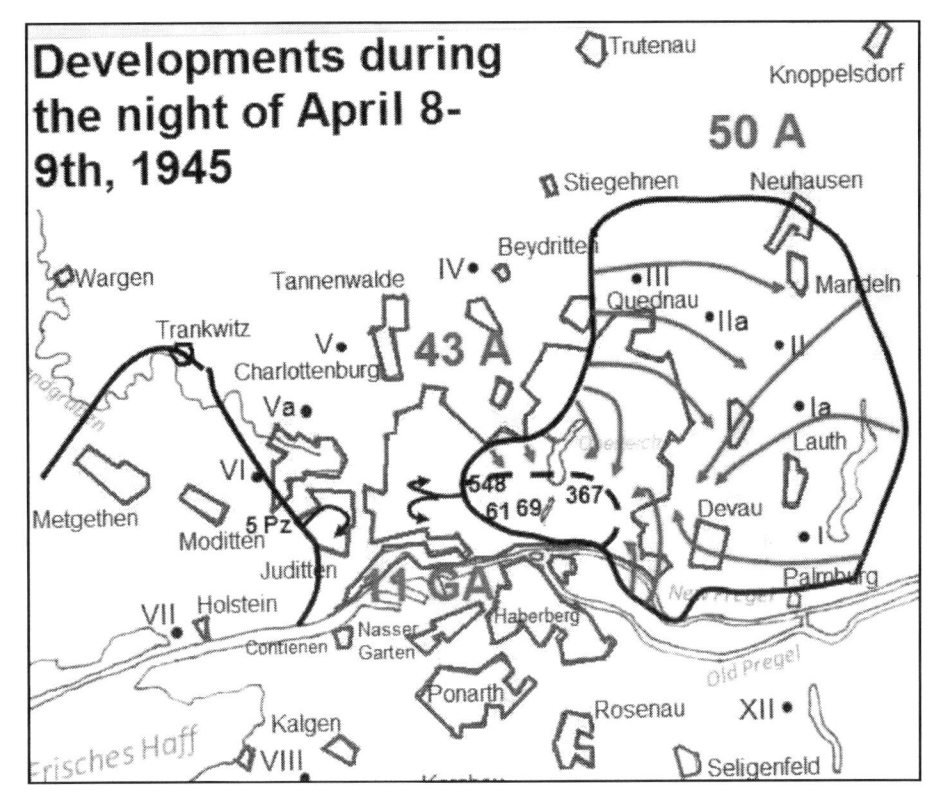

Developments during the night of April 8-9th, 1945

In Samland the 5th Panzer Division launched its attack at 0400 hours but could not even get off its start lines as it was brought under continuous air attack. Only with the greatest difficulty did it manage to push forward at all. As Novikov recalled:

> We employed the main forces of the 3rd and 18th Air Armies against the enemy troops concentrated west of the city. Bomber strikes were followed by strikes by attack planes and fighters. The sound of exploding bombs went on all day and night west of Königsberg.
>
> The fate of those still remaining in the Königsberg garrison was sealed. The final stage of the storming operation began on the morning of April 9, when several thousand guns and mortars

opened a devastating fire on the fortress and last strong points of German defence.[5]

The attacks by the 5th Panzer Division quickly petered out. It was as clear to Lasch as it was to the forlorn soldiers and citizens inside Königsberg that the break out attempt had failed. Nothing now remained but a desperate and bloody end against a vengeful foe.

As daylight broke over the doomed city, thick palls of smoke hung in the sky. The Germans knew the end was close. The remnants of the 61st Infantry Division was left with the task of blocking up the hole in the western perimeter which had been left by the failed breakout attempt. It held a half-mile front around the Sternwarte Bastion while z.b.V. Mikosch was to its south east, blocking the road into Steindamm. The survivors of Battlegroup Schuberth continued their battle along the northern shore of the Pregel and a mixture of stragglers and Volkssturm held the area around the Lithuanian Tower. The remnants of the 367th Infantry Division was around the Grolman Bastion and Dohna Tower. As the 43rd and 11th Guards Armies had overran the German defences from north and south, the 50th Army closed in on the weakened 367th from the east. It had transferred its command post to the Grolman Bastion in the centre of its new front line as it abandoned its positions to the east of the city. During the withdrawal Fort I and III fell to the Soviets. At Fort I the German commander, Major of the Reserve Heisel, refused a Soviet request to surrender but his men decided to take matters into their own hands and shot him dead before surrendering. Fort II surrendered at 0900 hours, Fort Ia at 1300 hours and Fort IIa at 1400 hours, the majority of the men in these forts having pulled back into the city during the night. The remnants of the 69th Infantry Division were deployed to the left of the 367th, holding the northern face of the perimeter.

At dawn the Soviets unleashed another artillery storm upon the tightly packed German soldiers and civilians in the city centre. Aerial attacks struck command posts and the surviving artillery positions. There was

THE BATTLE OF KÖNIGSBERG

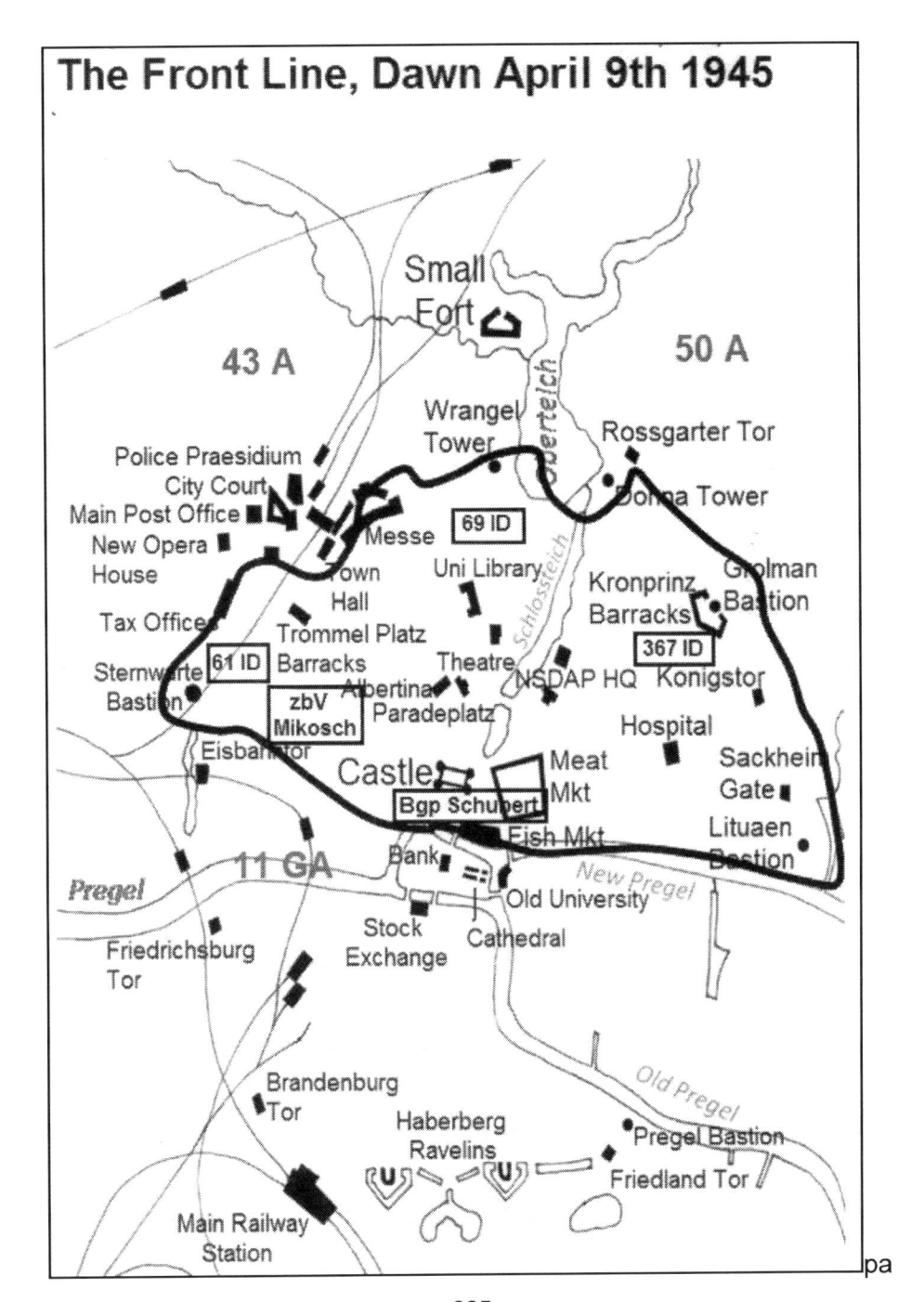

The Front Line, Dawn April 9th 1945

rticularly heavy artillery fire on the University. The Soviets inched their way through the city from north, east and south, avoiding the heavily defended bastions, working their way around them through the weaker spots in the German defensive perimeter. The 43rd Army captured the northern railway station and the cement factory after heavy fighting while the 50th Army had entered the suburb of Devau during the night and captured the airfield close by. The Dohna Tower was isolated by the advancing Soviet troops and came under heavy attack. Inside the tower men of the 61st Infantry Division and staff of the 974th Grenadier Regiment surrendered to the Soviets. The men in the Sternwarte Bastion also gave up the struggle late in the day and surrendered to the Soviet forces.

In the south, Battlegroup Schuberth held its positions along the river bank until late in the afternoon when Soviet pressure finally became too great. As one soldier here recalled:

> *At dawn the enemy strengthened his artillery fire on the northern parts of the city that were still held by us. Bombs rained down almost continuously on headquarters, gun positions and strongpoint's.... After the artillery and aerial preparation the enemy launched a concentrated attack on the northern part of the city centre, roughly the university area. There was constant street fighting all day between advancing enemy units and the garrisons of German strong points. One strongpoint after another was lost as a result of the enemy's superiority.*[6]

Numerous Soviet attempts to cross the Pregel were repulsed but eventually they were able to secure a foothold. The battle group was then threatened by a Soviet advance from the east, as they penetrated between the Königstor and Sackheim suburb.

The battlegroups' position was endangered as the enemy, advancing towards the Königstor and Sackheim, pushed close to the Rossgarten Market and Mittelanger. To stop this attack, the left flank of the 31st Regiment was pulled back to the New Market and extended along the Landhofmeisterstrasse as far as Königsstrasse. Retreating troops were rounded up and deployed as reinforcements. Early in the afternoon the enemy worked his way closer to the city centre from all directions. There was street and house-to-house fighting everywhere...The frontline was not clear and was very mixed up. No-one knew exactly which buildings we or the enemy occupied....Organised combat was no longer possible. The strong point garrisons were on their own.[7]

The Soviets attacking from the east were able to make significant gains in the Rossgarten area, closing up to the market. By the early afternoon they had closed in on the inner city, hemming the Germans into the Sackheim, Rossgarten, Tragheim and Steindamm areas. Bloody fighting was raging throughout the shattered and rubble strewn streets of the city centre. It was no longer clear where the front line was as the battle deteriorated into isolated engagements between pockets of defenders and attacking troops.

By this stage of the battle Lasch no longer exerted any further control over events. The various units still resisting did so in isolation around strong points and fortified buildings. Continuous Soviet artillery fire, infantry and armoured attacks, whittled away at the Germans, cutting them into smaller sections still.

Lasch was convinced that he, his soldiers and the civilians in the city had been abandoned by Hitler and the High Command. Their continued resistance served no purpose. No help would be coming to the fighters of Königsberg. The civilians inside the city cowered in their cellars and began to resist the efforts of the defenders to set up positions in their homes. Many houses flew white flags from their ruins and in some instances civilians tried to disarm soldiers who attempted to fight from their shelters. For the soldiers themselves the struggle was desperate. Ammunition was running out as supply dumps had been captured, food and water were in short supply and the sheer exhaustion of four days of intense fighting had taken its toll.

Lasch resolved to end the battle to save the lives of those who still survived. Meeting with his officers during the morning he informed them of his decision to accept the truce which had been offered by Vasilevsky. All those present agreed and so a radio message was sent to the German High Command informing them of their intention to surrender as ammunition and food had run out.

Lasch then despatched Lieutenant-Colonel Kerwien to deliver a hand written message to the Soviets requesting a ceasefire. He managed after some difficulty to establish contact with an enemy detachment on the Trommelplatz. The request for a ceasefire so that an embassy could be sent through the lines was agreed. Hours later Lieutenant-Colonel Kerwien returned to Lasch's headquarters, accompanied by a Soviet deputation. They made their way through the German lines and down into the bunker under the Paradeplatz. The Soviet officers agreed that if the Germans surrendered, the soldiers and civilians would be treated well, they would be given food and water and their wounded would be cared for. Not all of the Germans agreed with this course of action and one Party official, Amtsleiter Fielder, tried to break into the bunker to shoot Lasch and the Soviet negotiators. He was forcibly restrained by the guards Lasch had placed at the door as a precaution

At 1720 hours Lasch broadcast to those men who were still in touch with headquarters that, with both ammunition and stores finished, further resistance was pointless. At 2130 hours he agreed to the Russian terms of surrender, but such was the catastrophic state of the German force that not all got the message, and of those that did, not all wanted to give up.

The police and SS men of Battlegroup Schuberth, who had been fighting since the first day of the offensive, were now reduced to just 150

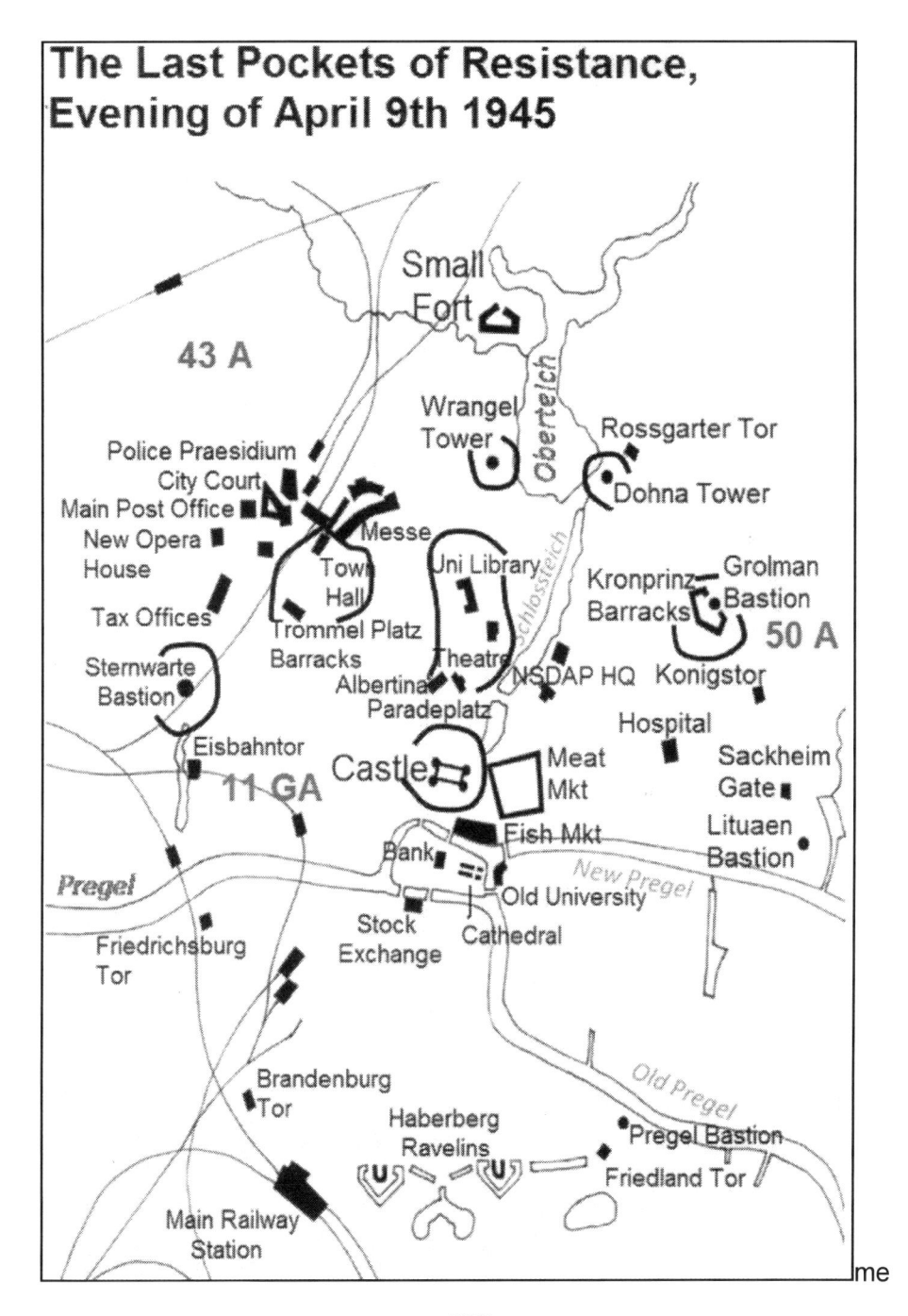

THE BATTLE OF KÖNIGSBERG

The Last Pockets of Resistance, Evening of April 9th 1945

43 A

Small Fort

Wrangel Tower

Rossgarter Tor

Police Praesidium
City Court
Main Post Office
New Opera House
Tax Offices
Sternwarte Bastion
Eisbahntor

Messe
Town Hall
Trommel Platz Barracks
Albertina
Paradeplatz

Uni Library

Dohna Tower

Kronprinz Barracks
NSDAP HQ

Grolman Bastion
50 A
Konigstor

Theatre

Hospital

Sackheim Gate

11 GA

Castle

Meat Mkt

Bank

Fish Mkt

Lituaen Bastion

Pregel

New Pregel
Old University
Cathedral

Stock Exchange

Friedrichsburg Tor

Old Pregel

Brandenburg Tor

Haberberg Ravelins

Pregel Bastion

Friedland Tor

Main Railway Station

239

n. When Böhme heard of Lasch's surrender negotiations he declared Lasch relieved of his command and proclaimed Schuberth as fortress commander. Schuberth, maybe sensing what a poisoned chalice was being offered to him, replied that he did not feel qualified to command and in turn nominated Major Voigt as commander of the fortress. Voigt duly accepted the command and announced to the assembled men that the battle would continue.

Bitter fighting in the city centre continued despite the call to surrender. Major Voigt ordered the abandonment of the positions in Löbenicht, intending instead to make a stand around the Castle. Here his group came under intense fire and, lacking heavy weapons of their own, were compelled to pull back around midnight. The group split up into smaller groups as Voigt told them to make their way west towards Pillau. Voigt did not make it out of the city, being killed in the confused fighting. The remnants of Group Schuberth attempted in various ways to escape met with a singular lack of success. Böhme attempted to make his way along the Pregel by boat but was caught by Soviet fire and he and his men were killed.

Figure 34 - Königsberg Castle after the battle

Major-General Schuberth, together with his Chief of Staff Lieutenant-Colonel Peschke and Ia, Police Major Denninghaus, had a little more success. They were able to press on to Juditten and at dawn took cover in a number of bunkers, intending to continue their march the following night. Unfortunately they were discovered by Soviet soldiers, who demanded that they surrender. The occupants of the first bunker duly surrendered and were told to tell their comrades in the other bunkers to surrender as well. Getting no answer the Soviets then threw grenades into the remaining bunkers, killing any who remained inside. Schuberth, Peschke and Denninghaus all died.

At 0100 hours on the 10th the defenders in the Castle also surrendered. Despite later stories of a harrowing final battle last many hours, no such evidence exists. Lasch himself was able to verify that these tales were false. The Volkssturm commandeer in the south of the city, Reserve Captain Wachholz, and his deputy Lieutenant Minckwitz, attempted a breakout from the Castle toward the Münzplatz but were killed by Soviet fire. The survivors and those left in the Castle cellars saw the hopelessness of the situation and surrendered.

Figure 35 - Fort V after the battle

The surrender of the remaining German forces in the city centre began in earnest during the early hours of Tuesday April 10th and continued on into the morning. The survivors of those elements of the 561st

Volksgrenadier Division who that had been trapped in the city lay down their arms around 0630 hours. The survivors of the 367th Infantry Division, holding out in the Grolman Bastion, also surrendered.

Lasch and the other senior German commanders were taken to Vasilevsky's headquarters, where Lasch was noted to be extremely downcast. News had reached him that he had been declared a traitor by Hitler and his family had been condemned to imprisonment. Lasch, who was interviewed by Vasilevsky and complimented the Soviet commander on the effectiveness of his attack, admitted:

> ...that on the second day of the assault he had completely lost control of his forces. The massive attacks by the Soviet Air Forces, and artillery fire caused so many fires in the urban area, with such severe damage that it was impossible to work through the streets. The last two days of the assault...showed the futility of any further resistance.[8]

Major Lewinski and his small group were among the few lucky ones who did manage to escape the city after the disastrous break out attempt in the early hours of April 9th. He and his men linked up with around twenty survivors of the 171st Infantry Regiment and a few men from the 548th Volksgrenadier Division. The latter informed Lewinski of the death of Major-General Sudau and the failure of the entire breakout effort. Lewinski recalled that on April 10th:

> ...we saw behind us a dying city. Covered in its mantle of smoke and fire it was lit up by the flashes of heavy artillery that was still landing. At 1700 hours the firing died down. There were still occasional bursts of machine-gun fire from a few positions, but eventually even these last signs of fighting died away. As dusk

fell the black clouds of smoke, lit by the unholy red glow of numerous fires, covered the dead city.[9]

Figure 36 - German prisoners being marched out of Königsberg after the battle

The city, and the thousands of civilians who remained, were now to face their worst fears, occupation by the Red Army. As Lasch was marched off into captivity at the head of his men, through the devastated streets he noted:

Smashed vehicles stood between burning tanks, clothing, equipment lay everywhere. Amongst this danced drunken Russians, shooting wildly...Weeping girls and women were dragged into houses despite their resistance. Children cried out for their parents. It was unbearable. We marched on. We saw scenes that cannot be described. The ditches by the sides of the streets were full of corpses, many of them clearly showing the signs of unbelievable maltreatment and rape.[10]

The Soviets claimed 42,000 Germans had been killed and another 92,000 captured during the fighting. Possibly as many as 25,000 civilians had also been killed. The Soviets also claimed the capture of ninety tanks and assault guns, 2,000 artillery pieces and 1,600 mortars. Soviet practice of rounding up anyone in uniform and counting them as combatants (even postal workers, foresters etc) meant the number of captured was greatly inflated.

That the number of killed and captured was grossly exaggerated is extremely likely. If Lasch's figures for those present at the start of the battle are to be believed there were around 30,000 military and 8,000 Volkssturm personnel in the city. The severity of the battle undoubtedly led to extremely heavy losses among the combat units, including the Volkssturm, which took an extremely active part in the battle. Among their number killed was Kreisleiter Wagner. It is impossible to say with any degree of certainty how many German troops died in the fighting. Similarly, tales of the mass murder of the Volkssturm in the city centre by Soviet troops[11] are equally difficult to verify, Lasch failing to mention this particular atrocity in his own book, despite giving comment on the terrible fate which befell the civilians.

Of Soviet losses it is equally difficult to determine. At the end of the East Prussia campaign Soviet casualties were given as a whole, the different phases not being recorded separately. From the beginning of operations in January to the surrender of the final German units in April, the Soviets admitted the loss of 126,000 killed or missing and 458,000 wounded. Königsberg though, was no more.

Figure 37 - The wreckage left after the fighting ended

[1] Thorwald, 1950, p200 quoted in Duffy, *Red Storm on the Reich*, p214

[2] Lasch, *So Fiel Königsberg*, p98

[3] Lasch, *So Fiel Königsberg*, pp99-100

[4] Lasch, *So Fiel Königsberg*, p100

[5] *Battles Hitler Lost*, 12. The Storming of Königsberg, Novikov, p181

[6] Lasch, *So Fiel Königsberg*, p92

[7] Lasch, *So Fiel Königsberg* p92

[8] Bagramyan, *So We Went to Victory*, p572

[9] Lasch, *So Fiel Königsberg*, p101

[48] Lasch, *So Fiel Königsberg*, p115

[11] Lucas, *War on the Eastern Front*, p59

Chapter Eleven - After the Battle

When Hitler learned of the fall of Königsberg, and that Lasch had not fought to the death, he was furious. In revenge, he condemned Lasch to death *in absentia* and had his family arrested. In the bloodthirsty final days of the war Lasch's wife and children were lucky to survive. General Müller, who had done so little to help and so much to hinder Lasch, was dismissed from his post as commander of the broken and shattered forces in the Samland. This responsibility was taken on by General von Saucken. Vasilevsky and Bagramyan meanwhile turned their attention to the destruction of this force.

The Samland Offensive was brief but bloody. Bagramyan's task was simple, to push the Germans back to Pillau and destroy them. It was thought that around 100,000 German troops were trapped in the peninsula, but the Soviet armies were still able to achieve a considerable concentration of force on the narrow attack sector. The offensive began on April 13th and within days saw a breakthrough in the XXVI Corps sector in front of Fischhausen. The 5th Panzer Division, which had fought so long and so hard in East Prussia, was encircled against the coast at Peyse and destroyed, its remnants surrendering to Soviet captivity. Just a few days later the Germans were reduced to a tiny bridgehead around Pillau itself. Amid heavy fighting the Soviets stormed the port, wiping out most organised resistance on April 25th, and extinguishing the final pockets of desperate defenders by April 27th. Army Detachment Samland was destroyed. German resistance now only remained on the narrow spits of land along the Haff coasts and in the Vistula Delta where desperate men fought on until the very last days of the war. Organised resistance in East Prussia though, was now over.

In those final bitter days Erich Koch had looked after his own safety above all others. He fled from East Prussia on April 23rd as the desperately fighting soldiers at Pillau faced their destruction. He sailed to the west aboard the icebreaker *Ostpreussen*, which had been kept in readiness for his escape. He eventually reached Flensburg in western Germany. True to form, Koch had refused to allow any civilians on board his sizable vessel and only he and his Party cronies took the journey. When Germany surrendered in May 1945 Koch went into hiding in Hamburg. He used false papers to try to evade detection but was quickly captured by the British. Despite Soviet demands that he be extradited to them, Koch was handed over to the Polish authorities in January 1950. Only after eight more years in prison was he put on trial, facing charges of war crimes against the Polish people. He was found guilty in 1959 and sentenced to death, although that sentence was commuted to life imprisonment. Koch spent the rest of his life in jail and died in November 1986 at the age of ninety, a far longer life than was granted to many of the poor people of East Prussia, men, women and children who he had abandoned so ruthlessly to their fate.

After the fall of Königsberg Otto Lasch was taken to the Soviet Union and was put on trial by the Soviet authorities in Leningrad. He too was sentenced to death but this was commuted to twenty-five years hard labour. The Adenauer negotiations a decade later saw Lasch, together with General's Mikosch, Sperl and Hähnle, who had also been captured, released from Soviet captivity in October 1955. Lasch returned to Germany and lived the remainder of his life in the West, dying near Bonn in 1971 at the age of seventy-seven.

Colonel-General Raus had left East Prussia when his Third Panzer Army headquarters had been removed to the west to defend Pomerania. Raus was dismissed from this command after a meeting with Hitler in early March 1945, and spent the short weeks that remained until the end on the Officers Reserve List. He was captured by the Western Allies and, after the war, wrote a number of influential documents on German tactics and the experience of fighting the Red Army. He returned to his native Austria, where he died in 1956.

General Hossbach, who had been dismissed from command of the Fourth Army in late January 1945, also survived the war to surrender to the Americans. The last few days of the conflict were dramatic for

THE BATTLE OF KÖNIGSBERG

Hossbach though. Warned that the Gestapo were about to come to his home in Saxony and arrest him, he held the agents of the state at bay with pistol fire. A gun battle ensued but the approach of Allied forces saw the Gestapo men flee. Just an hour later US forces arrived and took the General into their captivity. After a brief period as a prisoner of war he returned to his home and lived out the rest of his life at Göttingen in West Germany, where he died in 1980 at the age of eighty five.

Hans Schittnig, former commander of the 1st Infantry Division which had fought so long and hard in East Prussia, had left the province in February 1945 after he had been dismissed from his command. He was captured by the Western Allies in May 1945 but released in 1947. He died in Munich in November 1956.

Following his dismissal as commander of Army Group North at the end of January 1945, Colonel-General Reinhardt took no further military command. He was captured by US forces at the end of the war and was tried for various war crimes. Found guilty, he was jailed for fifteen years in 1947 but was released in 1952. He spent the rest of his life in his native Saxony, where he died in 1963.

Friedrich-Wilhelm Müller was captured by the Soviets forces in East Prussia at the end of the war. Unlike Koch, Müller did not run away, he stayed with the army and surrendered. He was quickly handed over to the Greeks for trial for his crimes in Crete. He stood on trial in late 1946 and sentenced to death for his actions. On May 20th 1947, Müller was executed by firing squad.

Marshal Vasilevsky went to the Far East after the destruction of the German forces in East Prussia. Here he presided over the annihilation of the Japanese forces in Manchuria, one of the cheapest but most effective of the Soviet campaigns of the war. The post war years saw him remain in his post as Chief of Staff of the Army, at least until Stalin's death. He continued to hold senior military appointments until 1959. He died at the age of eighty-two in 1977.

Bagramyan ended his war in the Baltic States, taking the surrender of the German forces in Courland. He later went on to command the Soviet forces in the Baltic States and in 1955 became Deputy Minister of Defence, at which time he also became a Marshal of the Soviet Union. Bagramyan retired in 1968 and died in 1984 at the age of eighty-four, the last surviving Front commander of the Great Patriotic War.

Kuzma Galitsky also remained in the army after the war and went on to command the Soviet forces in Poland between 1955 and 1958, and those in the Trans Caucasus from 1958 to 1961. He died in 1973 at the age of seventy-five.

Afanasii Beloborodov went to the Far East after the victory in East Prussia, taking command of 1st Red Banner Army. He helped to defeat the Japanese Kwantung Army in Manchuria, where he ended his war. He remained in high posts with in the Soviet Army for the rest of his career. He died in September 1990 at the age of eighty-seven.

Nikolai Krylov also headed east after the East Prussian campaign. He commanded the Soviet forces in the Far East after the war and then returned to command the Leningrad and Moscow Military Districts between 1957 and 1963. He died in February 1972, aged sixty-eight.

The end of the conflict in Europe brought with it not only the end of German rule in East Prussia, but the expulsion of the German populace. From April 1946 the northern portion of East Prussian formally became part of Russia, and in July of that year Königsberg was renamed Kaliningrad in honour of Mikhail Kalinin, who had died earlier in the year. Those few Germans who had remained, and those who tried to return after the hostilities ended, found their homeland was no longer a welcoming place. The occupying Soviet authorities expelled the remaining 20,000 Germans from the city in 1950, and brought in a new Russian populace. Many of the city's historic buildings were demolished. The Castle, around which the city had grown, was demolished in the 1950's and in its place the Soviet authorities built the monstrous concrete House of the Soviets, which remains empty and unfinished to this day.

The dismemberment of the region wiped out for ever its German heritage. German place names were erased, being replaced by Polish and Russian names. East Prussia, with its seven centuries of history behind it, was eradicated in the name of destroying forever German militarism. Even after the fall of the Soviet Union in the late Twentieth Century, Königsberg remained Kaliningrad, with its Russian populace now calling the city their home.

Selected Bibliography

Books

Bagramyan, I., So *We Went to Victory*, Moscow 1977

Buttar, P., *Battleground Prussia*, Osprey 2010

Clark, A., *Barbarossa*, Cassell 1965

Denny, I., *The Fall of Hitler's Fortress City*, Greenhill, 2007

Dieckert & Grossmann, *Der Kampf um Ostpreussen*, Lindenbaum Verlag, 1960

Duffy, C., *Red Storm on the Reich*, Castle Books, 1991

Ellis, J., *Brute Force*, Andre Deutsch 1990

    The World War Two Databook, Aurum 1993

Erickson, J., *The Road to Berlin*, Cassell Military 2004

Fleischer, H. (ed), *Combat History of Sturmgeschütz Brigade 276*, Fedorowicz 2000

Guderian, H., *Panzer Leader*, Penguin Classics, 2000

Kirosheev, *Soviet Casualties and Combat Losses in the Twentieth Century*, Greenhill 1997

Lasch, O., *So Fiel Königsberg*, Lindenbaum Verlag 1958

Lederrey, E., *Germany's Defeat in the East*, War Office 1959

Lucas, J., *War on the Eastern Front*, Greenhill 1991

Mellenthin, F.W. von, *Panzer Battles*, Oklahoma Press 1989

Mitcham, S.W., *Hitlers Legions: the German Army Order of Battle, World War II,* Leo Cooper/Secker & Warburg 1985

Plato, A.D. von, *Die Geschichte der 5 Panzer Division*, Walhalla & Praetoria Verlag, 1978

Seaton, A., *The Russo-German War 1941-45*, Presidio 1990

Shirer, W.L., *The Rise and Fall of the Third Reich*, Secker & Warburg 1984

Speer, A., *Inside the Third Reich*, Phoenix 1995

Taylor, B., *Barbarossa to Berlin Volume One: The Long Drive East*, Spellmount 2003

Barbarossa to Berlin Volume Two: The Defeat of Germany, Spellmount 2004

Tsouras, P., (ed) *The Anvil of War*, Greenhill 1994

Vasilevsky, A., *A Lifelong Cause*, Progress 1981

Ziemke, E.F., *Stalingrad to Berlin: The German Defeat in the East*, Washington 1987

Websites

www.armchairgeneral.com

www.axishistory.com

www.feldgrau.com

www.ibiblio.org

Index

1

103rd Panzer Brigade · 88, 90, 91
103rd Rifle Corps · 158
113th Rifle Corps · 82, 104, 146, 150, 158, 162, 165, 191, 205
11th Guards Army · 44, 80, 82, 86, 89, 90, 94, 96, 98, 105, 123, 125, 126, 128, 130, 133, 136, 137, 138, 140, 141, 145, 147, 157, 158, 160, 171, 177, 190, 193, 198, 199, 201, 207, 208, 209, 222, 235
11th Guards Rifle Corps · 158
124th Rifle Corps · 192, 205, 213, 221
128th Rifle Corps · 82, 105, 128
131st Infantry Division · 87, 96
13th Guards Rifle Corps · 146, 150, 158, 192, 203, 213, 223, 224
15th Air Army · 194
16th Guards Rifle Corps · 82, 89, 90, 131, 148, 160, 193, 208, 214, 218, 225
170th Infantry Division · 92, 96, 115
171st Grenadier Regiment · 154, 187
18th Air Army · 194, 211
1st Air Army · 83, 106, 117, 119, 194
1st Baltic Front · 34, 39, 43, 44, 45, 46, 70, 79, 103, 157, 164, 170
1st Belorussian Front · 101, 103
1st Infantry Division · 8, 21, 85, 86, 88, 89, 90, 91, 113, 118, 119, 121, 122, 125, 126, 128, 136, 137, 138, 140, 145, 161, 162, 165, 167, 168, 176, 205, 212, 249
1st Parachute-Panzer Division *Herman Göring* · 78, 95, 114
1st Tank Corps · 8, 46, 47, 72, 78, 105, 122, 123, 125, 128, 130, 136, 138, 142, 146, 148, 150, 157, 159

2

201st Security Division · 58
20th Rifle Corps · 82, 105, 118, 120, 128
21st Infantry Division · 60, 77, 84, 115, 131
236th Rifle Division · 8
286th Security Division · 113, 128

28th Army · 44, 82, 86, 95, 105, 118, 119, 120, 123, 126, 128, 136
2nd Baltic Front · 44, 102, 157
2nd Belorussian Front · 101, 102, 105, 120, 130, 137, 159
2nd Guards Army · 46, 47, 72, 75, 78, 79, 103, 105, 189
2nd Guards Tank Corps · 82, 91, 94, 96, 98, 104, 122, 123, 131, 136, 137, 138, 140, 141, 145, 148
2nd Parachute Panzergrenadier Division *Herman Göring* · 94, 95, 118, 131, 141, 145, 148

3

31st Army · 82, 87, 91, 92, 94, 96, 105
349th Infantry Division · 21, 22, 85, 140
349th Volksgrenadier Division · 85, 104, 120, 122, 123, 126, 128, 131, 136, 137
367th Infantry Division · 138, 140, 141, 143, 145, 146, 147, 160, 186, 205, 210, 213, 214, 229, 231, 235, 242
36th Guards Rifle Corps · 82, 89, 90, 128, 130, 136, 137, 148, 155, 160, 193, 207, 214, 218, 223, 224
39th Army · 47, 60, 75, 79, 80, 104, 118, 122, 123, 126, 128, 130, 135, 136, 138, 141, 142, 143, 145, 146, 148, 150, 152, 158, 159, 163, 165, 166, 185, 189, 191, 205, 212
3rd Air Army · 47, 70, 159, 166, 194
3rd Baltic Front · 43, 73
3rd Belorussian Front · 34, 37, 47, 60, 79, 83, 98, 99, 102, 103, 104, 116, 121, 126, 135, 157, 158, 164, 170
3rd Guards Rifle Corps · 82, 105, 118, 121, 128

4

43rd Army · 46, 47, 71, 73, 103, 104, 125, 126, 128, 138, 142, 157, 158, 159, 185, 189, 190, 192, 198, 199, 201, 203, 204, 212, 221, 222, 235

5

50th Army · 159, 189, 190, 192, 204, 210, 213, 221, 235
51st Army · 47, 74
547th Volksgrenadier Division · 87, 89, 90
548th Volksgrenadier Division · 59, 75, 77, 78, 113, 125, 128, 135, 140, 145, 148, 163, 167, 168, 176, 185, 186, 198, 203, 204, 210, 212, 213, 214, 229, 243

549th Volksgrenadier Division · 86, 87, 89, 90, 91, 105, 113, 118, 120, 121, 123, 126, 128, 131, 136, 137, 145, 148
54th Rifle Corps · 158, 166, 192, 204, 213, 221
551st Volksgrenadier Division · 58, 71, 72, 113, 146
561st Volksgrenadier Division · 87, 88, 89, 90, 95, 113, 125, 136, 138, 141, 143, 145, 161, 162, 167, 168, 185, 205, 212, 223, 227, 242
56th Infantry Division · 84, 85, 113, 125, 126, 128, 130, 136, 137, 140, 145, 148, 154, 187, 207, 208, 210, 215
58th Infantry Division · 74, 75, 132, 141, 163, 167, 168, 169
5th Army · 7, 80, 82, 89, 90, 104, 120, 122, 123, 128, 131, 136, 138, 189
5th Guards Rifle Corps · 80, 104, 146, 158, 191, 205
5th Guards Tank Army · 46, 47, 73, 75, 137, 171
5th Panzer Division · 60, 75, 77, 78, 94, 95, 96, 98, 113, 119, 120, 121, 122, 123, 125, 126, 128, 130, 136, 138, 141, 145, 148, 161, 162, 163, 165, 166, 167, 168, 169, 176, 185, 210, 212, 219, 223, 227, 234, 247

6

61st Infantry Division · 114, 118, 120, 126, 130, 131, 141, 186, 205, 218, 229, 230, 234, 235
65th Rifle Corps · 104, 120, 123
69th Infantry Division · 77, 113, 125, 126, 128, 131, 136, 137, 140, 141, 145, 148, 161, 187, 198, 207, 208, 209, 210, 215, 217, 226, 235
69th Rifle Corps · 192, 193, 205, 214
6th Guards Army · 46, 47, 71, 72, 73, 74

7

72nd Rifle Corps · 82, 104, 131
75th Security Regiment · 186, 204, 210, 214
7th Panzer Division · 58, 72

8

81st Rifle Corps · 192, 204, 213
8th Guards Rifle Corps · 82, 90, 130, 136, 147, 194, 209, 217, 225

9

90th Rifle Corps · 158, 192, 203, 213, 222
93rd Infantry Division · 163, 167, 169
94th Rifle Corps · 80, 104, 118, 119, 122, 141, 143, 145, 146, 158, 191, 205
95th Infantry Division · 77, 114, 141

A

Allenburg · 138
Altenberg · 180
Army Group Centre · 27, 29, 36, 41, 45, 46, 75, 78, 86, 110, 111, 114, 133, 137, 138, 158
Army Group Kurland · 138
Army Group North · 21, 27, 28, 29, 39, 40, 41, 45, 46, 47, 73, 74, 77, 79, 102, 138, 140, 158, 170, 249

B

Bäckerberg Mount · 143
Bagramyan, Ivan Kristoforovich · 39, 43, 44, 45, 46, 47, 70, 71, 72, 73, 74, 82, 83, 103, 117, 157, 158, 159, 162, 163, 164, 166, 170, 171, 190, 191, 193, 201, 203, 211, 243, 247, 250, 253
Balga · 172
Bärwalde · 166, 167
Battlegroup Schuberth · 187, 207, 208, 217, 225, 226, 234, 237, 239
Becker, Felix · 185, 205, 212
Beloborodov, Afanasii Pavlantevich · 46, 47, 71, 103, 125, 126, 128, 138, 142, 157, 158, 166, 192, 201, 202, 203, 204, 206, 212, 250
Beydritten · 178, 186, 205, 213
Böhme, Horst · 187, 208, 239, 241
Bormann, Martin · 18, 62, 68
Breitenstein · 113, 119, 125, 126
Burdeinyi, Alexei Semionovich · 82, 91, 94, 105, 122, 123, 140
Butkov, Vasily Vasilevich · 46, 47, 105, 122, 159

C

Chanchibadze, Porfirii Grigorevich · 46, 47, 79, 103, 105
Charlottenburg · 146, 178, 185, 192, 198, 204, 213
Chernyakhovsky, Ivan Danilovich · 47, 78, 79, 80, 82, 83, 88, 89, 90, 92, 98, 102, 103, 104, 106, 119, 120, 121, 122, 123, 126, 133, 135, 137, 146, 158, 159, 164
Chistyakov, Ivan Mikhailovich · 46, 71
Chuikov, Vasily · 31, 82
Courland · 74
Cranz · 132, 141, 143, 146, 147

D

Dargel, Paul · 115

E

Ebenrode · 87, 90, 91, 95, 104, 115, 116
Eighteenth Army · 21, 28, 36, 43, 45, 73, 86, 114
Elbing · 102, 120, 130, 137

F

Fischhausen · 138, 163, 221, 247
Fourth Army · 7, 37, 80, 83, 84, 87, 90, 92, 95, 104, 106, 111, 113, 114, 121, 125, 130, 131, 135, 137, 140, 148, 150, 156, 157, 158, 159, 160, 161, 171, 175, 176, 249
Fuchsberg · 146, 201, 202
Führer Grenadier Brigade · 95, 96

G

Galitsky, Kuzma Nikitovich · 82, 89, 90, 91, 92, 94, 105, 123, 128, 133, 136, 138, 147, 152, 157, 158, 193, 207, 209, 210, 214, 218, 223, 250
Gerdauen · 105
Glagolev, Vasily · 82, 87, 96, 105

Godrienen · 177, 193, 198
Goebbels, Josef · 99
Goldap · 79, 94, 95, 96, 98, 105, 114
Gollau · 177
Gollnick, Hans · 57, 73, 114, 132, 160, 161, 162, 169, 191
Gorn, Walter · 87, 113, 185
Gross Friedrichsburg · 132, 142, 144, 151, 170
Gross Heydekrug · 154, 168
Gross Lindenau · 140
Gross Ponnau · 130
Grossdeutschland Panzergrenadier Division · 58, 72, 73, 74, 75, 113, 148, 154, 155, 158, 160, 171, 172
Grossmann, Horst · 87, 91, 92, 105, 119, 172, 253
Grosswaltersdorf · 91, 96, 98
Guderian, Heinz · 27, 37, 68, 106, 107, 108, 109, 110, 111, 116, 125, 130, 131, 144, 253
Gumbinnen · 79, 83, 88, 91, 92, 94, 95, 96, 98, 99, 105, 114, 120, 121, 123, 126, 128
Gutenfeld · 145, 148

H

Haberberg · 10, 11, 12, 182, 183, 218, 225
Hähnle, Hermann · 138, 140, 186, 229, 248
Heavy Panzer Battalion 505 · 95, 98, 114
Heiligenbeil · 138, 157, 159, 161, 171, 172, 175, 186, 187, 188, 189, 196
Henrici, Sigfrid · 59, 75
Herman Göring Para Panzer Division · 92
Herzog, Karl · 77, 163, 165, 166, 167, 178, 185, 212
Himmler, Heinrich · 61, 62, 69, 133
Hitler, Adolf · 14, 18, 21, 22, 23, 25, 26, 27, 28, 29, 31, 32, 34, 35, 37, 41, 45, 61, 67, 68, 69, 74, 75, 83, 92, 101, 106, 107, 108, 109, 110, 111, 113, 121, 125, 130, 131, 132, 135, 137, 140, 141, 144, 145, 156, 172, 175, 186, 191, 194, 202, 203, 212, 223, 234, 238, 243, 247, 248, 253
Hossbach, Friedrich · 83, 84, 88, 94, 95, 111, 114, 115, 116, 130, 131, 132, 137, 138, 140, 156, 198, 249

I

Insterburg · 21, 79, 88, 91, 98, 104, 105, 123, 126, 128, 130, 136, 159
IS-II Stalin tank · 51, 52, 91, 191

IX Corps · 39, 60, 73, 77, 78, 103, 104, 113, 121, 122, 123, 159

J

Jaedtke, Alfred · 95, 96, 163, 165, 166, 168
Jank, Karl · 86, 87, 113, 118, 123
Jelgava · 41
Jodl, Alfred · 22, 107, 109
Juditten · 162, 165, 178, 203, 212, 223, 241

K

Kalgan · 154
Kalgen · 180, 207, 208, 214
Karschau · 154, 208
Kattenau · 113, 118, 119, 121, 122, 126
Katyusha rocket launcher · 50, 53, 71, 191, 230
Kelmy · 42, 47, 75
Kniephof · 10, 12, 19
Koch, Erich · 14, 16, 17, 18, 23, 99, 115, 132, 133, 142, 143, 144, 170, 198, 226, 245, 248, 249
Königsberg · 7, 9, 10, 11, 12, 14, 18, 19, 20, 23, 25, 46, 77, 79, 84, 86, 87, 98, 101, 102, 104, 105, 114, 123, 130, 132, 133, 135, 136, 137, 138, 140, 141, 142, 143, 144, 145, 146, 147, 148, 150, 151, 154, 155, 156, 157, 158, 159, 160, 161, 162, 163, 165, 166, 167, 169, 170, 171, 172, 173, 175, 176, 178, 180, 181, 185, 186, 187, 188, 189, 190, 191, 192, 194, 195, 196, 197, 201, 202, 203, 204, 205, 207, 208, 210, 212, 216, 217, 219, 221, 223, 225, 229, 230, 231, 232, 233, 234, 238, 243, 244, 245, 247, 248, 250, 251, 253
Königsberg Cathedral · 10, 19
Kosse · 222, 223
Kötz, Karl · 85, 113, 118, 123
Kreizer, Yakov Grigorevich · 46, 47, 74
Kreuzingen · 128, 130
Krylov, Nikolai Ivanovich · 82, 89, 90, 94, 104, 118, 136, 250
Kurseinai · 46
Kussen · 122, 123, 126

L

Labiau · 128, 135, 138, 141
Landgraben · 203, 212
Landkeim · 166
Lasch, Otto · 11, 13, 21, 22, 23, 85, 133, 138, 140, 142, 143, 144, 145, 146, 147, 150, 151, 152, 154, 155, 156, 160, 161, 162, 167, 168, 169, 170, 171, 172, 175, 176, 185, 188, 191, 195, 196, 197, 198, 199, 202, 207, 208, 210, 214, 216, 217, 218, 219, 224, 225, 226, 렘227, 229, 231, 232, 233, 234, 237, 238, 239, 242, 243, 244, 245, 247, 248, 253
Lauth · 11, 143, 152, 177, 178
Leningrad · 21, 27, 28, 36, 40, 43, 77, 86, 114, 189, 248, 250
Lewinski, Thorwald · 186, 230, 231, 232, 243
Leysuhnen · 172
Libau · 46
Liebenfelde · 128
Lippert, Rolf · 113, 119, 120, 122, 163
Lorenz, Karl · 58, 150
Lötzen · 131, 140
Löwenhagen · 141
Luchinksy, Aleksandr Aleksandrovich · 82
Ludwigswalde · 148, 177
Lyudnikov, Ivan Ilych · 47, 80, 82, 104, 118, 157, 158, 164, 166, 191, 192, 205, 206, 212

M

Malden · 143
Mandeln · 178, 214
Marauenhof · 204, 221
Masurian Lakes · 105, 130, 131, 137, 138
Matzky, Gerhard · 84, 85, 88, 113, 118, 121
Mehlsack · 164
Meiner, Ernst · 87
Memel · 46, 47, 58, 70, 73, 74, 78, 79, 103, 114, 132, 141, 142
Metgethen · 148, 150, 162, 165, 166, 167, 168, 185, 192, 213
Mikosch, Hans · 150, 151, 152, 168, 226, 234, 248
Minsk · 27, 37, 86
Moditten · 133, 143, 144, 145, 151, 165, 166, 223, 233

Müller, Friedrich-Wilhelm · 156, 161, 172, 175, 176, 196, 197, 198, 210, 219, 226, 227, 247, 249

N

Nasser Garten · 10, 214, 216, 217
Nemmersdorf · 94, 95, 98, 99, 105, 131
Neuendorf · 177, 180, 187, 208
Neuhausen · 141, 143, 146, 177, 186, 189, 193
New Pregel, River · 9, 186, 193
Nordenburg · 105
Norkitten · 131, 136
Novikov, Alexander · 175, 194, 201, 202, 203, 205, 211, 212, 221, 223, 234

O

Oberteich · 181, 182, 204, 221
Old Pregel, River · 9
Old Town, Königsberg · 9, 10, 19
Operation Bagration · 34, 36, 37, 44, 47, 77, 79, 84, 86
Ozerov, Fedor Petrovich · 159, 193, 204, 205, 206, 213

P

Palanga · 47, 74
Palmburg · 177, 178
Panther tank · 35, 51, 64, 104, 150, 160, 165
Panzer IV tank · 63
Parachute-Panzer Corps *Herman Goering* · 87
Paradeplatz · 11, 145, 170, 239
Pillau · 13, 132, 138, 143, 144, 150, 154, 163, 169, 192, 201, 203, 205, 221, 229, 232, 241, 247, 248
Plibischken · 131
Ponarth · 187, 207, 208, 209, 214, 216, 217
Powangen · 168
Powunden · 142, 143
Prappeln · 187, 207, 208, 209

Priess, Helmuth · 86, 87, 96

Q

Quednau · 147, 178, 214, 221

R

Rablacken · 165
Rastenburg · 22, 140
Raulitt · 177
Raus, Erhard · 40, 41, 45, 61, 73, 74, 75, 94, 111, 113, 115, 116, 117, 118, 121, 125, 130, 132, 133, 135, 198, 248
Rein, Siegfried · 77, 113, 125, 187
Reinhardt, Georg-Hans · 21, 36, 41, 42, 92, 110, 111, 113, 115, 121, 125, 130, 131, 132, 135, 137, 140, 141, 144, 249
Rendulic, Lothar · 141, 144, 145, 171
Riga · 21, 39, 41, 43, 45, 73, 77
River Pregel · 10, 178
Rokossovsky, Konstantin · 44, 101, 102, 103, 120, 121, 158, 159
Rosenau · 10, 209, 217
Rosenberg · 172
Rossgarten · 12, 19, 181, 237, 238
Rothenstein · 214, 221

S

Saalau · 131
Sackheim · 12, 180, 182, 226, 237, 238
Schillen · 126
Schillfelde · 85, 98, 113
Schirwindt · 85, 86, 89
Schittnig, Hans · 85, 86, 88, 113, 117, 122, 138, 140, 145, 161, 212, 249
Schlossberg · 86, 87, 91, 98, 104, 113, 115, 116, 117, 119, 121, 122
Schmalz, Wilhelm · 87
Schörner, Ferdinand · 39, 45, 73, 84
Second Army · 87, 102, 111, 120, 125, 130, 132, 171

Seerappen · 148, 150, 151, 162, 166, 168, 169, 176, 185, 192, 205
Seligenfeld · 180, 193, 207, 208, 209
Siauliai · 39, 40, 41, 45, 46, 57, 61, 70, 71, 88
Sixteenth Army · 36, 39, 42
Sperl, Rudolf · 186, 229, 248
Stalin, Joseph · 7, 25, 26, 29, 30, 31, 32, 33, 35, 36, 43, 44, 54, 72, 74, 101, 103, 116, 147, 164, 165, 171, 175, 191, 196, 197, 201, 232, 249
Stalingrad · 30, 31, 32, 34, 35, 40, 50, 69, 82, 152
Stavka · 32, 33, 34, 36, 39, 43, 45, 47, 79, 101, 157, 159, 164, 170, 171, 175, 189, 190
Steindamm · 238
Sudau, Erich · 59, 113, 125, 176, 185, 186, 192, 203, 204, 205, 212, 229, 230, 243
Suwalki · 88, 92

T

T-34 · 28, 30, 51, 63, 64, 104, 165, 191
Tannenwalde · 146, 177, 192, 204
Tapiau · 130, 135, 136, 138, 143
Third Panzer Army · 36, 39, 41, 45, 57, 59, 75, 77, 78, 84, 94, 104, 111, 113, 114, 130, 132, 133, 135, 137, 138, 144, 157, 160, 248
Tiger tank · 51, 58, 64, 65, 67, 95, 114, 141, 146, 150
Tilsit · 47, 78, 92, 94, 104, 113, 123, 125, 126, 128, 185
Tragheim · 12, 181, 238
Trakehnen · 94, 95, 105
Trankwitz · 148, 192
Trappen · 113
Truttenau · 142, 177
Tryskiai · 46, 58, 72

U

Üderwangen · 141

V

Vasilevsky, Marshal Aleksandr · 31, 33, 34, 47, 102, 164, 165, 170, 171, 175, 189, 190, 196, 197, 198, 199, 201, 202, 226, 239, 242, 243, 247, 249, 254

Verhein, Siegfried · 58, 113
VI Corps · 84, 87, 91, 105, 172
Virbalis · 86, 87, 88, 89
Volker, Kaspar · 187
Volkssturm · 18, 62, 68, 69, 70, 91, 92, 94, 125, 135, 141, 142, 143, 154, 161, 185, 186, 188, 195, 199, 234, 242, 245
Volsky, Vasily Timofeevich · 46, 47, 72, 73, 74

W

Wargen · 148
Warthen · 154, 160, 177, 207
Wehlau · 104, 105, 128, 136, 137, 138
Weidling, Helmuth · 87, 115
Weiss, Walter · 87, 102, 111, 120, 130, 171, 172, 176
Wormditt · 131
Wundlacken · 160
Wuthmann, Rolf · 60, 77, 78, 103, 113

X

XXVI Corps · 7, 39, 84, 86, 88, 89, 104, 113, 116, 247
XXVII Corps · 75, 84, 86, 87, 88, 94
XXVIII Corps · 57, 58, 71, 73, 84, 114, 132, 142, 150, 159, 160
XXXIX Panzer Corps · 39, 42, 45
XXXX Panzer Corps · 39, 42, 57, 59, 73, 75, 77, 94
XXXXI Panzer Corps · 37, 84, 87, 92, 94, 115

Z

Zhukov, Georgy · 28, 29, 31, 33, 34, 101, 102

Printed in Poland
by Amazon Fulfillment
Poland Sp. z o.o., Wrocław